The
American Quilt Story

The American Quilt Story

The How-To and Heritage
of a Craft Tradition

by SUSAN JENKINS
and LINDA SEWARD

Rodale Press, Emmaus, Pennsylvania

First published as *Quilts: The American Story* in 1991 by
HarperCollins Publishers, London

Text copyright © 1991 by Susan Jenkins
Project design and text copyright © 1991 by Linda Seward
Photographs copyright © 1991 VisionBank Limited
Illustrations copyright © 1991 HarperCollins Publishers

HarperCollins Publishers
Designer: Judith Gordon
Editor: Barbara Dixon
Photographer: Ray Daffurn
Technique Illustrations by: Tig Sutton
Project illustrations by: Esi Cakmakcioglu

Rodale Press
Editor in Chief: William Gottlieb
Senior Managing Editor: Margaret Lydic Balitas
Crafts Editor: Suzanne Nelson
Associate Crafts Editor: Mary Green

The author and editors who compiled this book have tried to
make all the contents as accurate and as correct as possible.
Illustrations, photographs, and text have all been carefully
checked and cross-checked. However, due to the variability of
materials, personal skill, and so on, neither the authors nor
Rodale Press assumes any responsibility for damages or other
losses incurred that result from the material presented herein. All
instructions and diagrams should be carefully studied and clearly
understood before beginning any project.

If you have any questions or comments concerning this book,
please write: Rodale Press, Book Reader Service, 33 East
Minor Street, Emmaus, PA 18098.

Library of Congress Cataloging-in-Publication Data
Jenkins, Susan, 1947–
  The American quilt story: the how-to and heritage of a craft
  tradition: step-by-step directions for 30 antique quilts/by Susan
  Jenkins and Linda Seward.
      p. cm.
  "First published as Quilts, the American story, in 1991 by
  HarperCollins Publishers, London"—T.p. verso.
  Includes bibliographical references (p. 252) and index.
  ISBN 0-87857-992-3 hardcover
  1. Quilts—United States—History.   I. Seward, Linda.   II. Title.
  NK9112.J4 1991   746.9'7—dc20   91-20619 CIP

ISBN 0-87857-992-3

Distributed in the book trade by St. Martin's Press
2 4 6 8 10 9 7 5 3 1 hardcover

Typeset by Ace Filmsetting Limited, Frome, Somerset
Color reproduction in Hong Kong
Manufactured in Great Britain by
HarperCollins Publishers, Glasgow

Front cover: **Cockscomb and Currant Variation**. This exquisite
quilt from Pewee Valley, Kentucky, c. 1850, is composed of nine
large blocks each bearing an unusual variation of the traditional
Cockscomb and Currant pattern. *Half-title and title*: Detail of
Bluebird Appliqué.

ACKNOWLEDGEMENTS

I'd like to thank our photographer and friend Ray Daffurn of
VisionBank, for taking such magnificent photographs of my quilts
for this book, and his wife, Katherine, for her continuing
encouragement and support. Many thanks also to my excellent
editor, Barbara Dixon, who thoughtfully and patiently guided me
over many a difficult patch, and to our designer, Judy Gordon,
who is responsible for the outstanding visual content of the book.
I am grateful for the untiring efforts of my research assistant and
friend, Ann Lee Landman, who was never too busy to track down
an elusive picture or obscure article. A big thankyou to my co-
author, Linda Seward, who has generously contributed so much
to every aspect of this book, from the selection of the quilts to
advice on editorial content. My agent, Araminta Whitley, deserves
a special note of thanks, as does my cousin, Goldie Eder, who
sent me packages of books and articles from America. Judy
Wentworth and Sarah Franklyn, of the Antique Textile Company
in London, have been especially helpful and supportive and I'd
like to thank them for sharing their knowledge about English
quiltmaking traditions with me, and for generously allowing the
publication in this book of photographs of three of their
outstanding English quilts. Many, many thanks as well to Betsy
Nimock, who has not only contributed her marvelous collage to
the book, but who took so much time to help locate a number of
quilts and their makers. I am grateful also to Nancy Gibson
Tuckhorn of the Daughters of the American Revolution Museum
in Washington DC, who helped to research the Album Quilt on
page 43; to Doris Beckham for providing the provenance of

several quilts; to Bo Wiechens and Ray Beckmann in St Charles,
Missouri; to Clare Rose, for information on English needlework
publications; to Harold and Ruth Williams; to Maureen Moriarty
for kindly lending several quilts to be photographed; and to
Dame Elizabeth Frink for allowing us to include her beautiful
Stars Quilt on page 38.
    I would also like to acknowledge the individuals and
institutions who have contributed to this publication: Megan
Hughes of Christie's, New York; Jill Sherman of the Missouri
Historical Society; The Library of Congress; Kathy Keist of the
Archive of Folk Culture of the Smithsonian Institution; Lorraine
Mayo and John Fleckner of the Archives Center of the National
Museum of American History, Smithsonian Institution; Jack Larkin
of Old Sturbridge Village; Martha Vestecka-Miller of the Nebraska
State Historical Society; Elizabeth Holmes of the Buffalo Bill
Historical Society; and Dr Joyce Storey of the Philadelphia College
of Textiles and Science.
    Special thanks, as well, to friends and family who have helped
in so many ways with the book – Hildegarde Heygate, Tory Weil,
Gideon Weil, John Weil, Jeannette Lasansky, Cuesta Benberry, Aly
Goodwin, Shelly Zegart, Darwin Bearley, Michael and Joley Malcé,
Suellen Meyer, Ron Simpson, Anny Evason, Doris Brady,
Dr Helane Rosenberg, Barbara and David Cooper, David
Landman, Dorothy Landman and Bea Garvan.
    Finally, a thousand thanks to Gareth, who has lived with this
book since its inception and who has never failed to offer
editorial advice and optimism when I needed it the most.

Contents

Foreword

Collecting quilts wasn't something I ever planned to do, it just seemed to evolve out of a strong but rather innocent interest in old textiles.

I have always loved vintage clothing and theater costumes, and in the late 1960s and early 1970s I haunted antique clothes shops and markets. These places were at the time also piled high with wonderful quilts, and you can imagine my delight upon discovering old fabrics and patterns. Since the top price was then $25, I bought a few, and kept buying them. In the mid-1970s, when I began to tour America with the Metro Theater Circus, the children's dance company I directed, my friends and I were never too tired after performances to visit local antique shops, buying up old clothing, shoes and quilts.

Later, in the early 1980s, after moving to London, I kept buying American quilts to give to friends and relations, always keeping a few to throw over sofas, chairs and beds. By 1985 I was an addict and regularly asked friends and quilt dealers in America to look out for special ones for me. I began to read avidly about quilts and quilting and to visit quilt exhibitions and auctions in America. I read a lot about American history, about the lives of the pioneer women, and about the beginnings of textile manufacturing. Slowly my collection grew. I found that the quilts I tended to like were ones which showed great spirit, humor or a special sense of design. I didn't restrict myself to the most well-preserved or eloquent examples of the quilter's art, preferring to leave that to the museums. I was more interested in the everyday quilts which expressed something particular or unique about the life of the women who had made them, and I didn't mind if they were a little torn or bleached from use. Each quilt was a kind of mystery to me. Who were the women who had made such wonderful quilts? How did they do it? They would not have had formal training. The more I learned, the more intrigued I became.

Eventually, by 1988, I started to organize selling exhibitions of American quilts in England, mostly with the support of two English textile enthusiasts, Judy Wentworth and Sarah Franklyn of the Antique Textile Company in London. Finally, in 1991, in the heart of London, I opened my own gallery devoted to American quilts, the Museum Quilts Gallery.

The quilts in my collection chosen for this book came from all over the United States and date from the early 1800s to the mid-1940s. They were specifically chosen to represent both the unusual, such as the appliqué Cowboy Quilt, and the everyday, like the Appalachian Tree of Life in rough blue denim. Particular quilts were also chosen which represented the work of women from sects, such as the Ohio Amish purple and black Crown of Thorns, and from particular regions, like the Pennsylvania Dutch Quilt worked in traditional reds and greens. I wanted to select quilts which were both idiosyncratic, like the Union Army Encircled Star, and humorous, like the Sailor's Quilt. Above all, both Linda Seward and I were anxious not only to feature the best examples of American quilts, but rather to catalogue the remarkable diversity of American quilt styles, techniques and patterns.

I hope you enjoy seeing the beautiful photographs of this quilt collection, reading about the history of quilting in America, and perhaps making a quilt based on one of the original patterns, as much as I have enjoyed collecting both the information and the quilts.

Introduction

*Every individual is part and parcel of a great
picture of society in which he lives and acts, and his
life cannot be painted without reproducing the
picture of the world he lived in.*

Harriet Beecher Stowe, *Old Town Folks*, 1869

Quilts have been a high-spirited artistic expression of American women over the past two hundred years. Although, in the nineteenth century, American quilts were ignored by the arbiters of national taste, later generations have now come to recognize their remarkable craftsmanship and graphic sophistication. Quilts are today being reappraised by historians, art critics and a growing international public as a unique and valuable legacy of American folk art.

For the first time, the extraordinary creativity of generations of American women is gaining recognition. No longer are quilts stored away in moth balls, or used to keep out draughts, pack furniture, or protect vegetables from winter frost. Instead, they are finding their way to the walls of some of the most important galleries and museums in the world. Since 1971, when the Whitney Museum of American Art in New York launched a major exhibition entitled 'The Pieced Quilt', quilts have come to represent a remarkable design tradition which has developed in the United States since colonial times.

It is the aim of the first part of this book to try to define that quiltmaking tradition within the broader context of the American social experience; and, in particular, through the experience of American women. On finding a wide diversity of quilts during my early years of collecting, I would ask myself questions such as, why was a particular quilt made at a particular time, and why did quiltmaking, derived from a European heritage, become so popular and so distinctly American?

This led me to wonder about day-to-day life during the early years of America's history – what were the thoughts and beliefs of people creating this new nation, and what were they influenced by? I also questioned the larger role of religion, politics and culture in American life as well as social attitudes towards women and the institution of the family. The quilts illustrated in this book, as well as being aesthetically exciting in their own right, provide fascinating historical signposts for this 'American Story'.

The second part of the book, written by Linda Seward, is an articulate and imaginative guide to making many of these historical quilts. With great insight and skill, Linda gives practical step-by-step instructions for 30 quilt patterns, some of which have never been named before, and many of which have never before been published. The projects range from easy quilts which anyone can tackle, to intermediate and more advanced patterns for quilters with some experience.

Quilts, fashioned out of everything from rough homespun to elegant silk, and made in every territory and state, are a vital expression of the hopes, desires, frustrations and sorrows of American women over the last 200 years. The story of the American quilt, from both a historical and technical point of view, reflects a rich social experience which is uniquely American.

—1—
Colonial America

They fell upon their knees and blessed the God of heaven, who had brought them over the vast and furious ocean, and delivered them from all the perils and miseries thereof, againe to set their feete on the firme and stable earth, their proper elemente . . . they had no friends to wellcome them, nor inns . . . no houses or much less townes to repaire too, to seek for succoure . . .[1]

These were the words of Governor William Bradford, who witnessed and reported the landing of the Mayflower passengers. The early settlers who came to the shores of the New World were, within a few short years, caught up in the routine of everyday life – the crop season, maintaining the house and family, and basic survival. From the first landings at Jamestown, Virginia, in 1607 and Plymouth, Massachusetts, in 1620, America was dominated by scarcity and small-scale production. Life was regulated by the weather and seasons and most families were tied to the local agricultural calendar. Yet after only 150 years, this uncivil land had prospered enough to emerge as a new civilization, and by 1750 the colonists came to be greatly affected by much larger events and ideas. Religious attitudes, political uprisings, economic growth, cultural trends and the quality of domestic life were all

critical factors in shaping the beliefs and concerns of successive generations. The women who created the unique legacy of the American quilt, from those living in East Coast mansions to those in frontier log cabins, expressed in their needlework a social history which reflected the rapidly changing character of American life.

Recent writings indicate that not many quilts were made during the early Colonial years. Despite strong English quilting traditions, in pre-Revolutionary America conditions were generally unfavorable for quiltmaking. Houses were small, cramped and dirty. Imported material was scarce and expensive and homespun fabric was mostly used for other household items rather than for quilted bedcovers. In addition, the commercial manufacture of cloth was strictly prohibited, although fabric, flax, seed and sheep were smuggled into the country by various shippers, despite severe penalties.

Examination of probate inventories and wills from New England and the Eastern coastal regions confirms that quilts were 'few and far between' in the seventeenth and early eighteenth centuries. They were 'the most expensive item of bedding inventoried and were almost certainly imported rather than home-made'. There was plenty of cheaper bedding available, including woolen blankets, coverlets and bed rugs.[2] Nonetheless, the harsh New England winters and the scarcity of fabric undoubtedly encouraged women to patch clothes and blankets in a rudimentary way for extra warmth. What passed for 'quilts' were often filled with corn husks or grasses and tied together with twine.

The earliest pioneers – the Puritans who settled in New England – were imbued with the new Protestant belief which taught that commerce and material pursuits were secondary to ethical and religious ideals. This first generation was intent on creating a 'New Zion' in the wilderness, but based on the social European hierarchy of family, church and community with its emphasis on privilege and rank.

The Quakers, who arrived in 1682, fifty years after the Puritans, settled in the Delaware Valley to carry out their 'Holy Experiment' under William Penn. The Quaker 'Friends', who dominated Pennsylvanian political life for nearly a century, advocated egalitarian beliefs, spiritual pursuits and social service.

In these early settlements church leaders were also civic leaders and wielded tremendous influence as moral arbiters. Their sermons, based on Puritan and Quaker ideals which stressed industry and frugality, had a powerful effect in shaping the outlook and ethics of Colonial America, and no rural or mountain cabin was too poor or too isolated to be without its Bible. Religious ideas and fervor were perpetuated by religious circuit riders on horseback who, with saddlebags to hold their few possessions, would spend years riding through miles of dense wilderness, bringing religion to the pioneers. These traveling ministers and bishops were often the only sources of news from the outside world.

The majority of the first settlers lived in one or two rooms in primitive conditions. These houses had tiny windows, little or no decoration and were dirty, bug infested and smoky from the continuously burning hearth. Refuse and slops were thrown directly out of the doors or windows, and farm animals often wandered about freely.

From the earliest days, women played an essential role in the domestic economy. Survival depended on the strength and cohesiveness of the family unit, and women spent hours performing the necessary household chores related to sustaining the family. This included raising a good portion of the provisions, all food preparation and cooking, sewing, spinning and weaving, the making and cutting of the cloth from wool, linen and cotton, rearing children and making household items like candles and soap.

For ordinary families fabrics were scarce and were used, re-used, saved and salvaged. Homespun fabric was painstakingly worked on the spinning wheel and loom by Colonial wives

---

PREVIOUS PAGE: *HEWSON PANEL*
This remarkable panel was made at the end of the eighteenth century by textile printer John Hewson of Philadelphia. The large urn and flower motifs, as well as the birds and butterflies, were patterns typical of popular textiles during the period.

Courtesy: Paley Design Center, Philadelphia College of Textiles and Science, Dr Joyce Storey

While this rough-and-ready rural setting might seem to be colored with a hint of caricature, it probably conveys, with the exception of the two storeys, a somewhat realistic appraisal of early American life; hardly a setting for an intricate or beautiful quilt.

Old Sturbridge Village Photo. by Henry E. Peach

and daughters. This was a primary domestic task requiring a high level of skill, as described in an article from The Museum of American Folk Art:

To turn flax into linen took sixteen months from planting to finished fabric: sowing, weeding, pulling up the ripened stalks, de-seeding, drying, retting (or rotting) them with a five day water treatment; cleaning still again, re-drying, and beating several times to remove the woody center . . . then carded with a heavy comb called a hetchel, and recarded several times to refine it into fibers fine enough for spinning into thread for weaving. Wound into skeins, the thread was bleached in ashes and water for a week, rinsed, washed, dried, and rewound onto bobbins and shuttles. The final fabric itself had to be bleached for weeks in the sun before it was cut, sewed, or embroidered.

Wool processing wasn't any easier, although it wasn't always necessary to raise the sheep themselves; fleece could sometimes be bought through trade. After shearing it was cleaned of burrs and twigs, washed and dried, and then carded: the wool was rubbed with melted swine's grease, then pulled through the fine wire teeth of carding combs, sometimes dyed at that point, sometimes spun first, wound into skeins, and then dyed.[3]

Home-made dyes were no less arduous to produce, and before the availability of dye books in the nineteenth century the art of 'coloring' was nearly as important as clothmaking. Roots,

berries, leaves, nuts and barks were continually gathered for dye making and home-made recipes carefully guarded or exchanged. The real secret was to create stable colorfast dyes which would survive many washings. However, the stench from the dye vat which contained chamber-lye (urine) needed to set the color was an unfortunate addition to the family hearth.

In these conditions there was neither the time, the space, nor the money for most women even to consider making a beautiful quilt. Those quilts which were made during this period were plain, rough affairs used by successive family members until they simply fell apart or were recycled as linings for other bedcovers.

The earliest quilt documented in America is in the 1685 inventory of the house of Captain George Corwin in Salem, Massachusetts, which mentions 'a quilt of calico, colored and flowered . . .'[4] There is also a reference from 1692 in the estate of the famous pirate Captain John Kidd to 'featherbeds, pillowfeathers, tablecloths, linen sheets, napkins, ten blankets and three quilts'.[5]

The New Middle Classes

Although America was primarily still a land of small farmers, the potential for the creation of wealth occasioned the development of a new class of merchants, artisans and professionals, and slowly the character of domestic life altered. By the 1750s, houses were still fairly bare but a few more domestic touches had been added; chairs, rugs, painted floors and curtains became more affordable, as did painted pottery, glasses and even mirrors. Beds with fancy counterpanes or quilts became showpieces and had place of honor in the parlor, where they represented the prosperity attained by a family.

A worldwide trade network had developed in the East Coast ports and a large range of goods and fabrics were becoming available to these growing middle classes. Costly furnishings and expensive imported fabrics began to grace the rooms of newly built, 'fancy' houses. Newspaper advertisements for imported quilts began appearing; in 1746, the *Boston Gazette*, for example, listed 'English goods (including quilts), a great variety imported from London, in the last ships, and to be sold'.[6]

The Revolutionary period of the 1770s saw the beginnings of small-scale manufacturing, with the war itself creating opportunities for expansion. One of the most important new industries, along with iron manufacturing, pottery and glassworks, was textile manufacturing, particularly cotton, which was to play a substantial role in the development of the American quilt. Prior to the nineteenth century most raw cotton was imported from either Egypt or the Caribbean.

A new breed of professional, European-trained dyers and chintz and calico printers, such as John Hewson (see page 13), started to emerge in more densely populated areas like Pennsylvania and New England, and by the last quarter of the eighteenth century women were able to save hours of labor by having their fabric professionally dyed and by purchasing less expensive domestic fabric.

Fashion and Style

The new affluent classes, especially in the growing cities, sought to emulate European society and were less and less influenced by strict church dictates and attitudes. Money was to be made and Americans were interested in acquiring European culture. They ordered European books, watched European plays and, if they could, sent their children to be educated in England. Fashion and good taste were considered essential in all things, which meant that elegant furnishing and dress materials were ordered in greater quantity, and large amounts of Indian chintz, which was all the rage in Europe, were imported despite the cost. Calicos, silks, quality cottons, good woolens, furniture and decorative items all found their way to more and more homes, through the new road and waterway systems.

During the second half of the eighteenth century, the creation of leisure time, the abundance of imported materials and a new social emphasis on domesticity made quilting widely popular. Women lavished much time creating elaborate pieced and appliquéd quilts. They were strongly influenced by the styles and methods of England, where the ability to sew and do fine needlework was a feminine priority. Newly established American 'Dame Schools' and 'Young Ladies' Schools' – types of finishing school for the middle classes – gave needlework prominence as a paramount accomplishment and a testimony to good breeding. Girls were often taught to sew from the age of three, and by the time they were five they had probably made their own four- or nine-patch quilt. Boys were also taught how to sew and cut patterns.

There are records from this period of the occasional 'quilting party' and of professional quilters. According to quilt historian Barbara Brackman, written accounts of quilts during this period may also refer to quilted petticoats as well as bedquilts. For example, in the mid-eighteenth century, fashion in England and America dictated a skirt split to reveal a decorative quilted petticoat. Like the bedquilt, the cloth was often silk or glazed wool quilted with designs such as feathers and flowers.

Certain social conventions governing quilting were established early on. The piecing and appliqué work that decorated the top came to be the work of a single maker, while the quilting, a separate step, might have been done either by the woman who pieced the top, by a professional quilter, or jointly by a group of friends.[7]

The earliest preserved example of an American quilt comes from Maine and is inscribed

JOHN HEWSON – CALICO PRINTER

Following the growth of the textile industry in America, in 1773 John Hewson, an English textile printer, was invited by Benjamin Franklin to come to Philadelphia to start up a block printing shop. His designs soon became sought after and he embraced America as his new home. During the Revolutionary War he fought the British and later, in 1787, he and his family took part in the parade through Philadelphia that was organized to celebrate the adoption of the Federal Constitution.

Hewson's technical achievements were well recognized and, soon after the War, he received a state subsidy from the Pennsylvania legislature to expand his business. His designs featured block-printed neoclassical, flower-filled urns, surrounded by smaller flowers and other natural motifs. Hewson's prints, many designed especially for making quilts, were often cut apart to be used as the central frame motif.

Very few examples of John Hewson's work remain, although some of his quilts are in the collections of the Philadelphia Museum of Art, Winterthur Museum and St Louis Art Museum. The center panel pictured on page 9 is a recently discovered original Hewson print found quite by accident in a Philadelphia textile factory. The Paley Design Center was given this centerpiece through the generosity of John Seder and Robert Blum of Craftex Mills, Philadelphia, and it was displayed at the Center for the first time, after restoration, in May 1984.

Another example of Hewson's work is the quilt top, below, which, like the fine centerpiece, has borders made from many patchwork pieces, all of which are late-eighteenth century and very early-nineteenth-century printed cottons.

The botanically correct motifs which John Hewson printed on this magnificent coverlet appear to have been influenced by older Dutch books of engravings, as well as by the birds and leaves which appeared on popular Indian chintzes of the period. Both English and American fabric manufacturers of the time created individual panels specifically for use in elegant domestic bedcoverings.

Courtesy: The Philadelphia Museum of Art

CHINTZ MEDALLION APPLIQUÉ COVER
*This charming English appliqué cover dates from 1815 to 1825. The
cotton ground has two outer printed flower borders and the main
field is decorated with motifs of bird and flower sprays. The central
lattice fruit basket is contained within a printed flower and fruit
surround. It was one of the fabrics specially printed to be the
centerpieces of patchworks, a practice which was popular from
about 1795 to c.1820.*

Size: 114 × 114″ /
289 × 289 cm

Courtesy: Sarah Franklyn and Judy Wentworth,
Antique Textile Company of London, England

'Anna Tuels her quilt given to her by her mother in the year Au 1785'.[8] It has a central square made up of a segmented circle, multiple inner pieced borders and a very wide, scroll-quilted wool outer border. Another quilt from the period, made in the central medallion style from a copperplate chintz fabric and depicting William Penn's treaty with the Indians, is in the collection at George Washington's home at Mount Vernon. It is reputed to have been made by Martha Washington. Both these quilts, like the others preserved in American museums and historical societies, are clearly in the English style and made with European fabric.

English Traditions and American Borrowings

Because there are very few known eighteenth-century quilts that have survived in America, knowledge of English influences is somewhat clouded. It is, however, known that the earlier sixteenth- and seventeenth-century English traditions of quilted wholecloth bedcoverings, block-patterned piecework quilts and appliqué and pieced central medallion style quilts were popular in mid-eighteenth-century England. The framed medallion quilt exhibited a strong design element placed firmly in the center of the quilt which was often surrounded by successive layers of elaborate borders. The Chintz Medallion Appliqué cover illustrated on page 14 is beautifully designed and proportioned, with airy spaces in between carefully stitched chintz pieces.

Many of the wholecloth quilts which are recorded or preserved are commonly called linsey-woolsey after Lindsey in Suffolk, England, where they originated. These quilts were very much the household staple and were made of a linen warp and a wool weft, creating a rather stiff heavy fabric. They were stuffed with unbleached wool and finely quilted with loosely spun linen thread in fanciful arabesque and scroll designs. Brilliant shades of indigo blue, red and brown from home-made dye vats created admirable colors on otherwise bulky utilitarian items.

After 1750 much more elegant wholecloth or pieced quilts were made from expensive fabric printed in the traditional hand-blocked method or with engraved copperplates. These would have been in either the popular pastoral style or the French-inspired toile de Jouy materials which depicted lavish historical or mythological scenes.

The *Guide to English Embroidery* in the Victoria and Albert Museum, produced in London, discusses the popularity of pieced quilts:

A technique which assumed prominence at this time was patchwork. Early pieces are usually very simple, consisting of rectangles of printed cottons joined together to make a quilt or coverlet which might be further embellished with simple embroidery . . . Towards the end of the century there arose a fashion for cutting shapes or motifs out of printed cottons and applying them to a plain ground, a technique often combined with patchwork.[9]

One of the most fashionable textile designs of seventeenth- to mid-nineteenth-century Europe was the Indo-European flowering tree motif. Large hand-painted or block-printed cotton panels known as palampores were produced to order in India for a European market. These lush designs, ordered through the East India Company, incorporated Hindu, Islamic, Chinese and European motifs. The introduction of such gaily colored cottons revolutionized the English textile trade in woolen and linen manufacture. Their cheapness and color took the public fancy and women, who had previously dressed in woolen cloth, were 'now clothed in calico and printed linen'.[10]

These painted and glazed colorfast Indian chintzes featured outsize flowers, exotic birds, trees, and colorful leaves and vines and were, by the end of the eighteenth century, in great demand for dresses and tasteful furnishings. However, import restrictions, fueled by the hostility of English silk and woolen manufacturers against both imported and English cottons, inflated the prices of these 'charming chintzes'. Pamphlets warned of 'this low priced thing called Callico . . . made by heathens and pagans that worship the devil . . .'

Nonetheless, fashion and taste prevailed and despite years of bans on chintzes in Europe they were still affordable to 'society', and the highly valued 'leftovers' came to be ingeniously stitched into bedcovers and counterpanes. The earliest surviving set of pieced bedhangings made from Indian prints is the Levens Hall Patchwork. This intricately stitched, appliquéd and pieced quilt, made mostly from red and blue chintzes which may well have been imported during the mid-seventeenth century, is rumored to have been made in the early years of the eighteenth century. Today, it is part of the collection at Levens Hall, Cumbria, England.

Figurative portions of the chintz – the birds, flowers, leaves or animals – were often cut out and then stitched directly onto a fine white wholecloth background, the overall pattern perhaps inspired by the popular Tree of Life motif. This appliqué style was known as broderie perse, or Persian embroidery, and may have been developed as a quick way to achieve the look of stylish embroidery or crewel work.[11] The broderie perse style actually created a new design entirely out of pictorial patches.

The Tree of Life broderie perse quilt illustrated on page 17 is composed solely of hand-blocked English and Indian chintzes on a fustian (a combination of linen and cotton) background. While at first sight it appears to be of English origin, the scale of the design and the somewhat chunky pieces suggest that it is more likely to have been made in America.

According to English textile authority Judy Wentworth, by the mid-eighteenth century there were three distinct English needlework traditions which had found their way to American shores. First there were the appliqué covers – often made to cover daybeds in English country houses – with their characteristic spaciousness of design, large central flower panels (often cut from bold chintzes), or specially printed medallion centers. These often sported swag, ribbon patterns or bows employed as border motifs. Then there were the pieced patchworks composed entirely of stitched shapes – hexagons, diamonds, squares and rectangles, sometimes with a central medallion panel. Finally, there was the quilted wholecloth covering, as elaborate or simple as time and circumstance dictated.[12] The beautifully stitched English hexagon quilt (Grandmother's Flower Garden) pictured on page 18 reflects the preoccupation with detail typical of many fine

English mosaic-style pieced bedcoverings of the early 1800s.

English fancy stitching, embroidery and elaborate quilting, which had evolved from ecclesiastical and later aristocratic traditions, became a distinguishing hallmark in fashionable bedrooms and parlors of the early thirteen American colonies. This tradition existed in parallel with the plainer wholecloth or patched quilt which was made more for practicality and less for aesthetic or social reasons. These quilts would have been made out of wool or linen, or the mixture of the two (linsey-woolsey). Another popular material for the wholecloth quilt was calamanco, an imported fine worsted fabric which was sometimes glazed. The only design on these plain quilts was that formed by the often elaborate quilting patterns.

The Revolutionary Period

Up to 1775 most Americans had still considered themselves English, Dutch, Scottish or German, and maintained close ties with Europe. However, powerful religious and political forces were at work which translated into a growing spirit of Republicanism and prepared the way for the Revolutionary War.

The character of the new American army and later of its government was strongly influenced by the religious basis of the original settlements. The Puritan and Quaker Protestant ethic, which encouraged hard work, frugality and egalitarian sentiments, became secularized into a patriotic rallying cry for democracy among the producing classes, which included the small farmers. To

---

TREE OF LIFE
This English appliqué cover with a narrow zigzag border dates from the last quarter of the eighteenth century. Made in the style of an Indian palampore out of furnishing cottons and chintzes, it is stitched into a background fabric of fustian – a combination of linen and cotton. This cover is a true broderie perse in that the printed fabrics create a totally new design, one which is in this case, as in many, buttonhole stitched.

Courtesy: Sarah Franklyn and Judy Wentworth, Antique Textile Company of London, England

Size: 94 × 74″/238 × 188 cm

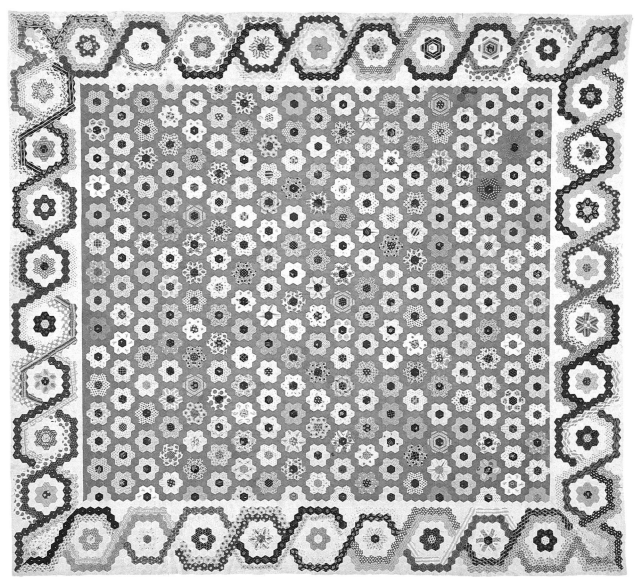

Size: 100 × 110″/250 × 275 cm

GRANDMOTHER'S FLOWER GARDEN
This fine English patchwork, carefully designed and beautifully executed, has, unusually, a light-brown ('tea') colored ground. The fabrics used are dress prints from the period 1780–1800 and, like many English patchworks of this period, the piece was not quilted. Each of the 'flower beds' has a darker center surrounded by carefully arranged lighter pieces. The minutely oversewn seams joining the hexagons each measure 1″/2.5cm.

Courtesy: Sarah Franklyn and Judy Wentworth, Antique Textile Company of London, England

these early Americans democracy meant not just a rejection of monarchy in favor of a government responsive to the people, but also new voting rights, the growth of a free market economy, and social mobility. Restrictive British legislation fueled a new spirit of American nationalism and the wearing of American 'homespun' fabric became a badge of patriotism.

By 1787, when the Constitution was ratified, America had become an agrarian democracy of small farmers, artisans and merchants guided by an enlightened class of patrician lawmakers and politicians. The Constitutional Convention had hammered out a federal policy which would both encourage the small farmer and mildly restrain industrial development. By the end of the eighteenth century America had begun to think of itself as a nation.

Changes in Religion

After the Revolution, the widespread expansion of trade presented many families with new economic and social opportunities. The transition had begun from the medieval guild outlook, which had dominated American Colonial life for nearly 200 years, to a new commercial mentality. The restrictive doctrines of the church, which frowned upon material acquisitions, lost ground in the emerging Republic. Strict puritanical ideas became less influential as the accumulation of wealth accelerated.

In the 1790s a religious revival movement called 'The Great Awakening' emerged as a counter-offensive to austere Calvinist thinking, offering a more generous and loving picture of God. Well-known preachers stressed God's mercy, humanized the church's view on children and acknowledged that limited wealth could contribute to the enrichment of spiritual life. By 1800 church membership had increased dramatically, with women constituting the majority of the new membership.

This 'awakening' was important in the story of quilting because it transferred the responsibility for moral and religious education directly from clergymen to women in the home. Women were called upon to establish a domestic environment where suitable training would be offered to America's future citizens. Thus began a cult of 'domesticity' which in the early years of the nineteenth century encouraged the creation of a well-ordered and comfortable domestic setting.

This new Republicanism – a legacy of European ideas in a New World setting – thus came to dominate nineteenth-century life in America and mediated between the world of commerce and the world of religion, between wealth and piety.

The family came to be seen as the moral repository of the nation and home life to be associated with virtue.

Attitudes towards Women

Such sweeping religious and political changes in the years after the 1776 Revolution engendered important shifts in public attitudes towards women. Women's education was taken more seriously, prompted in part by the new domestic thinking whereby women assumed the mantle of moral guardianship of the family and also became the religious educators of their children. A range of seminaries and academies were established as women were called upon to disseminate 'mental nourishment' to the young.

This new cult of domesticity was the main reason for the widespread development of needlework and quilting as occupations thought suitable for women. By 1800 it was considered necessary and proper for a young lady not only to acquire a thorough knowledge of needlework, but also to gain an insight into a science, such as botany, in order to become a better home-maker, companion and conversationalist. *Curtis's Botanical Magazine*, an English periodical featuring botanical engravings, was widely distributed in the United States in the late eighteenth and early nineteenth centuries, and many flowering specimens consequently found their way into needlework done during that period.[13]

This new attitude towards women was accompanied by a dramatic change in dress style. A high-waisted 'empire' look allowed women to do without confining layers of corsets and petticoats. It also meant that women were freer to go out and socialize, and new 'middling'- (middle) class women began to do needlework and quilt together in groups. As a distinct American identity began to assert itself in all aspects of economic and cultural life, the quilt came more and more to express the aspirations of a growing nation.

—2—
A New
Democracy

Until the mid-nineteenth century, the population in the new American republic was in general homogeneous, most settlers coming from the British Isles and the remainder coming either from Germany or Holland. Many also came as indentured servants or slaves. Although most families tended to live in isolated rural conditions, they shared, for the most part, a common cultural heritage and were able to socialize and exchange goods, information and ideas on a regular basis. This was particularly true for New England where 80 per cent of the population came from England.[1] These social conditions played an important role in popularizing a tradition of quiltmaking.

In 1800, some twenty-four years after the end of the Revolution, the area of America had doubled to 18 million square miles. The pace of westward expansion accelerated and by 1820 more than 2.2 million people had settled in the Missouri Valley. The frontier ran in a long irregular curve from Michigan to Arkansas[2], and the technological and social advances which had led to the development of quiltmaking in the East were slowly finding their way westward where quilting was taken up by local communities.

A rapidly developing transportation system of waterways and roads, itinerant peddlers,

religious circuit riders, medicine shows and social gatherings facilitated the exchange of information and ideas. Sewing bees, 'get-togethers', agricultural fairs, 'ladies' fairs' and church bazaars were common events. Also, greater literacy among both women and men, especially in the New England area, allowed a wider scope for the circulation of news and ideas. By 1800 more than 180 newspapers were being published throughout the states, as well as important broadsides, magazines and books, and the almanacs of the early 1800s carried quilt patterns for the benefit of their female readers. These factors strongly contributed to the spread of new quilting methods and patterns which seemed to emerge at random, and yet simultaneously across the growing nation.

Increasing Popularity of Quilting

After the Revolutionary War, and again after the War of 1812 against Britain, over disputed shipping rights, British merchants, anxious to make up the profits they had lost during the years of conflict, flooded the American market with manufactured goods. These included a great deal of fabric which was purchased by well-to-do families and used for furnishings, fine clothing and quilts.

At the same time, new Republican policies dictated a fresh set of domestic and moral responsibilities for women which encouraged the role of quilting and needlework. Because few rural households were fully self-sufficient, it was customary for families both to barter with the local store (exchanging produce for nails, rum or cloth etc.) and to exchange goods and services

---

PREVIOUS PAGE: *NINE-PATCH*
The extraordinary border on this very early-nineteenth-century quilt features a romantic lute player in an abundant floral setting. The depth of field in this fabric was probably achieved by the use of English engraved copper plates. The center of the piece is richly endowed with a glorious combination of glazed chintzes and elegant dress prints.

Size: 92 × 102″/233.7 × 259 cm

CHARLES H. TAYLOR,
DRAPER AND TAILOR,
RESPECTFULLY informs the inhabitants of Auburn and its vicinity that he has taken a shop in Genesee street two doors east of Robert Muir's Store, and he flatters himself that he will be able to secure a liberal share of public patronage. All orders in his line will be promptly attended to, and the work executed in the best New-York style. All kinds of Country produce will be taken in payment.
Auburn Oct. 20th, 1828   30m6

---

with each other. The primary reason for the national lack of cash was that up to the mid-nineteenth century imports greatly exceeded exports. This resulted in a continual shortage of gold and silver currency, since money was sent to Europe to pay interest on loans and to purchase manufactured goods.

It became a broadly followed tradition for neighborhoods to interact through mutual visiting and 'frolics'. Such examples of cooperative labor as 'log-rollings' for clearing timber, 'stone-bees' for ridding fields of rocks, and even 'dunging frolics' for spreading manure on fields, were common events.[3] Most important of these gatherings were the house- and barn-raisings, and the get-togethers – often composed of women only – for needlework and textile production, in particular the 'quilting bees'.

The women who made these quilts were making something which was most likely for their own families or close friends, something which represented a labor of love. The quilt may have been beautiful or comforting, or simply warm and practical, but it also represented a new interpretation of women's roles as mothers and wives. For by 1830 it was the wife who had become the moral and spiritual provider for the family.

Quilting also took on a wider social aspect and often involved the entire family:

Everyone seemed to participate in the making of quilts, whole families were involved. Husbands and fiancés drew complex patterns on a quilt top or cut out templates from which patterns were cut. Grandmothers and children threaded needles and cut out patches while mothers sewed pieces together and quilted the top. A quilt in some instances represented the creative efforts of an entire family.[4]

THE QUILTING BEE

Of all the romantic quilt stories, none is so cherished as the tradition of the 'Quilting Bee'. Some quilting bees lasted several days, especially when people came long distances, and guests often brought food. Frames would be set up and two or three women would sit on each side and one at each end. The hostess would usually supply the thread and scissors. 'The failure to ask a neighbor to a raising, a clearing, a chopping, a frolic, or his family to a quilting, was considered a high indignity. Each settler was not only willing but desirous to contribute his share to the general comfort and public improvement, and felt aggrieved and insulted if the opportunity to do so were withheld.'[6]

Francis Underwood, a social historian of the time who was Associate Editor of *Atlantic Monthly*, describes in a well-known book from the 1830s how a dozen farm wives would 'dress in their best gowns, cambric collars and lace caps' and come for a 'quiltin''. They sat around the quilting frame 'that so nearly filled the room that there was little space behind the chairs. As their fingers flew through stitches they would exchange information in regard to measles and whooping cough. They would then stop for tea.'[7]

There was a strong sense of mutual dependence among women in this period and 'young women routinely spent months preceding their marriage almost exclusively with other women – at neighborhood sewing bees and quilting parties'.[8] A young woman was expected to have made a trousseau of twelve quilt tops in the years prior to her marriage; the thirteenth, reserved as the special wedding quilt, was generally all-white and stitched with hearts. These tops would have been quilted by friends and family at bees and were often displayed at the wedding:

Part of the entertainment provided for the feminine guests at a girl's wedding was the display of the quilts and coverlets she had made, the visible proof of her accomplishments as a needlewoman. But the bridegroom also brought to the new establishment a certain amount of similar gear as the contribution of his own family. Though perhaps somewhat lacking in fancy and intricate stitchery of twin hearts which the bride-to-be lavished on her best quilts, the dowry gift of quilts and coverlets furnished by the bridegroom's mother represented a tradition which was likewise never ignored. They too were always exhibited before the appraising eyes of the feminine wedding guests, equally expert needlewomen.[9]

The Swedish novelist Fredrika Bremer wrote in a letter home in 1849:

I have been at a 'Bee'. And if you would know what this creature is in society here, then behold! If a family is reduced to poverty by fire or sickness, and the children are in want of clothes or anything else, a number of ladies of the neighborhood who are in good circumstances immediately get together at some place and sew for them. Such an assembly is called a bee![10]

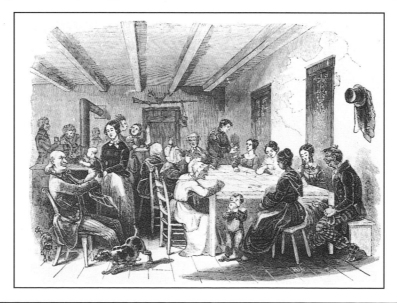

23

Girls and women began to write of their quilting experiences in their diaries. Lucy Larcom, a New England mill girl in the 1830s who became a well-known poet and writer, noted in her autobiography:

We learned to sew patchwork at school while we were learning the alphabet; and almost every girl large or small had a bed quilt of her own. I was not overfond of sewing, but I thought it best to begin mine early. So I collected a few squares of calico and undertook to put them together in my usual independent way, without asking direction. I liked assorting those little figured bits of cotton cloth, for they were scraps of gowns I had seen worn, and they reminded me of the persons who wore them. One fragment, in particular, was like a picture to me. It was a delicate pink and brown sea-moss pattern, on a white ground, a piece of dress belonging to my married sister, who was to me bride and angel in one.[5]

Domestic Life

By 1830 there were significant contrasts between the houses of ordinary and well-off families. The small farmers and settlers venturing westward continued to recreate earlier conditions of domestic life. Log cabins were the primary housing unit. They were small, with peeling bark, and cracks that needed to be continually filled with mud. Indeed, worn-out quilts were often cut into strips and stuffed into the chinks in the walls. Framed houses were rarely painted and were quite unlike the picture we have of tidy white Williamsburg dwellings. Open fireplaces, dirt roads and the proximity of the barnyard meant that houses were dusty and dirty, and most housewives engaged in a daily struggle against dirt.

These houses had no real physical partitions, but there were appointed spaces for eating, sleeping, working and socializing. At night the space would contract as families gathered by the hearth or oil lamp, and by day the workspace expanded to include the yard.[11] Houses with more than one room would be separated into private and public space, with one room for working and the other, the parlor or chamber, for both sleeping and entertaining. In New England this was the parents' bedchamber and also the formal entertaining space.

While most of the family might have slept under a woolen bedcover, perhaps patched or roughly quilted, the 'parlor' wasn't considered well furnished unless it had a 'best bed' covered with an appropriately 'best' bedcover or quilt. This may have given rise to the dual tradition of the 'plain' and the 'fancy' quilt: the former strictly utilitarian, the latter more decorative.

Conditions were, of course, very different among the wealthy. The English traveler and novelist of the time Frederick Marryat wrote that over their 'immense amount of territory . . . Americans lived in a great diversity of conditions running from a state of refinement in cities such as Boston and Philadelphia, down to one of positive barbarism in the backwoods'.[12]

Although by the early 1800s thousands of ordinary Americans had learned the techniques of log construction, most farmers expected to be able in a few years to move up to timber-framed houses; these were usually built by skilled craftsmen and were similar to those of earlier generations. But by 1830 a faster, more economic building technique called 'balloon framing' was developed.

'Balloon Framing' revolutionized the way Americans lived. This new construction method was fast and cheap and allowed a family of moderate means the luxury of a reasonably sized dwelling or barn. For the first time, women of the middle classes might have a proper room in which to entertain and to hold 'bees' or 'quiltins'.

Old Sturbridge Village Photo By Henry E. Peach

Size: 76 × 76″ / 193 × 193 cm

This method, which used a simple construction of two-by-four beams in a frame, was rapidly taken up in the growing cities and later in the countryside, and allowed for a greater democratization of housing.

By 1840, for the first time a family of average means had the opportunity to live in a house with more than two rooms. Such a house would have been furnished with factory-produced furniture and many other decorative items, including quilts. Goods that had been considered the

MARINER'S COMPASS
A circle with radiating points is a familiar idiom associated with many cultures. The earliest documents which call this design a Mariner's Compass come from eighteenth-century England and may refer to the wind roses found on sea charts. The pattern itself, often also called Sunburst or Rising Sun, was popular along the Eastern coastal region and reflects the close relationship between the colonists and the sea. This quilt was made in New York State in the 1860s. A pattern for it appears on pages 195–99.

trappings of luxury in earlier Colonial days gradually became more widespread. A larger living space and more chairs also provided the necessary physical space for larger gatherings, including quilting bees.

The New Pieced Block Quilt Style

While early quilts and coverlets made by the colonists were planned with consideration to the design as a whole, by the early 1800s more and more women were making individual blocks and then setting them together with strips or latticework, or with alternate white blocks. Although the central medallion-style quilt continued to be popular, this new block technique allowed for more experimentation with traditional design elements. Squares and triangles were pieced together in innovative ways. Stars grew more elaborate and 'sprouted serrated edges called feathers and grew to cover an entire top in the Star of Bethlehem design. Squares were organized into Irish Chains, and triangles into sawteeth. Circular patterns fractured into Mariner's Compasses and Sunflowers.'[13] The Mariner's Compass Quilt on page 25 is beautifully composed in the new pieced block style, with strong sashing framing each block. It was one of the most popular designs of the period.

Traditional appliqué designs in the central medallion tradition incorporating trees, flowers, leaves or vines became stylized into repeated patterns and were often encircled with elaborate borders. New patriotic designs such as the Federal Eagle were used as decorative elements on

household furnishings and quilts. No one knows who originated any particular design, or what these patterns were first called. But something new was happening – more women were making quilts and these quilts looked different and were made differently from the early English quilts that came before.

Much has been written about the character of the pieced block quilt, a design motif which distinguishes the American quilt as we recognize it today. Jonathan Holstein, a quilt historian, writes:

It is my feeling that two English styles were transmitted to America in the second half of the eighteenth century, and these furnished the ideas from which the block quilt sprang. The first style . . . was the high appliqué quilt, one modeled on the overall format of Indian quilts and palampores. In the borders and corners of such quilts we find regularly arranged design elements which are the direct ancestor of the block style. The other was the continuous mosaic piecedwork style . . . In such quilts the basic design is of a repeat block jammed together with others of its kind and arranged helter-skelter . . . This is most likely the other half of the block style's parentage, the two design ideas eventually combined in the overall block style.[14]

Earlier researchers had expressed the view that this new design motif was probably more functional since at the time rooms were too small and fabric too expensive for a complete quilt to be worked on as a whole. Other accounts speculate that the new American spirit of growth and energy was translated into inventive quilt designs. While these suggestions all ring true, probably no one explanation accounts for the emergence of this new type of quilt.

However, there were also more technical factors which help to account for the development and popularity of the pieced block quilt, and one of the most crucial of these was the growth of a native textile industry.

Factories and Technology

In England textile manufacturers had mechanized their operations by 1770, brought their workers together under one factory roof and used water, and later steam, power to develop new methods for spinning and weaving. This process revolutionized the textile industry and created an international market for British fabrics which had two powerful effects on America. Firstly it created a growing market for cheap raw cotton which American farmers in the South rushed to fill. Secondly, it created a desire by

Size: 75 × 80″/190 × 203 cm

American manufacturers to try to duplicate the new mechanized processes and establish a textile industry in their own country.

In 1790 an Englishman named Samuel Slater came to America in answer to an advertisement placed by a Philadelphia firm which was looking for an engineer to design cotton rollers. Slater had been trained as an apprentice cotton spinner in a mill in Derby owned by the inventor of the cotton-spinning machine, Sir Richard Arkwright. Slater was able to reproduce entirely from

COCKSCOMB AND CURRANT VARIATION

This exquisite quilt, from Pewee Valley, Kentucky, c.1850, is composed of nine large blocks, each bearing an unusual variation of the traditional Cockscomb and Currant pattern. The Wild Goose Chase geometric central design of each block is intriguing as a counterpoint to the floral appliqué surrounding it. An overall sense of focus is subtly retained by the maker who used a darker pink fabric to set off the center block.

CHINTZ AND APPLIQUÉ QUILTS

Traditional chintz and appliqué-style quilts continued to be popular well into the early nineteenth century, when many quilts were made out of fashionable dress materials, such as Chinese export and plain Quaker silks. 'Seventeenth-century French prints of flowers arranged in baskets, vases and bouquets as well as botanically correct eighteenth-century English prints established a decorative tradition that strongly influenced textile and wallpaper design during [this period].'[15] Many quilts from the southern states, including Maryland and particularly Baltimore, used a motif of flower-filled baskets. This tradition was strongly influenced by an Anglo-French heritage.

Appliquéd chintz cut-outs (broderie perse) became so fashionable that fabric printers in both America and London created special squares of cloth with popular motifs of birds, butterflies and flowers specially for the central medallion portion of these quilts.

Apart from the fancy furnishing prints and fine silks, many quilts were made using English dress fabrics of the 1810–30 period. These were for the most part small-scale, finely etched prints 'with minute leaf, flower and feather patterns among others, with mushroom, green or lilac as favorite colours'.[16] Such quilts would have been pieced using a simple variation of designs such as the Four-patch, Nine-patch, Star of Lemoyne, Double Irish Chain, Variable Star and Wild Goose Chase. The Nine-patch Quilt on page 21 displays the vivid imagery created by the juxtaposition of dress and furnishing prints. It was all the rage for both Euro-pean and American women to dress in the lively colors of these new chintzes. The patches in this quilt (see detail below) still retain their original glaze.

Fancy needlework was always encouraged on good quilts and there were a number of published needlework guides (mostly English) which gave directions for both plain and fine needlework. Miss Lambert's *Book of Needlework* of 1842 was one of the most popular manuals and was republished several times in Philadelphia and New York following its original London edition.[17]

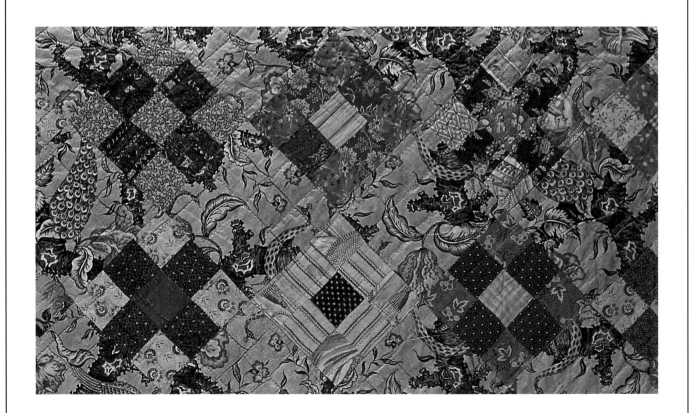

memory the plans for Arkwright's factory. Financed by a group of Boston businessmen, he designed and supervised the building of carding, drawing, roving and spinning machines in a wooden factory in Pawtucket, Rhode Island.[18]

In 1793, the same year that the Rhode Island wheels began turning, Eli Whitney invented the 'cotton gin' which mechanically removed the seeds from the cotton balls. The combination of these two processes effectively produced America's first national industry and by 1831 there were 800 cotton mills operating in America. Five

NINE-PATCH WITH FLYING GEESE BORDER
Imported English cottons were used to make this quilt, the earliest fabric on it dating from 1810. The design, with its squares and triangles, is typical of the many kinds of variations which were done during the period, while the rich madders and brown dyes, too, were popular colors in use at the time. The flying geese border adds richness and warmth to the delicate tones of the main body of the quilt.

After Eli Whitney invented the cotton gin in 1793, cotton production rose from its previous level of about 3,000 bales in 1790, to 10,000 bales in 1801. Despite this increased level of production, cotton prices remained high and the South boomed. However, while this stimulated the rest of the nation's economy, it also revived slavery, which had declined after the Revolution.

Courtesy: The National Museum of American History, Smithsonian Institution

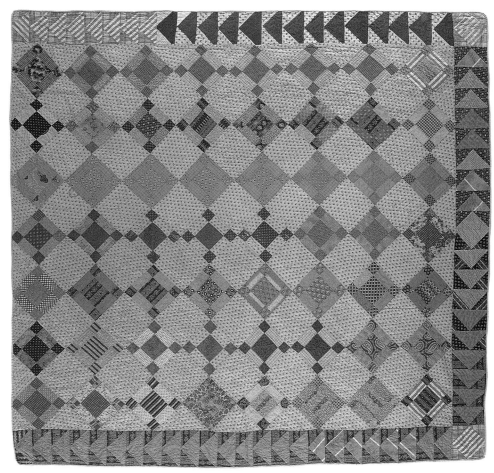

Size: 74 × 78″ / 188 × 198 cm

THE WHITE WORK QUILT

As fine white cotton and cotton thread became more widely available, White Work Quilts took the place of the older wholecloth quilts. These all-white quilts called for refined stitching techniques which could only be executed by the most experienced needlewomen. Elegantly quilted and often corded and stuffed, their overall design motif continued to utilize the central medallion. Often such quilts took years to complete and would most likely only have been worked on during daylight hours.

White Work Quilts were frequently associated with marriages, and in the early part of the nineteenth century white work represented the apogee of good taste.

While paying a visit to her aunt's house in Newburyport, Massachusetts, in the early 1800s, Caroline King described the bedroom:

The room was furnished in white painted furniture, the dimity drapery of windows and bed were white, the straw matting on the floor was white . . . The great white bed stood like a snowdrift, crowned with a thick white 'comforter' or 'blessing' as we called the 'down-puff' of those days.[19]

years later the industry produced 120 million yards of calico.

There were three major social effects of this early industrialization, the first being that demand for cotton turned the South into a one-crop economy and created a strong need for the cheap manpower necessary to raise such a labor-intensive crop. From the 1830s, slavery, which was already part of the Southern economy, grew at a record rate.

Secondly, because New England provided the appropriate physical conditions for industry – the small streams and swift-running rivers necessary for water power, and the coastal port facilities for transportation – it became the site for the nation's first industrial factories.

Finally, the abundance of cheap cotton prints made it possible for women of all social classes to take up quilting and ensured that the quilt would be made of cotton. This contributed to the democratization of the quilt.

This technical achievement coincided with the

growing social emphasis on home and family in force by 1840. A favorite magazine of the period, *The Young Lady's Friend*, expressed the popular middle-class sentiment that: 'All sorts of cotton fabrics are now so cheap that there is no excuse for any person's not being well provided.'

However, despite the abundance of domestic cotton prints, higher-grade English and French cottons continued to be imported. The early 1800s Nine-patch with Flying Geese Border Quilt pictured on page 29 is a good example of the variety of imported English cottons which were still being used in American quilts.

Home and family had become an important element of American life and quilting became closely associated with domesticity. As it increased in popularity, quilting began to reflect a new and very American style.

Women's Roles in the New Republic

The *New England Farmer* noted in 1835 that flax was hardly grown any more, being superseded by 'the extensive and daily use of cotton',[20] and by 1840 women in the Northeast were abandoning one of their main traditional household tasks – the manufacture of cloth – as factory production got under way. The loom and wool wheel were stored away, and farmers' wives and daughters used their newly freed time for sewing, making shirts, dresses, curtains, sheets and quilts in far greater quantities than their grandmothers had done. These changes came more slowly in the West and the South, where the production of cloth still remained an important part of the domestic economy.

The growth of the factory system and the expansion of cities diminished the importance of the family as a primary unit of economic production. This occurred first in the Northeast and then in the West, where non-agricultural jobs such as factory and office work occupied a growing percentage of the workforce. Because the husband was away for long hours, often in a new urban setting, it fell to women to take over day-to-day control of household affairs. Economic developments changed the domestic living patterns of early-nineteenth-century American women, especially among the growing white middle

classes. More household goods were made in factories, there were more servants and women tended to marry later and have fewer children. And whereas in the eighteenth century all crafts and trades practiced in early America included at least a few women, in the nineteenth century these occupations came to be viewed as unsuitable for women, or incompatible with their work in the home.

Economic conditions created a new domestic model for women popularly known as 'The Cult of True Womanhood'. The family became the repository of moral virtue for the new nation and the 'Mother' its curator. The concept of the 'home' was elevated into a Republican virtue which was celebrated in novels such as *Home* (1835), songs such as 'Home, Sweet Home', and paintings featuring domestic settings by painters like William Sydney Mount and Ernst Fischer.

Evangelists, novelists and politicians of the time elevated the concept of 'the Republican home' as a 'refreshing oasis of idealism in the barren desert of the commercial and industrial world'.[21] Women were advised that their true place was in the home and that 'in the home women were not only the highest adornment of civilization, but they were supposed to keep busy at morally uplifting work'. Such work necessarily included housework, and in particular needlework. America, in the throes of unheard-of material advance, called upon women to maintain a well-ordered home life as a stabilizing influence in society.

In the early part of the nineteenth century a new idea of motherhood had evolved. Evangelical preachers maintained that motherhood prepared the child for salvation and that the country depended upon the strength of character and self-control that only mothers could instill in their children.

The dual concept of a woman's place being in the home and the necessity of her subordination to her husband was a message repeated in thousands of churches across the country. 'Ministers used the concept of "women's sphere" to esteem female importance, while at the same time containing it. In their sermons of the 1830s the theme of order in the family and society took precedence, vividly emphasizing the necessity for women to be subordinate to and dependent on their husbands.'[22]

It became a well-applauded feminine talent to make something beautiful out of a basket of old scraps, and the creation of a hand-made quilt symbolized the apogee of womanhood. 'The model Republican woman was competent and confident. She could resist the vagaries of fashion; she was rational, benevolent, independent, self-reliant and dedicated to the service of civic virtue.'[23] Her home was to be a warm, comforting and beautiful sanctuary away from the harsh world of trade and commercialism.

There was a spate of literature on child-rearing and domesticity, which found a broad following among well-to-do and 'middling' women. Lydia Maria Child, one of the most important authors of the day, whose books went into dozens of editions, and whose articles appeared in every major magazine and periodical, wrote in *The American Frugal Housewife*:

The true economy of housekeeping is simply the art of gathering up all of the fragments of TIME as well as MATERIALS. Nothing should be thrown away so long as it is possible to make any use of it, however trifling that use may be; and whatever be the size of the family, every member should be employed either in earning or saving money. In this point of view, patchwork is good economy.[24]

This separation of society along lines of gender created a unique sociological setting for the early- and mid-nineteenth century:

The attributes of true womanhood, by which a woman judged herself and was judged by her husband, her neighbors and society could be divided into four cardinal virtues – piety, purity, submissiveness and domesticity. Put them all together and they spelled mother, daughter, sister, wife-woman.[27]

When Sarah Joseph Hale, another popular author of the day, assumed the editorship of Boston's *Ladies' Magazine* in 1827 she proceeded to disregard the traditional emphasis on saccharine love stories and sentimental poetry and converted it into an organ for 'female improvement'. In mid-1830 when Louise Godey suggested to Hale that they merge the *Ladies' Magazine* with her own

'The Attributes of True Womanhood'

periodical, *Lady's Book*, Hale accepted and became the editor for *Godey's Ladies' Magazine* for the next forty years. This publication was to be one of the most influential magazines of the century, promoting the concepts of enlightened domesticity to a growing readership throughout the country.

Thus, with the emphasis on the home and domestic skills, the hand-made quilt came to be an important expression of national sentiment. As the American idea of democracy took root, and more families were able to acquire those material and cultural possessions which had for centuries been the domain of the rich, so the possession of a beautiful quilt became an accepted social aspiration.

There was, however, a new development in American life in the early nineteenth century which gave rise to another role for women. The growth of the cotton industry in New England occasioned the recruitment of children and farm girls to work as factory operatives. The experience of one mill in particular, at Lowell, Massachusetts, deeply affected the way many young women thought about both their personal and public roles in American society.

DOMESTIC ECONOMY

Catherine Beecher, sister of the novelist Harriet Beecher Stowe, wrote in her treatise on domestic economy in 1841:

When a little girl first begins to sew, her mother can promise her a small bed, as soon as she has sewed a patched quilt for it, and then a bedstead, as soon as she has sewed the sheets and cases for the pillows; and then a large doll to dress as soon as she has made the undergarments; and thus go on till the whole contents of the babyhouse are earned by the needle and skill of its little owner. Thus, the task of learning to sew will become a pleasure; and every new toy will be earned by useful exertion.[25]

Harriet Beecher Stowe, in one of the most popular nineteenth-century novels entitled *The Minister's Wooing*, writes even more specifically about quilts:

The good wives of New England, impressed with that thrifty orthodoxy of economy which forbids to waste the merest trifle, had a habit of saving every scrap clipped out in the fashioning of household garments, and these they cut into fanciful patterns and constructed of them rainbow shapes and quaint traceries, the arrangement of which became one of their few fine arts . . . Collections of these tiny fragments were always ready to fill an hour when there was nothing else to do; and as the maiden chattered with her beau, her busy flying needle stitched together all those pretty bits which little in themselves were destined, by gradual unions and accretions, to bring about at last substantial beauty, warmth and comfort.[26]

The Lowell Idea

The Boston associates who financed the early mills developed a particular system of employment which corresponded to earlier enlightenment beliefs. They aimed to set up 'model' factories which allowed a young woman both to earn money and to improve herself. The women stayed in company-run boarding houses, each presided over by a matron who looked after her girls, insuring that they 'show that they are penetrated by a laudable love of temperance and virtue'.[28] This carefully planned manufacturing community was designed to bring together the ideals of Republican simplicity and industrial capitalism.

The most well known of these factories was the one established in 1822 by the Merrimack Manufacturing Company at Lowell, Massachusetts. Here, girls from all over New England would come to work for a year or two at the mill. They earned between $2.50 and $3.25 a week, half of which went to room and board. An early promotional pamphlet for Lowell reads: 'The manufacturing works are interspersed with groves and woodlands so as to afford a prospect sublime and beautiful.'

The company offered many cultural and educational opportunities: a lyceum arranged free lectures on various topics and there were circulating libraries and 'improvement circles' to promote writing and public discussion. Yet although 85 per cent of the factory workers were female, not one of them held a supervisory position.

Charles Dickens was impressed by his visit to Lowell and by the female workers. He wrote: 'They were all well dressed . . . they were healthy in appearance . . . and had the manners and deportment of young women . . . the rooms in which they worked were as well ordered as themselves.'[29]

Lucy Larcom, whose mother ran one of the boarding houses in Lowell, entered the mills at the age of thirteen. Later in her autobiography she recalled the generally pleasant conditions where the girls put plants on the mills' window-sills, told stories and gossiped during the day, and read Shakespeare and Milton in the evening.

Through public readings and well-attended lectures, the mills had inadvertently introduced these young and impressionable New England farm girls to many of the important political ideas of the day. They heard talks given by the abolitionist poet John Greenleaf Whittier, signed anti-slavery petitions and developed a wide inter-

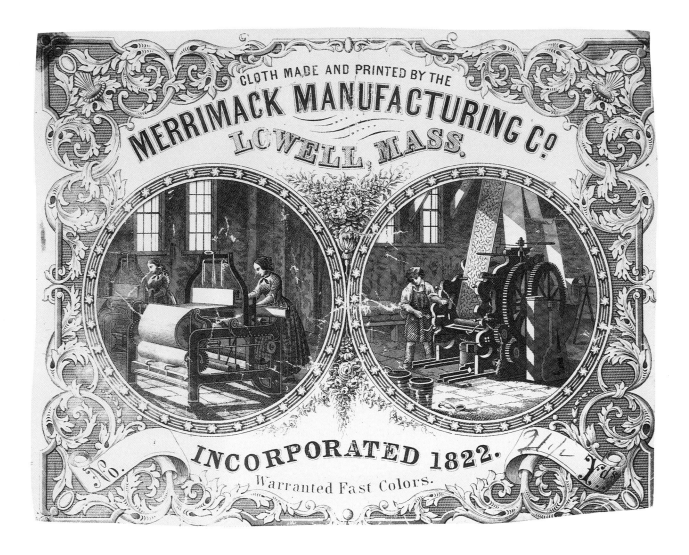

In Lowell, Massachusetts the first workers in the new cotton manufacturing industry were women and children, and despite the idyllic setting of pretty red factories in landscaped grounds, complete with potted plants on the windowsills, early mill girls experienced the impersonal nature of work that came with industrial development. In the journal which these young women published, The Lowell Offering, *many wrote about the continually ringing factory bell. One young worker, Hannah Gordon, gave this account:*

The factory bell woke her at 4:00 in the morning. Taking her breakfast along, she readied the looms by 5:00, when the bell signaled the start of work. At 7:30 it announced the breakfast break . . . At noon it rang the half-hour lunch period, and at 12:30 it summoned them back. It dismissed them at 7:30 each evening . . . At 10:00 the bell rang for bed and lights out. Sundays it called them to church. [30]

Many millworkers also wrote songs and poems about the bell for the journal:

It was morning and the factory bell
Had sent forth its early call,
And many a weary one was there,
Within the dull factory wall.

And amidst the clashing noise and din
Of the ever beating loom,
Stood a fair young girl with throbbing brow
Working her way to the tomb. [31]

est in popular reform movements of the period.

However, in 1834 and again in 1836, there were strikes over wage cuts and rent increases, and in 1845 a Female Labor Reform Association was formed at Lowell to effect a shorter working day. But despite the protests, which aroused a substantial degree of national attention, conditions at Lowell slowly deteriorated and began to bear a grim resemblance to the factory towns in England.

The authors of *Hearts and Hands*, a recent American book which analyzes the influence of women and quilts on American society, note that the experience of the New England mill girls marked the beginning of a major change in the relationship of women to textile work. In the 1845 *Lowell Offering*, a literary journal which the mill girls wrote and produced, an essay was published called 'The Patchwork Quilt'. This essay, one of the earliest descriptions of quiltmaking in American literature, is described as 'both a celebration and a eulogy to pre-industrial work processes'. In it the author describes the quilt as something which was personal and lovingly made, thus contrasting with the impersonality of factory work.[32] It is from this period on that the American quilt became associated with a nostalgia for bygone pioneer days.

The Lowell experience also demonstrated that the paternalistic and enlightened views which led to its founding were irreconcilable with the demands of an expanding economy. The mill owners and managers were not able to provide both good wages and extra services for their female employees and make a profit. Rapid industrial development began to outstrip the old agricultural order and change the character of American life. The days of Republican democracy, based on farming and outlined by Thomas Jefferson, were beginning to fade. America's new wealth had created a new social hierarchy, and with it came the need for a new cultural setting reflecting a distinct American heritage.

New American Culture and Quiltmaking

By the 1830s, artists, writers and popular entertainers began to look at and celebrate the legacy of American, rather than European, history. James Fenimore Cooper helped to create a native mythology with novels such as *The Pioneers* (1823) and *The Last of the Mohicans* (1826). Washington Irving produced in his world-famous *The Sketch Book* (1819) a memorable group of folk characters from the Hudson River Valley, including Rip Van Winkle and Ichabod Crane, who were later depicted by a number of major artists. There was also a cast of more true-to-life popular frontier heroes such as Davy Crockett, the rough and ready Tennessee backwoodsman, and Mike Fink, the legendary riverboatman. Stories and songs about these two and their exploits and colorful language were published in popular almanacs, newspapers and broadsides.

This celebration of regional types was also portrayed in the work of serious artists like George Caleb Bingham, who painted works depicting scenes from everyday life in Missouri. Popular plays featuring local 'types' such as *The Yankee in England* and *Yankee in Time* as well as popular songs like 'Green Mountain Boy' became part of the new American vocabulary.

This aesthetic principle which sought to emphasize the new, the characteristic and the original, created a national consciousness and culture which was, for the first time, distinct from Europe. Its influence was part of the American woman's everyday experience and as such must have played an interactive role in her own artistic endeavors. For what women were expressing through the creative act of quiltmaking, in the stylistic innovations which they were spontaneously introducing, was reinforced by a new cultural independence. A host of imaginative new patterns and designs, many based on local folklore and regional characteristics, were to flourish by the middle of the nineteenth century.

—3—
A Country in Transition

T he mid-nineteenth century saw an increase in the popularity of quiltmaking. Women in all parts of the country, from the East coast through the Ohio and Mississippi valleys, to the plains and prairie states in the West, stitched a variety of new types of quilt. Quilting had come into its own.

This was due to specific technological and social developments; innovations such as the sewing machine, the improvement in roller printing for fabrics, and the development of dye chemistry continued to create better quality and more affordable material. At the same time, a revived spirit of Protestantism among the growing middle classes engendered an increasing network of women's sewing circles, often associated with the church, as well as benevolent and reform associations. Quilts were made to benefit worthy causes. This, coupled with a continuing tradition of bees, quiltings, get-togethers, fairs and auctions, endowed quilts with new social meaning.

The functional, everyday, plain, patched or tied quilt was reproduced in the conditions of scarcity which existed in frontier life. The lure of

Size: 88 × 94″ / 223 × 238 cm

PREVIOUS PAGE: *UNION ARMY ENCIRCLED STAR*
This complicated and unusual pattern was designed
by someone with a remarkable sense of geometry
and proportion. The quilt is rumored to have been.
made c.1860 at a 'Bee' in the North to raise money
for the Union cause. A pattern for it appears on
pages 230–34.

Size: 72 × 76″ / 183 × 193 cm

ABOVE: *STARS*
This rare, if not wholly individual pattern was made
in Texas in 1855. The quilt is intricately pieced with
a galaxy of small stars surrounding a central lone
star. The fabrics, some imported from England,
others from American mills, appear as a stunning
array of colors which are linked by the overall
strength of the design.

Courtesy: Sculptor, Dame Elizabeth Frink

On careful examination, one can still read the 1880s newspaper advertisements in this nineteenth-century English hexagon quilt. English silk template constructions continued in the mid-nineteenth century to be published in many best-selling American magazines.

Courtesy: Màureen Moriarty

cheap land had drawn hundreds of wagon trains over the Appalachian Mountains, thus constituting the first major wave of westward migration. Despite the isolated living conditions, records indicate that whenever possible women also continued to get together to make more intricate quilts in these western territories. East of the Mississippi, however, the wealth created through the expansion of industry suggested new domestic possibilities. Homes became more elaborate and 'style' in both furnishing and dress became an important consideration.

The majority of quilt patterns from this period reflect the changing domestic circumstances in the eastern states. New designs bearing imaginative and romantic-sounding names such as Philadelphia Pavement, Rose Wreath and Princess Feather were created in colorful calico prints. However, some patterns related to the westward migration, and names such as Rocky Road to Kansas, Prairie Rose and Indian Hatchet are equally evocative of the time. Innovation was highly valued and women spent many hours developing interpretations of popular designs. The Cockscomb and Currant Quilt on page 27 is a charming example of the original variations which were developed around specific patterns.

Influential publications such as *Godey's Ladies' Magazine* – which had reached a circulation of 150,000 by 1850 – published mostly English hexagon quilting patterns which recommended silk template construction (see page 79). But despite the advice from magazines such as these, American piece block quiltmaking traditions flourished

Size: 76 × 74″ / 193 × 188 cm

PRINCESS FEATHER
The feather design has been a well-known quilting pattern in England and America for generations. The Princess Feather quilt, particularly set out in fashionable reds, greens and yellows, enjoyed enormous popularity in the United States during the nineteenth century. This fascinating example, which comes from New England, has an added flourish of beautiful stuffed work in both the vine border and center nine blocks. A pattern for it appears on pages 172–77.

and patterns and ideas continued to be exchanged locally among women.

Rapidly shifting patterns of geographical settlement during these years, coupled with more clearly defined social roles for men and women, drew women together both physically and emotionally. 'Most eighteenth- and nineteenth-century women lived in a world bounded by home, church, and the institution of visiting. Women helped each other with domestic chores and in times of sickness, sorrow and trouble. Urban and town women were able to devote some of virtually every day to visits, teas or shopping trips with other women. Rural women developed a pattern of more extended visits that lasted weeks and sometimes months.'[1] The strong ties between women within a community or family setting were often expressed in needlework. An Album or Friendship Quilt, for example, where friends or family members each signed a block (either by embroidery or in indelible ink) to serve as a lasting memory, was often given as a memento to a family embarking on one of the overland trails.

The place of the quilt in the hearts and minds of the American people was thus confirmed in the middle of the last century. Despite the influence of English patterns, the quilt was now defined not by European traditions but rather by a new American spirit of growth and optimism.

The Album Quilt

An Album Quilt is composed of a number of separately designed blocks incorporated into an overall quilt. The blocks themselves are often pictorial (although there are examples of pieced Album Quilts), stitched in the appliqué technique and generally sewn by individual members of a family or group contributing jointly to the project. There is a special social significance in the Album or Friendship Quilt in that it was made to commemorate or celebrate a particular social event which was important to its makers.

During the period 1840 to 1860 several types of Album Quilt were popular. These included the Friendship Quilts, Presentation Quilts, Bride's Album Quilts and Autograph Quilts. The remarkable Album Quilt on page 43 highlights the life of an entire family and is beautifully composed, featuring a combination of highly stylized, folk-like and symbolic blocks.

The most well known of this type of quilt is undoubtedly the Baltimore Album Quilt. According to historian Dena S. Katzenberg, Baltimore Album Quilts are:

. . . prized for their unusual designs, exquisite craftsmanship, and striking beauty representing floral motifs, ships, churches, Baltimore monuments, and historic events. These designs in printed cottons have been applied to individual cloth squares, measuring 16 to 18 inches, which are then sewn together in series to form quilts as large as ten feet square. It is the assembling of these blocks, many of which are inscribed with the contributor's name, that lead to the appelation 'Album Quilts', since each quilt square is similar in spirit to the pages of an autograph album. The most distinguishing characteristic of the finest of these quilts, made in Baltimore between 1846 and 1852, is the imaginative manner in which the printed cottons were pieced together to suggest texture, shading, and contour.[2]

Baltimore, Maryland, was the third largest seaport in the United States at the time. It was also the most important East Coast port used for exporting domestic cotton and for importing a wide variety of English, French, German and Swiss fabrics and trims. Baltimore therefore amassed a great deal of wealth quite quickly, and these conditions gave rise to a leisured class of women who had sufficient time, money and materials for the creation of such intricate needlework. In addition, professional needlewomen in Baltimore offered their services for a fee to both design and make the intricate blocks which would be stitched into Album and other types of quilts.

These included the Presentation Quilt, which dates from the early 1800s and would have been made specifically to present to some well-known or respected figure as a suitable testimonial to his or her good deeds or work. Also, the Friendship Quilt, examples of which – often with identifying names, dates, locations and informative quotes and sayings – have provided a rich field for quilt scholars. These quilts, recalled from the usual realm of anonymity, have offered tangible evidence about the lives, relationships and concerns of particular women or groups of women at a particular time. Historian Ricky Clark, drawing on a study of Friendship Quilts, argues that 'by studying large numbers of such quilts we learn that mid-nineteenth-century women valued religion, the family and female communality, sentimentalized friendship, commemorated events and dreaded separations'.[3]

Barbara Brackman has traced the spread of Album Quilts in a detailed study. She notes that 'the album quilt craze surfaced in the mid-Atlantic area from Trenton, New Jersey, down through Philadelphia and Delaware to Baltimore, Maryland. By 1845 the signature quilt spread north to New York and New England and south to Virginia and the Carolinas, and later to the rest of the country.'[4] After 1860, however, the fad for jointly made Album Quilts faded, and those made in the period following the Civil War are often the work of a single woman and would be autographed by the maker's friends and relations.

The thematic element central to these various forms of the Album Quilt is clearly a social one, which strongly addresses not only a woman's role in a changing society but more precisely her perceptions of and responses to that role. These quilts were more than simply a creative expression involving the juxtaposition of colored fabric and design. Quilts had become, for thousands of women, both an artistic and a personal statement reflecting the demands of a society in transition.

ALBUM QUILT

This remarkable Album Quilt was made largely by members of the Ketcham family from Pennington, New Jersey, in 1862, and through state census and biographical records, the following information on the provenance of the quilt has been traced.

Three Ketcham brothers originally emigrated from England to Long Island, New York sometime in the eighteenth century, one of whom moved to Pennington. Most names on the quilt are familiar New Jersey names and include George and Louisa Ketcham. George was a native-born New Jersey farmer, and it is known that in 1860, when he was thirty-five and Louisa was thirty-eight, they lived in Mercer County, N.J., with their two children, Margaret and Mary. Among various other Ketchams inscribed on the quilt is the widow Catherine, possibly George's aunt or mother, who lived on the farm next to theirs.

Each block of the quilt is composed of different motifs, and several are inscribed in indelible ink with sayings, poems and biblical references. Many of the blocks are signed 'from your Aunt', 'from your cousin', or 'from your Mother' or 'Father'. The fabrics used are a combination of fine chintzes and glazed and plain cottons, often featuring intricate trapunto work. There is elaborate detail in the gold embroidery thread, for example, which outlines the baskets and the 23rd Psalm, as well as in the black embroidery surrounding the Federal Eagle.

There is some speculation that this quilt was made for a young Ketcham who was going off to war, and this is borne out by the central block which reads:

My son, hear the instructions of thy Father and Forsake not the love of thy Mother

On other blocks there are also references to death:

May angels twine for thee
A wreath of immortality

And references to poetry:

May your life be like a
Summer cloud floating in brightness
Until it floats in heaven

This stunning work testifies to the national penchant for documenting in quilts the close bonds which existed among families and communities during the nineteenth century.

Size: 80 x 90"/203 x 228.6 cm

This oil painting is entitled 'Madonna of the Prairie', and the beatific figure of the young woman sitting in a Conestoga wagon, presumably heading to a farm out West, expresses the kind of romantic sentiment that has been historically associated with pioneer America. What most people didn't realize, however, was that, in reality, the 'Madonna' was hard-working and long-suffering. In 1862, for example, the Department of agriculture published a study on the condition of farm women: 'In plain language, in the civilization of the latter half of the nineteenth century, a farmer's wife . . . is a laboring drudge . . . it is safe to say that on three farms out of four, the wife works harder, endures more, than any other place; more than the husband, more than the farmhand.' In such relentless physical conditions, it is all the more remarkable that these women found the time to sew quilts with such care, and often eloquence. Yet stitchery often provided them with a much needed creative outlet.

Courtesy: Buffalo Bill Historical Society, Cody, Wyoming

Pioneer Women

Many different ethnic groups played a role in the settlement of the West, including families from Germany and Scandinavia, while the very poor and dispossessed tended to settle in crowded urban centers. Traveling west in a Conestoga wagon with a yoke of eight oxen and supplies for a year took a considerable investment and those Americans who chose to undertake the arduous journey tended to be members of the middle classes.

While traveling across the prairies, plains and mountains – remarkable journeys which were fraught with hardship and death – women considered it important to wear freshly ironed and starched white aprons in an effort from day one to transplant their established ways and lifestyles to the new land. Although there was little time to make a quilt on the journey, nonetheless a few records exist of wagon train quilts. A recent publication, entitled *Ho for California: Pioneer Women and Their Quilts*, records a quilt called 'Road to California', which was made by Mary Margaret Hezlep during a seven-month trip to California by covered wagon in 1859. Inked into the fabric are the names of members of the wagon train from Iowa, Illinois and Ohio, as well as notations such as 'Left Hamilton, April 15, 1859' and 'Crossed the Plains'.

For the most part, however, quilts would have been assembled by family members and friends back home for the settlers to use in their new homes; they 'did heroic service on the journey itself. Thick comforts and quilts were used to line wagons. They were wrapped around fragile china, used to pad and soften the wagon seats and to protect the exposed sides of the wagon during Indian attacks. And they were used to bury the dead.'[5]

Lillian Schlissel, who has documented and researched the lives of thousands of pioneer women from diaries and other original sources, concludes that 'there is scarcely a diary written during the 1840s which does not record the death of a father or husband or child or wife along the way'.[6] Wrapping a loved one in a quilt and burying them in a grave which would, it was hoped, go unnoticed by the Indians added to the

storehouse of sentiment and emotion attached to the quilt.

It was considered a woman's duty not only to maintain the stability of the family unit in the new environment but also to provide a measure of refinement and domestic comfort to their crude homes. Rather than leave behind aspects of life that they regarded as civilized, women tried to recreate them on the prairie. 'They would often add rag rugs, wallpaper the sod walls with newsprint, crochet dainty covers for slop jars, and hang curtains fashioned from newspapers, old sheets or petticoats.'[8]

It is clear from many diary entries, as well as from romanticized folklore, that like their counterparts in New England, frontier women spent hours stitching the curtains, table linens and quilts which would add a touch of domestic and psychological comfort to the home – which might be a log cabin or sod hut. Remembering her mother's quilts, India Simmons from Kansas wrote:

Such quilts! Appliquéd patterns of flowers and ferns, put on with stitches so dainty as to be almost invisible, pieced quilts in baskets or sugarbowl or intricate star pattern, each one quilted with six or more spools of thread, the patterns of the quilting brought out in bare relief by padding with cotton each leaf or petal or geometric design . . .[14]

The Homestead Act of 1862 required a settler to live on his claim for five years in order to perfect his title. This gave a character to farm life in the West which was very different for the old-world peasants who had lived in tightly knit villages. The average distance of half a mile between farms meant isolation and loneliness for many women, and in order to adjust to their new lives, pioneer women worked to establish their own schools and churches and created a network of associations which would provide female companionship. Both get-togethers to make a quilt and the quilt itself served important social functions and provided women with a material means to soften the harsh reality of the frontier. The popularity of the Album and Friendship Quilts during this period testifies to the importance of personal bonds, both within families and among women.

Courtesy: Solomon D. Butcher Collection, Nebraska State Historical Society

Central to pioneer survival and success was the institution of the family, wherein each individual was forced by circumstance to work in a continuous and cohesive way. This carefully staged photograph displays the material possessions of a successful Nebraskan family. The wagon, horses and outbuildings, as well as the striking quilt thrown over a hitching post, would all have been acquired over the years and are here proudly exhibited.

This piece of 'boomer' literature speaks for itself: Missouri Is Free. Advertisements like this helped to attract over 2.5 million immigrants, who by 1860 had fled from the hardships of Europe, as well as settlers from the eastern states. Alexis de Tocqueville, a well-known European diarist who published popular accounts of his travels in America, noted that 'In America, men never stay still.' Many of the people who came to Missouri, in fact, were Germans who learned farming methods from their American neighbors. German women also learned to quilt, and thus began a longstanding tradition of quiltmaking.

Courtesy: The National Museum of American History, Smithsonian Institution

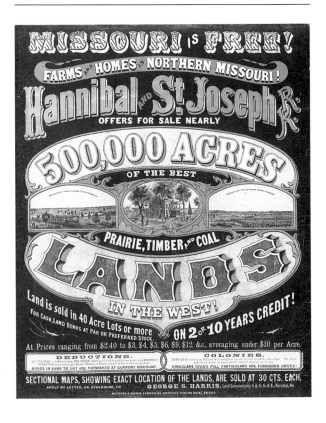

Frontier women were responsible for every aspect of clothing manufacture, from planting the seeds of the flax or cotton, to carding and spinning the yarn and dyeing, bleaching, cutting and sewing the cloth. Spinning was a skill which involved a high degree of hand and eye coordination and this skill was passed down through generations from mother to daughter. Even after the development of manufactured cotton in the mid-nineteenth century, many women in the frontier states and territories continued to spend long hours spinning and weaving cloth.

Courtesy: Missouri Historical Society

Country and agricultural fairs, where quilts were prominently displayed and judged in contests, became an important feature of mid-nineteenth-century life. Initially, fairs tended to be livestock shows for the benefit of local farmers. Then, early in the nineteenth century, women were encouraged to enter examples of their domestic efforts in competitions, and by the middle of the century quilt competitions came to take pride of place in fairs. The *Dollar Missouri Journal* of 1855 reported:

The number of quilts and counterpanes greatly exceeded that of last year, showing that our fairs are a healthy stimulus to the hands of our fair ones.[15]

Domestic Life

Women on the frontier continued to spend long hours on mundane traditional tasks. During the first half of the nineteenth century, domestic manufacture of thread and cloth had given way to industrial production. However, while home manufacturing declined in the Midwest and East from 1840–60, it remained an important activity for frontier women, and spinning wheels and looms were used universally in the western states. Martha Minto, recalling her first winter in Oregon in the mid-1840s, wrote in her diary:

I think there was only one bolt of Calico in Oregon when we came here. That was all the cloth we had for dresses at that time. That was sold for fifty cents a yard. It was very poor quality calico . . . The next summer . . . [I] got a little piece of blue drilling that made . . . a covering. And that was about all; it could not be considered dresses, but it was so [I was] covered. [I] did not have any ruffles . . .[16]

AUNT JANE OF KENTUCKY

Eliza Calvert Hall, in the popular series of nostalgic reminiscences, *Aunt Jane of Kentucky*, which were published in the late nineteenth century, writes about quilting:

You see, you start out with just so much caliker; you don't go to the store and pick it out and buy it, but the neighbors will give you a piece here and a piece there and you will have a piece left every time you cut a dress, and you take out what happens to come and that's like predestination. But when it comes to cuttin' out, why, you're free to choose your pattern. You can give the same kind o' pieces to two persons, and one'll make a 'nine patch' and one'll make a 'wild goose chase', and there'll be two quilts made out o' the same kind o' pieces, and jest as different as they can be, and that is just the way with livin'. The Lord sends in the pieces, but we can cut 'em and put 'em together pretty much to suit ourselves.[13]

According to accounts published in Glenda Riley's book, The Female Frontier, *the prices for some of the goods in this advertisement of the 1850s were as follows: 100lbs of flour: $2.25; 1 yard of gingham: 30 cents; 1 neck ribbon: 23 cents; 1 gallon of molasses: 60 cents; 5 spools of thread: 15 cents; 5 yards of calico: 37 cents; a calico dress: $1.25.*

Courtesy: The National Museum of American History, Smithsonian Institution

GOOD NEWS

—— FOR THE ——

PEOPLE!

The fact that there is a place in Franklin

County where Ready Pay buyers of Goods do not have to pay fifteen per cent extra to cover bad debts.

A. L. TYLER

Has made his arrangements complete for doing a READY

PAY BUSINESS EXCLUSIVELY; believing that to be the true way of doing business at the present day. The time has come in these days of Steam Power when the old Credit System can be done away with, and a new order of things take its place, as almost everything in the country is ready cash. I think my old customers and the public generally will acquiesce in my arrangements and will prefer to pay for their goods when they purchase them, and not be compelled to pay for long credits and poor debts, and thereby save themselves a handsome profit by so doing; as I can afford to sell goods at a much less price than those who follow along in the old way of doing business.

I am now receiving and opening a very large STOCK of FOREIGN and DOMESTIC

DRY GOODS,

which have been selected with great care and with due regard for the wants of this community. It will be kept up with such additions from time to time as sales may require.

The following is a list of some of the articles kept on hand.—
For particulars call at the Store and examine Goods and Prices.

Rich and Medium Price Black and Fancy Dress Silks; Black Silk and Bay State Shawls; Dress and Cloak Trimmings, all widths and qualities; Gloves and Hosiery in great variety. In Dress Goods everything new and desirable: Thibets, Wool Plaids, Cotton and Wool do, All Wool DeLaines, Cotton and Wool do, in Plain Stripes, Plaids and Figures from 12 1-2c. upwards; Alpaccas, Lyonese Cloths, Cashmeres and DeBieges; Prints, a splendid assortment from 4 1-2 to 11c. per yard. A good assortment of Mourning Goods, Ladies' Collars and Under Sleeves, Opera Hoods, Bleached and Brown Sheetings; and prices that defy all competition. Denims, Tickings, Tweeds and Doeskins, Fancy Cassimeres and Vestings.

READY-MADE CLOTHING,

Consisting of OVER COATS, DRESS, SACK and FROCK COATS, Pants and Vests, made at one of the best Clothing Establishments in New Hampshire. Also, Merino Under-shirts and Drawers, Gents' COLLARS, Suspenders, Buck Gloves and Mittens, Hats, Caps, Trunks and Valices, Buffalo Robes, Umbrellas, &c., &c.

Crockery, Glass and Hard Ware of almost every variety.
BENNINGTON STONE WARE.

GROCERIES.

Head Quarters for everything in the Grocery Line. Sugars, Molasses, Teas, Coffee, Saleratus, Ginger, Pepper and Allspice; Oils, Salt, Codfish, Flour, constantly on hand at the lowest market prices. The fact is, I will sell a good Tea less than any man does sell the same quality in this County.

I AM BOUND TO SELL AT THE LOWEST POSSIBLE PRICE.

All kinds of Produce taken in exchange for Goods at cash value.

I wish to be distinctly understood that I shall keep no Books
to charge Goods, consequently I can deliver no goods until paid for.

My Motto is "READY PAY" on delivery of Goods, as my present prices will not allow me to take any risk.

All persons in want of Goods are requested to call and examine Goods and Prices before purchasing elsewhere, and satisfy themselves of the benefits of the READY PAY SYSTEM.

Charlemont, Nov. 18, 1855.

Most clothing at this time was made out of hand-carded wool and hand-spun linen. If cotton was available it was woven with wool warp to make jean. 'The finest homespun, the pure linen bleached scores of times, was reserved for coverlets, tablecloths, appliqué and stitchery.' If store-bought cloth was available – cotton or woolen broadcloth, gingham or calico – it was used for 'dress-up' clothing, and quilts, which were considered, even in isolated and often primitive living conditions, as the highest material expression of a woman's culture.[17]

While most women on the frontier didn't have the luxury of seriously considering fashion and had to contend with a shortage of new garments and fabrics, they managed either to trade trinkets with the Indians for moccasins, use buffalo hides for robes or shoes, or recycle old clothing or household items.

Alzada Baxter, emigrating to Kansas in the late 1850s, used some amusing ingenuity, as recalled later by a family friend:

The problem of trousers was another thing to be taken care of. When the Baxters came to Kansas they expected to have large grain crops and consequently brought a large number of grain sacks with them. The name 'Baxter' was stamped in red across the sacks. Mrs Baxter cut them up and made trousers for her husband from the material. There was no danger of him being lost with his name brightly stamped across the seat of his trousers.[18]

Nonetheless, many of the women moving westward tried to uphold the standards and ideals of mid-nineteenth-century domestic life. Successful farming and trade allowed second-generation settlers a certain degree of social mobility. Lucy Malick, whose family had migrated to Oregon, wrote in April 1852 to her sister in Ohio: 'I shall be pleased to send you patrns of every new thing that comes in fashion such as wearing aparal . . . I have got me some peach Cambric of which I am making a sun bonet . . . and a small peace of dark Calico for aprons.' [sic] In February 1853 she wrote of how she was now moving in social circles and attending 'grand quiltens' with as many as '15 ladeys'. She and her husband were living like 'the highest grandees'.[19] Quilting on the frontier had come to symbolize the highest tradition not only of domestic but also of social respectability.

A MEMORIAL QUILT

Throughout the nineteenth century quilts were made in remembrance of a lost loved one, and might be used during a period of mourning. Often such quilts were made in black or gray, decorated with appliquéd coffins or with a dart motif (symbolizing the black darts of death), or they were sewn from pieces of the deceased's clothing. In Nebraska, Dorothy Boettner told of her grandmother's experience in the late nineteenth century when her baby daughter died:

Grandmother was so laid out by the death, that she was unable to go on with her life. And so Grandpa ran or took a horse over to the neighboring couple, an older couple, who had lost their only child many years ago. [The neighbor] gathered up scraps of velvet and silk and old linsey-wool and strands of thread and showed Grandma how to fashion pieces and then embroider flowers, birds and so forth on it. [Grandma] patiently put them together . . . She tacked the flowers or fruit from a seed catalog and then embroidered over it, then picked out the paper behind. That's how they did, they didn't have any patterns in those days you know . . . Each night she would work by the light of the lamp . . . Gradually she got better . . . Grandma got hold of her life again and finished the quilt and folded it up and put it away. . . When we'd ask to see the quilt, she'd get it out, but she never used it because the memory in each scrap would tell her about her baby daughter.[7]

AFRO-AMERICAN QUILTS

In the frontier towns, the same standards held true for other groups as for the predominantly white settlers. Black families had migrated West as early as 1794. The highest concentration of blacks was in Missouri, which was admitted to the Union as a slave state in 1821. All the other prairie areas – Iowa, Indiana, Illinois and Minnesota – prohibited slavery. Anti-slavery sentiment ran high in many of these areas and the underground railroad, which facilitated the escape of slaves from the South, flourished.

The work that allowed the most upward social mobility for black males and their families in non-slave states seems to have been barbering. This and other occupations generated the income necessary for a black woman to have the leisure time to participate extensively in church and other benevolent activities.[9] Wherever blacks lived on the prairies they tended to form their own communities and, like white farm women, black women too managed to find the time to make quilts. This was also true for many southern black women. Whether in a separate town or a community within a larger town, members of the black enclaves established their own schools, social service agencies and churches.[10] For example, 'By 1849, San Francisco blacks had formed a "mutual Benefit and Relief

Society" of their own. By 1854, the city had three black churches . . .'[11] According to Lillian Schlissel, there is evidence that the black women 'strove to make the western territories a more hospitable environment in which to raise their families'.[12]

The Album Quilt pictured right, dated c. 1860–70, was made primarily by Mary E. Rutland, a black woman in the Smithville District of Brunswick County, North Carolina. It bears a substantial resemblance to white Album Quilts of the period, and is signed on several blocks, the name 'M. Rutland' being the most prominent. Each block would have had special significance for its maker. The two blocks with appliquéd crosses might testify to the importance of the church and religion; another block is stitched with a cotton ball design. One of the most descriptive blocks portrays what appears to be a soup kettle (see above). Other blocks share another common link with white Album Quilts in their reliance on floral appliqués. Interestingly, all the applied stitching is done by machine, while the binding is hand-sewn. The predominant quilting pattern featured in each of the sixteen blocks is hearts, which strongly suggests that this quilt may have been made for a wedding. There is evidence of cotton seeds still in the quilt lining.

The Era of the Association

While conditions on the frontier provided a unique domestic setting for pioneer families, industrial development in the East and Midwest ensured the funds to support a fast-paced social mobility for many families. Mid-nineteenth-century evangelists were quick to bemoan 'money getting', which was seen as disruptive to family ties. Congregationalists, Presbyterians, Unitarians, Methodists and Baptists organized a diverse array of ecumenical societies in order both to bring about moral reform and to teach Republican virtue and Christian piety in this new society.

This period has been referred to as the 'era of the association', for along with the church and the family, the 'association' became the third pillar of middle-class life.[20] Many of these associations, spurred on by the spirit of reform, were created to promote good causes such as establishing schools and institutions for the deaf and blind, helping orphans, or to combat social evils like drinking and slavery. Many had female auxiliaries which ultimately were more active than the men's branches, especially the Temperance (first formed in 1808) and the Anti-Slavery societies. The movement for women's rights was forged in parallel with these societies as gradual discontent and resentment of women's second-class citizenship emerged.

Civic leaders, merchants, ministers and lawyers helped to create a number of these voluntary associations, which were intended to persuade people to believe and to behave. An anonymous article from a newspaper of the period gives a graphic illustration: 'Matters have come to such a pass that a peaceable man can hardly venture to eat or drink or go to bed or get up or correct his children or kiss his wife, without obtaining the permission and direction of some . . . society.'[21]

Women were called upon to play the dual role of keeper of the hearth and virtuous reformer. This led to the creation of a number of benevolent societies associated with women and the church. There were Sewing Circles, Sewing Societies, Female Prayer Groups, Women's Guilds, Fancy Work Improvement Clubs, Ladies' Aid Societies and African Dorcas societies in black churches.

These groups took it upon themselves to do needlework and, in particular, to make quilts for worthy causes. Many of these quilts were made to send to western missionaries or to auction for some charitable purpose. Symbolism in needlework reached new heights and female anti-slavery societies held fairs and bazaars where they sold needlework products to raise money for the growing abolitionist movement. In this pre-Civil War period, quiltmakers developed specific patterns that dealt with the question of slavery and abolition, such as Slave Chain (earlier called Job's Tears), and Underground Railroad. The fundraising quilt became an important concept which assumed a national urgency during the Civil War when quilts were auctioned to raise money for the troops, and thousands of quilts were made by women across the country and distributed to soldiers in desperate need of proper bedding.

New Romanticism and the Quilt

In the period leading up to the Civil War, American society experienced record economic and social growth. Communities were brought into a national network with the coming of the railroads and steamboats. Industrial development re-defined political ideas and habits of domestic consumption. The old agrarian order of Republican simplicity gradually gave way to a new economic liberalism and, for the first time, political parties became powerful institutions. The Democratic Party, which brought Andrew Jackson, the liberal reformer, to office, drew support from every social class, and in particular from the now well-defined middle class. While the Whig Party, in 1840, with its repeated emphasis on the 'common man', managed to put General William Henry Harrison, the hero of Tippicanoe (the victory in 1811 of General Harrison over the Indian leader, Tecumseh), into the White House. The now-famous slogan 'Tippicanoe and Tyler Too' (Tyler was the vice-presidential candidate) was part of a 'Log Cabin and Cider Barrel' campaign which quoted Harrison as 'a plain man who lives in a log cabin and eats hog meat and grits'.

Size: 84 × 84″/213 × 213 cm

These national campaigns influenced many women who endeavored to make quilts which reflected their political sympathies. There is a Baltimore Album Quilt, for example, in the Smithsonian Institution collection which has a picture of a log cabin under an American flag intricately stitched into one of the central blocks. Thus, the popular symbol for the William Henry Harrison presidential campaign, the humble everyday log cabin, found its way into domestic needlework.

This emphasis on the 'common man' coincided with the rise of the common school movement, the growth of colleges and universities and a heightened national identity. As the United States grew larger, richer and more centralized, it began to evolve a more distinctive culture which found its most embracing definition in Romanticism. This romantic view of life permeated American society and was expressed in a literary and artistic renaissance as well as in domestic taste. A host of thoroughly romantic quilt titles like Dove

BASKETS WITH CHINTZ BORDER
This extraordinary visual quilt is from North Carolina and dates from the 1860s to 1870s. It boasts an unusual broderie perse border and very accurate piecework. The random quality of the fabric selection, including a few swatches of chrome orange, creates a spontaneity often characteristic of quilts prior to the turn of the century.

at the Window and Flowering Almond came to be circulated among women.

The great figures of American literature of the period – Edgar Allan Poe, Nathaniel Hawthorne and Walt Whitman – also fostered romantic thought, and this caught the mood of nineteenth-century America. Their general themes highlighted the diminishing role of the individual within an impersonal society and glorified nature, primitive peoples and folk culture.

The idea of 'art' became a popular notion for

the first time also and was encouraged as a way of elevating Republican taste and character. The widespread public confirmation of the 'moral' value in art and design had two important effects on quilting. Firstly, it helped to reaffirm a woman's belief in the intrinsic value of her own creative handiwork. Secondly, the romanticism which permeated American culture encouraged in general the continuation of traditional quilting techniques which existed alongside newer methods. The Baskets Quilt pictured on page 53, with its border of oversewn chintz-flower patches, is a romantic interpretation of a traditional pattern.

Impact of New Technology

Synthetic Dyes

The discovery of synthetic dyes by the English chemist William Henry Perkin in 1856, and their subsequent production in Germany, stimulated the output of the commercial textile industry which now began widespread roller printing of brightly colored cotton fabric. Although various kinds of wools, including twills and challis, continued to be used along with cotton-and-linen combinations, cotton became the predominant material for quilts. There were widely varied patterns on the cotton fabrics, which included rainbow prints, prints with small-scale sprigs and berries, polka dots printed in vibrant reds, blues, greens and browns, and new and more decorative color combinations of pistachio, lavender and various shades of lime. This new palette of color and design allowed women to create quilts featuring contrasts of increased subtlety in their overall patterns.

The Sewing Machine

One of the most important inventions which contributed to the growth and continuation of the quilting tradition was the sewing machine, which eventually saved women hours of time-consuming hand piecework. It was developed during the 1840s and 1850s and, together with the earlier technological developments of commercial cotton manufacture and synthetic dyes, ensured the enduring national popularity of quilting.

In 1830 a French tailor, Barthelemy

Credited as the primary inventor of the sewing machine, Elias Howe Jr was confirmed in a host of trade cards of the 1860s as a modern-day hero. By the 1870s, over 700,000 machines were being produced every year with cut-throat competition among dozens of companies who filed for patents. The Singer Sewing Machine Company took the lead, however, and by 1880 claimed that they sold more than three quarters of all machines purchased.

Courtesy: The National Museum of American History, Smithsonian Institution

Thimonnier, had patented the first effective sewing machine, while in America at the same time Walter Hunt was one of many sewing machine inventors who had created a rudimentary machine with a revolutionary idea – an eye-pointed needle which moved by a vibrating arm, and a shuttle to make an interlocking stitch. He didn't pursue the idea, however, and in 1846 the mechanic Elias Howe Jr patented a machine similar to Hunt's. After unsuccessfully trying to market the machine in Boston (where he held sewing races with seamstresses in Quincy Hall), Howe sold his patent in England to a corset

NEW DESIGNS AND COLORS

It is possible that the individual creative effort which went into the design of a block for an Album Quilt may have in itself inspired new pieced patterns. 'The majority of the standard appliqué patterns, Rose Wreaths, Fleurs-de-lis, Whig Roses, Tulips and Pineapples, developed during the Album Quilt fad.'[22] During the mid-nineteenth century women began to experiment with complex new designs made from an increased number of small pieces; one such pattern is the Missouri Folk Art Lily (a variation of Wild Goose Chase) pictured below. Other quilts featured curved seams; examples include Whigs' Defeat, Feathered Star, New York Beauty and Rocky Mountain. Appliqué pieces were now cut out of domestic calico and plain cotton rather than imported chintz and were almost always done in blocks or repeat designs rather than in the central medallion style.

Two-color quilts, either in red and white or blue and white, became fashionable, due in part to the availability of a new colorfast 'Turkey' red. The other popular style of the day was the red, white and green appliqué in patterns such as Wreath of Roses, Princess Feather, Turkey Tracks, Whig Rose and Rose Wreath. The Princess Feather on page 40 is a charming example of the kind of care and detail lavished upon these early appliqués.

MISSOURI FOLK ART LILY
This quilt was made in Missouri during the middle of the last century, and is wholly original in its intricately pieced design. It is typical of the almost idiosyncratic character of American quilts during this period, where the pattern was based on a combination of the maker's technical skill and imagination. A pattern for this quilt appears on pages 235–39.

Size: 64 × 82″/162.5 × 208.3 cm

maker for next to nothing. While he was in Europe, however, sewing machines which incorporated his design features were being produced by others in America and Howe fought bitterly in the courts to uphold his patent. The surrounding publicity aroused the public's interest in the machine.

By the 1840s, the inventor Isaac Merrit Singer had come up with another version of the sewing machine, and after a three-year court battle all the patents were pooled into a single franchise and the owners of all the patents shared the fees. The Singer Sewing Machine Company was one of the many companies formed and Howe was persuaded to take a fee for every machine made.

The high price of the sewing machine precluded its widespread distribution and most sales went to clothing manufacturers. However, at the end of the Civil War in 1865, the sewing machine companies, anxious to establish a domestic market, recognized that they needed to counter two widespread beliefs which stood in the way of sales: 'the first that women couldn't control machinery, and second, that, freed from some of their arduous labors, women would go wild . . . people believed that men had the intelligence and temperament for machines; women, those delicate creatures, could use tools (needles, brooms, washboards) but not machines'.[23]

The battle to 'domesticate' the sewing machine was taken on by its manufacturing companies and one of the first national advertising campaigns was the result. The machine was seen in thousands of pictures and trade cards as a labor-saving device which would free women from hours of unnecessary toil.

Following the success of this campaign, the sewing machine slowly became affordable to the average family, due in part to the development of new 'credit' facilities. The ownership of a sewing machine became a symbol of prestige. Bedding as well as clothing came to be stitched on the machine and more and more women experimented with machine sewing on quilts. Nonetheless, it was not until the end of the century that the sewing machine was a standard item in both middle-class and poor homes. According to historian Suellen Meyer, perhaps as many as 10 per

NEW HOME SEWING MACHINE CO.
ORANGE, Mass. —:— 30 UNION SQ. NEW YORK
BARKER & ...LLOGG,
80 TRUM... ...T.,
HARTFOR... ...CONN.

Because women weren't thought capable of operating machines (the idea being incompatible with domesticity), sewing machine manufacturers had to work hard to convince the populace otherwise. In this trade card, the message explains that the sewing machine is so simple to use that even a child – or a pet, for that matter – can operate it. Often companies would offer free machines to the wives of clergymen or leading citizens in an effort to show how respectable it was to use a sewing machine.

Courtesy: The National Museum of American History, Smithsonian Institution

cent of all quilts during the period from 1865 to 1900 bear evidence in some areas of machine appliqué or quilting.[24] The Carpenter's Square Quilt on page 190, although made some thirty or forty years after this period, illustrates the use of the sewing machine to create elaborate quilting patterns.

Professional photographers regularly traveled across the plains and prairies taking pictures of settlers, and these pictures were frequently sent back East to other relatives and friends. The sewing machine, often the most expensive possession of the household, was regularly hauled outside where family members proudly posed around the 'Singer'. The interiors of these simple houses (called 'soddies') were creatively, and often ingeniously, furnished by women, who made every effort to create a civilized home in the unrelenting wilderness. They cut up wedding dresses and scraps of cheesecloth or feed bags to make curtains, plastered old newspapers on the walls, and planted flowers in the sod roofs.

Courtesy: Solomon D. Butcher Collection, Nebraska State Historical Society

The Civil War

With the onset of the Civil War in 1862, thousands of women turned their hands away from making domestic furnishings and fashion to devote their time and talents to the war cause. Both Union (northern) and Confederate (southern) women participated in relief efforts, supplying food, clothing and bedding to the armies. Hope chests and linen closets were raided as women went around door-to-door collecting sheets, quilts and blankets. Quilts that had been family heirlooms, as well as roughly quilted or tied everyday bedcoverings, were turned over to army supply units. The profound impact of the war saw quiltmaking taken up by thousands of women as a patriotic responsibility, and in the North new quilting patterns for the Union army were published in several important women's magazines, such as *Godey's* and *Graham's*.

U.S. Sanitary Commission

In the North, the Federal government, which rapidly called up a huge number of men, found itself unable to furnish the necessary supplies. A private agency called the U.S. Sanitary Commission was established to help find the private means

This photograph was taken at a Sanitary Fair in St Louis in 1864. It is remarkable to think that fairs such as this, organized by women in the Sanitary Commission, raised a total of nearly $5 million for Northern war relief. Women who had given up doing fancy needlework for quilts and other items during the war, took it up again in order to create pieces which would fetch a high price at the Fairs. Note the quilts displayed both on the front counters and at the back.

Courtesy: Missouri Historical Society

necessary for essential troop maintenance. A history of the Sanitary Commission, written in 1866 by Charles Stille, asserts that 'about 7,000 of the local soldiers' aid societies served as auxiliaries of the U.S. Sanitary Commission, the largest private national agency channeling donated supplies to soldiers.'[25]

These aid societies included many run by women. In her illuminating study *Quilts for Union Soldiers in the Civil War*, Virginia Gunn draws the link between women's societies and women's war efforts:

WOMEN IN THE WAR

The groups of women who stitched clothing, rolled bandages, prepared and preserved foodstuffs and packed boxes of supplies were often organized around a particular person, place or ethnic identity. In Cedar Rapids, Iowa, Mary Ely, a conductor on the underground railroad, converted her home into an aid station, where her friends and family formed a group. In Metamore, Illinois, young women whose boyfriends and fiancés had volunteered their services for the war effort, joined together in a group called The Girls of 1861. And in Minnesota, a number of German women formed the German Sewing Society.[27]

Not only did small women's groups like these make over 125,000 quilts[28] among other items which were sent to the front lines, but in many areas women took over and managed the distribution of food, clothing and bedding, assuming major organizational responsibilities throughout the Civil War.

Northern women had long been used to group work for worthy causes. Therefore, with the framework for service already in place, home mission societies, church sociables, sewing circles and various benevolent organizations were converted into Soldiers' Aid Societies without change in organization.[26]

The Union Army Encircled Star Quilt pictured on page 37 is typical of the type of quilt which might have been made at a northern quilting to raise money for the troops.

Similar groups were also formed by southern women. In an article on South Carolina quilts, Laurel Horton quotes a letter written by Alexander Fewell, who enlisted in 1861, from camp to his wife:

Martha we are speaking of getting a uniform having it cut out and sent home to be made. I shall send you mine and there will be others sent to the Society [The Ladies' Aid Society of the Ebenezer Presbyterian Church] if they will have them made which I have no doubt they will do with pleasure.[29]

The scarcity of material in the South, due in part to the Union blockade of southern ports, led women to get out the hand loom and the shuttle to weave home-made fabric for Confederate soldiers, who were in desperate need of clothing and bedding. In addition, the widespread desertion of black slaves from southern plantations diminished the South's ability to supply its army. Initial southern optimism had turned to despair and this change of mood was reflected in the quilts which were donated. The elaborate 'Secession' Quilts in white work, and the fancy appliqué Album Quilts, which had been presented to departing soldiers in the early years of the war, gave way to the rough affairs composed of remnants and salvaged scraps which were supplied to Confederate soldiers as the war dragged on.

There is some evidence of black women sewing quilts for the Confederacy. Kate Cumming, who worked in a Confederate hospital, wrote that 'a number of negro women are at work quilting comforts'.[30] Black women also moved with the Union army as it marched through the South, helping their husbands and most likely sewing clothing and bedding, among other things. In Washington D.C., Elizabeth Kekley, a black woman who earned her freedom from slavery through her sewing skills, organized the Contraband Relief Association for the benefit of freed but suffering blacks.[31]

Great fundraising Sanitary Commission fairs were organized by women in cities like Chicago, St Louis, Brooklyn, Long Island and New York City. These fairs became well-attended social events, held in elaborately decorated halls containing booths and exhibition spaces. Home-made products which included all varieties of food and fancy needlework (most prominently the quilt) raised a remarkable total of $4,500,000 for northern war relief.[32] Virginia Gunn describes how at the Brooklyn Fair there was a replica of a

At first glance this appears to be a political broadsheet . . . but no, it's an advertisement for a New York dry goods business. Closer inspection reveals the widespread Northern belief that the Civil War would be over by 1863.

This engraving from Frank B. Goodrich's The Tribute Book *shows a 'Quilting Party', one of the most popular features of the Sanitary Commission Fairs. The women are dressed in the Colonial costumes of 100 years earlier. This scene demonstrates that even as early as the Civil War period quilting was linked with nostalgia, patriotism and domesticity.*

Courtesy: The Library of Congress

New England farmhouse complete with tableau events which included an old-fashioned quilting party, and New York City's Metropolitan Fair presented a quilting party tableau.

The fairs, along with other fundraising events organized by women, created a widespread national impact. Newspapers, which had ignored women's activism at the beginning of the war, began to carry regular announcements and reports of the meetings of Ladies' Aid Societies. When Burlington, Iowa, staged a successful benefit concert in 1863, the local newspaper reported it in full, commenting that 'the ladies . . . not only deserve the gratitude of the soldiers but the thanks of the community'.[33]

By the end of the war in 1865, many of the women who had been organizers and fundraisers under the auspices of the U.S. Sanitary Commission continued to work for community education and reform.

Fashion and the Quilt

After the Civil War, fashionable American women were looking back at quiltmaking as an activity linked to the romance of rural life and bygone days. The development both of a ready-to-wear clothing market and factory-produced goods created an association between the hand-made quilt and the past. However, the buoyant middle classes preferred to look to the future.

Textile manufacturing, now well established, 'greatly cheapened and multiplied almost every species of clothing worn' and gave rise to a host of other related industries. One such industry was clothing manufacture, helped in part by uniform size standardization during the Civil War.[34] As clothing became democratized it led to an associated business, the fashion industry, and the beginnings of the ready-to-wear clothing market.

The new middle classes were obsessed with dressing well; the popularity of women's fitted apparel, the availability of good inexpensive cotton cloth and finally the emergence of printed paper patterns in the 1850s had all contributed to a heightened sense of style. Innumerable magazines, bursting with advertisements and glowing articles, testified to the advisability of purchasing a ready-to-wear frock in the latest Paris fashion. Slowly, the differences between dresses and suits made by 'city' dressmakers and tailors and those sewn at home were eliminated.

But the new democratization of dress had a double-edged effect. On one hand it stimulated the continuation of a tradition of dress and custom among women in thousands of small towns and farms on the prairies and plains of the frontier – these women could now order a ready-made calico gown or bonnet from new mail order catalogues. On the other hand, it played a role in creating a society increasingly concerned with fashion, style and money; middle- and upper-class women living in prosperous urban centers and southern plantations insisted that their wardrobes be created out of imported silks. The silk dress became the fashionable and desired attire in which to entertain in one's elaborate Victorian-style parlor. By the last quarter of the nineteenth century the quilt, made of both calico and silk, was also expressing these two trends.

—4—
The Age of Expansion

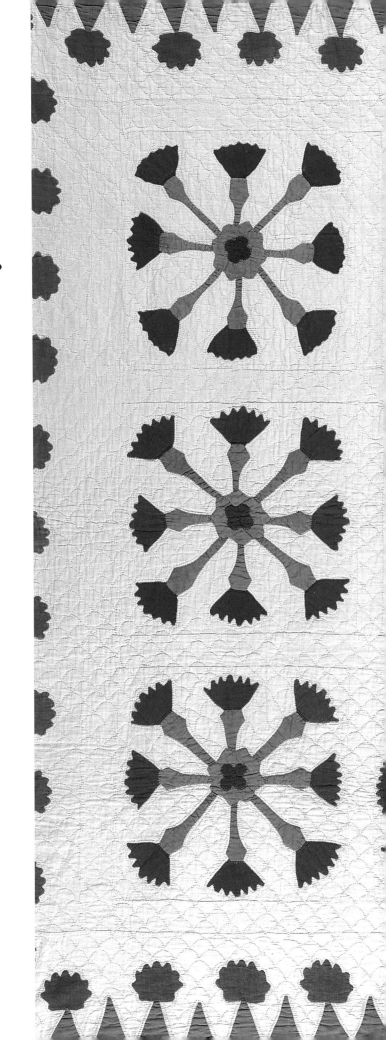

A merican concepts of taste and design during the final years of the nineteenth century reflected larger social and economic events. A wide geographic media network of newspapers, periodicals, broadsides and magazines – many targeted at a female readership – guaranteed the spread of new ideas. The development of mail order houses like Sears and Roebuck and Montgomery Ward insured that women, even in remote rural environments, could receive through the mail the latest fashion, fabric or appliance, including the majority of materials necessary for making a quilt – from a thimble to a sewing machine.

Prior to 1860 the population of America was made up largely of farmers of Anglo-American stock, slaves, or freed men with African roots. The dominant culture was for the most part white, Protestant and Republican middle class. But enormous shifts in the economy after the Civil War, great waves of immigration and rapid industrialization created substantial differences within American society – between Fifth Avenue and the Lower East Side in New York City, between the industrial East and the frontier West, between the shattered rural South and the great railway cities of the North and Midwest, and

Courtesy: The National Museum of American History, Smithsonian Institution

ABOVE: *More than any other institution, the mail order houses helped to consolidate American domestic taste. Both ethnic and regional differences faded as farmers from Kentucky to Oregon, as well as city dwellers, sent in orders for millions of dollars-worth of standardized, manufactured goods. Around the turn of the century, the new Montgomery Ward or Sears and Roebuck catalogues became the most important books in America after the Bible. In fact, many rural schools regularly used the Sears catalogue as a textbook for reading and arithmetic lessons.*

PREVIOUS PAGE: *CENTENNIAL EAGLE*
This quilt was made in Philadelphia to commemorate the Centennial Exposition in 1876, and its central Federal Eagle was copied from the Great Seal of the United States. Beautifully proportioned, the quilt has a wonderful childlike quality which is emphasized by the two little birds in the center and by the border treatment. The color combination of red, white and green was much favored by appliqué artists in the late nineteenth century. The quilting is extremely fine, with small, closely stitched clamshells.

Size: 70 × 88″ / 178 × 223 cm

between non-English-speaking immigrants and the white middle classes.

The complexity and pace of American life had increased dramatically during the 1870s and 1880s, and these profound changes contributed to the new and often contradictory way America thought about itself. The old Jeffersonian democracy was transformed into a modern, mechanized, continental nation. The many thousands of American women who continued to make quilts, or who took up quiltmaking, in the last quarter of the nineteenth century interpreted these changes in an enormous variety of quilt styles, fabrics and patterns.

New Directions in Quiltmaking

By the last half of the nineteenth century quiltmaking had evolved in two main directions, both fueled by a growing emphasis on artistic taste, fashion and patriotism. On one hand, there was a widespread development of ingenious new designs as calico piecework became increasingly complex. Intricate patterns like Ocean Waves and Drunkard's Path, and sentimental and figurative patterns such as Little Red Schoolhouse, Tree of Life, Horseshoe and Butterfly Quilts were made out of a wide variety of cotton prints. 'The cut of the late-nineteenth-century fashion styles – with their large sleeves, flowing skirts, and bustles – created leftover fabric scraps, and since women continually updated their wardrobes, they accumulated a large variety of these pieces. Thrifty and practical women utilized them in pieced quilt block designs, even though they could purchase inexpensive fabric.'[1] The Ocean Waves Quilt pictured on page 200 reveals the kind of detailed piecework which was becoming popular at this time.

On the other hand, silk had become paramount in the fashion world and women found it imperative to have at least one good silk dress. The opening of treaty ports with China and the domestic production of silk made this a realistic desire, and soon the high status of silk was applied to furnishings, and women all over America aspired to display fancy silk needlework in their homes.

The Decorative Arts Movement, transplanted from Britain, had re-established earlier English traditions of detailed and inventive embroidery as a praiseworthy feminine pastime, and stimulated the development of a new genre of quilt altogether. The Crazy Quilt was a random assortment of irregular silk, velvet or rich brocade patches (fabrics now readily and cheaply available) which were rather eloquently stitched together with brightly colored silk embroidery thread, often with over 100 different kinds of stitches in one piece.

Technological developments also continued to play an important role in enriching American quiltmaking. Advances in colorfast sharp dyes and roller printing created a vivid assortment of new fabrics and colors, and even though increased factory output sometimes meant a decrease in fabric quality women continued to be stimulated by the 'Calico Craze'. Charm Quilts, which were composed of 999 pieces cut out of the same template but in which there were no identical fabrics, became very popular, as did the Postage Stamp Quilt made out of thousands of squares which were less than one inch apiece.

The Growing Middle Classes

The advances in science and technology fostered a rapid growth of industrial development from 1870 which was supported by an infrastructure of steamboats, railroads and telegraph lines. Immigrants from all over the world poured into the United States eager for the opportunity to get jobs in the new coal or iron mines, the steelworks, or on the railways. Others were attracted by popular 'boomer' literature which promised cheap, plentiful and rich land in the West, or gold in Colorado and California. Still other immigrants came to make their way in the growing urban centers. The industrial revolution created a new era of big business, big cities and big money. But at the same time the booming economy not only widened the division between the very rich and the very poor, but also accelerated the growth of the middle class, for whom, in this so-called 'Gilded Age', the domestic setting was characterized by material opulence. Silk and velvet embroidered work became, by the 1880s, a clear signal of middle-class status.

By the late nineteenth century, child-care and homemaking had become a full-time job for the urban middle-class woman. She was no longer expected to make a direct contribution to family income, but was to be supported by her male relatives. Being able to support a woman in comparative leisure and not needing to depend on her wages became a significant criterion of a man's membership of the middle class. The immigrant who prospered to the point that his wife no longer went out to work for wages moved up the social ladder. The ready availability of domestic service, often supplied by immigrants such as the Irish in New York, meant that middle-class women had far more time to devote to domestic activities, thus enhancing their roles as wives and mothers.[2] The preoccupation with the beautiful and artistic home was continually encouraged by the popular media.

The national concern about design was informed in part by new scientific discoveries, and in particular by the investigation of optical illusion which accompanied advances in photography. This preoccupation is reflected in quilts of the period in which a two-dimensional surface

Size: 74 × 75½″/188 × 191 cm

TUMBLING BLOCKS
The beautifully pieced silks and taffetas of this 1870s Victorian-style
quilt create a visual metaphor which suggests everything from
precious gems to a kaleidoscope. The well-defined optical quality is
achieved by the careful placement of light and dark fabrics.

appears three-dimensional. Patterns such as Stairway to Heaven and Windmill Blades were fashioned out of silk and velvet, cottons and wools. The jewel-like Tumbling Blocks Quilt on page 66 illustrates what was probably the most popular optical design of the period. This particular quilt is said to have been made out of the ballgowns and fancy dresses from one Louisville, Kentucky, family in the 1870s.

National taste was also strongly influenced by exposure to Eastern cultures, resulting in a host of decorative objects such as wallpaper and textiles resplendent with Oriental motifs. Quilts such as the Fan Quilt and the Quill Quilt, made up of brightly colored scraps, approximately two inches wide and one inch deep, sewn into overlapping rows of quills, are examples of a strong Japanese influence.

These rather severe-looking women, working on an Irish Chain Quilt, reflect the tenacity of spirit which was echoed in thousands of pioneer settlements throughout the nineteenth century.

Courtesy: The Missouri Historical Society

Divisions in Society

As American society grew more stratified and less homogeneous it became riddled with corruption and labor unrest. Powerful political bosses, such as those in New York's notorious Tammany Hall, big land speculation deals in the West, and national financial scandals, all contributed to the growth of a liberal-thinking opposition.

Protestations against the acquisition of money and the trappings of wealth were aired by popular artists, writers, intellectuals and churchmen. Mark Twain, in an article entitled 'The Revised Catechism', published in the *New York Tribune* in 1871, caught the national mood when he wrote: 'What is the chief end of man? – to get rich. In what way? dishonestly if he can; honestly if he must. Who is God, the one and only true? Money is God.'[3]

Popular entreaties to return to simple ideals as expressed by old-fashioned family life were interpreted artistically by all classes and groups who continued a longstanding tradition of domestic needlework. Women settlers, particularly in the western states and rural areas, carried on stitching functional quilts as well as others which were more fashionable. Settlers from particular communities made quilts which adapted American quilting ideas to an already existing religious and folk heritage: the Amish and Mennonite

sects, the Pennsylvania and Missouri Germans, Hawaiians, Scots-Irish descendants in the Blue Ridge Mountains area, and Afro-American women, all made quilts influenced by their own distinctive cultures. The red and green Pennsylvania 'Dutch' (German) Quilt on page 69, for example, uses colors and symbols which were typical of the German settlers in that area and of that period.

Among lower-class and rural women, as well as among certain sects such as the Pennsylvania and Missouri Germans, the ordinary sturdy woolen comforter, or hap quilt (see page 68), continued in everyday use. Jeannette Lasansky, in an article in *Uncoverings*, describes the construction of such quilts:

Scrap material, usually wool but sometimes cottons and on rare occasions velvets and corduroys, are sewn on a foundation and block by block are assembled in either a random or patterned design. The fabric sandwich is often tied together with knots of wool or thick cotton thread placed at regular intervals across the quilt. Sometimes they are quilted instead of being tied (tacked or knotted) but the needlework is always coarse, about five stitches per inch, due entirely to the thickness of the batts as well as the coarseness of the material used for the top and back . . .[4]

Size: 78 × 76″/198 × 193 cm

LOG CABIN-STYLE HAP QUILT
This late-nineteenth-century, sturdy Log Cabin Quilt
is made out of a variety of what appear to be scraps
of old wool, cotton shirts and suits. It is also
commonly referred to as a Hap Quilt or comforter
by people in Pennsylvania, as well as by some Eng-
lish North Country groups. The well-matched blocks
are beautifully interrupted by the regular placement
of contrasting squares of faded red tartan plaid.

Voices of Dissent

The traditions and age-old customs of the small
rural communities continued alongside the
growth of large urban centers and national cultural trends. The liberal and enlightened social
tendencies of the day were closely associated
with the Fundraising Quilt. For example, after the
Civil War in 1865, a Log Cabin Fundraising Quilt
was made in St Louis to aid needy families of ex-
Confederate soldiers and is embroidered with
the words 'Feed the Hungry'. (This quilt is now
owned by the Missouri Historical Society.) The
most popular kind of Fundraising Quilt from the
1860s to the 1930s was the Signature Quilt where
women paid to have their names embroidered
onto the quilt.

Although attitudes to women and domesticity
largely remained the same throughout the nineteenth century, women nonetheless carried out
their reform activities with growing confidence.
The industrial forces which had given scope to
the development of a large leisured and educated female middle class also provided the
social conditions necessary for a mass movement
of women. This movement, which was closely
associated with moral reform and with the growing temperance movement, made good use of
the Fundraising Quilt. Later, such activities were
directly linked to the growing suffrage campaign,
where women were one voice among the many
calling for political reform.

Broad-based public dissent against the widespread corruption, both in industry and in
society, was voiced by a group of middle-class
citizens called Mugwumps. They were the
spokesmen for the American conscience of their
time, and though they had little political power,
they managed to have a great deal of influence.
President Grover Cleveland, who came to the
White House in 1884, identified and imple-
mented many of the Mugwump programs, which
included the introduction of the secret election
ballot which ended years of corrupt practices, the
spread of the free public school system, and the
reform of the civil service.

Although the serious problems presented by
business, labor unions, Indian wars, violent
racism and strong sectional interests were not
solved by Mugwump policies there was considerable lip service paid to Mugwump principles.
Personal ambition was idealized in a host of 'rags
to riches' stories and American society clung
onto renewed ideas of religion, morality and
patriotism. A quilt which is now in the Museum
of American Folk Art in New York City was made
to commemorate the term and achievements of
President Cleveland. Stitched out of pieced
cotton scrap prints, it has a central panel made
out of a kerchief picturing the President surrounded by stars.

Patriotic Fervor

The American Centennial in 1876, the huge
exposition in Philadelphia which celebrated 100
years of nationhood, ignited a commercial and
domestic fashion for American symbols. Special
cotton prints were manufactured which dis-

Size: 72 × 92″ / 183 × 233.7 cm

PENNSYLVANIA DUTCH FOLK ART
German settlers in Pennsylvania, commonly referred to as the Pennsylvania Dutch (a corruption of Deutsche), brought with them a strong cultural heritage which was reflected in the decorative aspects of their homes and barns. This remarkable mid-nineteenth-century quilt, with its red and green color scheme, appliquéd hearts and folk motifs, reverse appliqué, rickrack and oak leaf border, is a testimony to the ingenuity and skill of an anonymous Pennsylvanian woman. A pattern for it appears on pages 244–51.

played commemorative patterns such as liberty bells, liberty caps, profiles of George Washington and 'bombs bursting in air'. Patriotic quilts proudly bearing Federal Eagles, stars, stripes, pictures of presidents and names of states were enormously popular. The Centennial Eagle Quilt

pictured on page 63 was made in Pennsylvania in 1876. With its simplicity of design and 'folksy' character it typifies the response by ordinary people to the Centennial fever.

Quilts, as in earlier years, symbolized domestic and public events. Marriages, births and deaths were commemorated in innumerable Brides' Quilts, Crib Quilts and Mourning Quilts. Quilt patterns were named after war heroes, such as Dewey's Dream for Admiral Dewey in commemoration of the Spanish-American War. Others, like the T-Block, were associated with causes such as the temperance movement. Outline Quilts, also inspired by the decorative arts craze, depicted in bright thread against a white background a pictorial or historical motif.

Backed by tremendous financial gains and a growing overseas trade network, America began to have a strong voice in foreign affairs. For the first time, Americans saw themselves as part of an

LOG CABIN QUILTS

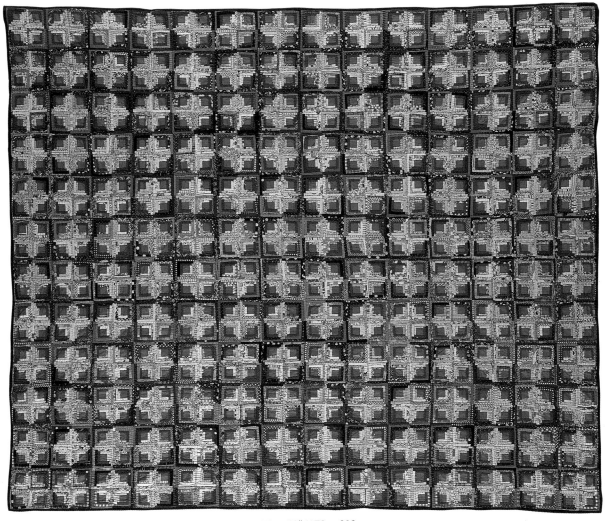

Size: 70 × 80″ / 178 × 203 cm

LOG CABIN

The Log Cabin motif became popular in the 1870s, a decade after Abe Lincoln's 'Log Cabin' presidential campaign. It was identified with rugged pioneer ideals and achieved such widespread popularity that country fairs began having special prize categories for Log Cabin quilts. This piece, made sometime at the end of the last century, is unusual in that it features a bright blue, rather than the traditional red, center. A pattern for it appears on pages 154–58.

Another important style of quiltmaking which became popular during this period was the Log Cabin Quilt, which was made with a type of pressed foundation whereby strips of light and dark fabric were sewn directly onto a block of another foundation fabric. The name of this type of quilt does not refer to the log cabin itself, but rather to the manner in which the design is created, the thin strips of cloth being assembled in the same way that logs are layered in the building of a cabin.

These quilts, characterized by at least six different design interpretations, were made in the popular fabrics of the day, including mohairs and woolens from the mid-century, cotton prints and wool challis from around the Civil War period, and Victorian silks and lush brocades at the turn of the century. The Log Cabin Quilt pictured above is rather atypical in that it uses a blue rather than the traditional red center.

international community. The 1876 Centennial celebrations not only featured impressive displays extolling American advances in areas such as electricity, internal combustion and steam power, but also hosted tremendously popular exhibitions by fifty-six foreign nations. The Japanese Pavilion, an elaborate and sumptuous display of textiles, bronzes, embroideries and silks, and the exhibition of the Royal School of Art Needlework from Kensington, England, were two of the best received events. Both were to have an enormous influence in setting new standards of taste for the American home.

Other European arts also found a growing following in the United States. The first English production of Gilbert and Sullivan's *H.M.S. Pinafore* which successfully toured major American cities, well-attended European grand opera at the newly opened Metropolitan Opera House, and excitement about French 'impressionist' painting all contributed strongly to national taste and design.

These influences were quickly translated into a domestic setting through magazines like the newly formed *Ladies Home Journal, Home Beautiful*, and new journals devoted to household and decorative arts. Women were advised that good taste and artistic discernment need not be limited to the wealthy, and that women of all stations could, by their own labor and handiwork, create a beautiful and artistically furnished home.

Although these magazines were intended for the intelligent middle-class housewife, the ideas which they espoused found their way to a much wider readership of lower-class and rural women. The calico quilt, which had featured so strongly in the lives of countless American women, was deemed unworthy in the 1870s and 1880s for consideration in the well-appointed home. An article in *Household Magazine* in 1875, entitled 'Beds and Bedrooms', makes the admonishment clear: 'Neither the unhealthy thing called a comfortable nor the unsightly covering known as the patched quilt should be seen on a bed in this day.' A host of articles and features designed to illuminate women's understanding about the tasteful Victorian style and to raise standards of housekeeping rejected traditional calico patchwork in favor of decorative embroidery. The silk quilt or 'show' quilt which followed is considered

A remarkable 1898 Sears catalogue cover.

to be a grass-roots response to the fervor surrounding the Decorative Arts Movement. These sumptuous quilts, more decorative than to be used for warmth, often sported intricately embroidered motifs such as names, butterflies and flowers, and included beading, ribbons, sequins and chenille appliqués.

Nonetheless, despite the frequent admonishments of the popular media, quiltmaking continued to flourish, though in new and often extravagant forms.

Quilts and the Decorative Arts Movement

The Decorative Arts Movement, an English phenomenon inspired by the writings and work of William Morris, John Ruskin and their followers, was embraced by American society with great enthusiasm. Formally introduced during the Centennial Exposition in 1876 through an exhibition of decorative needlework presented by the Royal School of Art Needlework, this aesthetic movement popularized the concepts which united domesticity, morality and art. The ideas presented by William Morris, whom many considered the greatest designer of his age, asserted that shoddy commercialism had subverted the work of the individual craftsman. He felt that the manner in which products were made was integral to the quality of the product itself. Emphasizing that decorative objects for the home must demonstrate 'clearness of form coupled with the mystery that comes from abundance and richness of detail'[5], Morris and his followers restated the craftsmanship of the Middle Ages in late-nineteenth-century artistic terms. Traditional skills of tile glazing, woodcutting, engraving, bookbinding, weaving, tapestry and embroidery were revived as influential sections of society willingly turned away from the opulent trappings of Victorian England.

The women who founded the Kensington Royal School of Art Needlework in 1872 intended both to recreate the tradition of ornamental needlework and to provide needy gentlewomen with suitable employment. This idea had a strong appeal in America where the economic crisis during and immediately after the Civil War had created short-term financial difficulties for many middle-class women.[6]

A year after the Centennial, in 1877, a New York socialite organized the New York Decorative Art Society which encouraged women from all classes to create beautiful ornamental needlework influenced by both English and the now popular Oriental styles. These pieces of 'art needlework', featuring intricate designs lavishly embroidered with brightly colored thread, were sold through special stores set up by the Society.

The success of this organization inspired the formation of a host of sister groups in cities around the country and allowed the Society to produce its own publication, *Art Interchange*. Virginia Gunn, in a well-documented account of the Decorative Arts Movement and the Crazy Quilt, quotes a number of period documents which state that *Art Interchange* was to be 'devoted to the subject of art as applied to household adornment' and gave 'instruction, in silk,

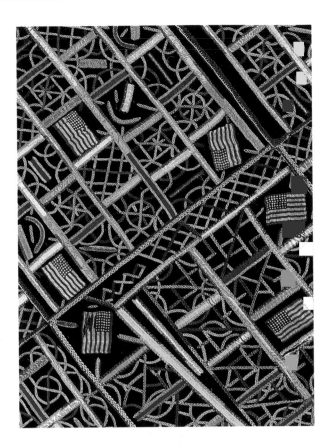

Part of the Patriotic Crazy Quilt on page 74, richly embellished with brightly colored embroidery and silk ribbons.

crewel, tapestry, and medieval embroideries . . . and full descriptions of all novel fancy work'.[7]

The societies had become the arbiters of national taste and magazines outdid themselves in an effort to produce articles, stories and poems about how women could achieve the new artistic look in their homes. An article from a periodical entitled *Art Amateur* observed this trend:

Art societies have sprung up all over the country. It is the fashion to talk about art and, in a fashionable way, to practice it. Young ladies, instead of spending their mornings at the piano . . . take lessons in painting on china, in oils or watercolors, or ply their nimble fingers in the production of 'art needlework'.[8]

Decorative Arts in England

English publications of the same period, featuring step-by-step, 'how to' instructions for needlework, made their way across the Atlantic.

Weldon's *Practical Shilling Guide to Fancy Work*, published from 1885 to 1890, is typical of this kind of manual which, although published in London, found an enthusiastic audience in America. An issue on Appliqué Work notes:

Chain stitch, feather stitch, buttonhole stitch, French knots, cross stitch, coral stitch, satin stitch, outline stitch, couching, and spike stitches will all be found requisite for the different kinds of appliqué work, and give beautiful effect if applied with taste and skill according to the design that is to be worked and likewise according to the materials used, as any readers would find.

A later volume of Weldon's (Volume II, 1887) indicated that English women were also advised to adapt fancy Art Needlework techniques to the patchwork quilt:

As a change from the accustomed routine of Art Needlework . . . Artistic Patchwork will be found an agreeable variation . . . Patchwork . . . instead of being a childish occupation, and only resorted to as a means of using up scraps that would otherwise be wasted, it has become quite a favorite work . . . All the best patchwork is carried out with silk, satin, and velvet . . .

While American magazines encouraged women to do needlework for reasons of art and good taste, English publications often emphasized the morally uplifting effects of patchwork. *Cassell's Household Guide*, published in London during 1869 to 1872, notes:

The advantages of making patchwork, besides the useful purposes it is put to – and indeed, to be reckoned before those purposes – are its moral effects. Leisure must either be filled up by expensive amusements, 'mischief', or by listless idleness, unless some harmless useful occupation is substituted. Patchwork is, moreover, useful as an encourager of perfection in plain work, because it must be very neatly sewn, especially if made of silk pieces and sewn with white sewing silk . . . patchwork often plays a noble part . . . and idle time is advantageously occupied.

The American Crazy Quilt

American quiltmaking traditions, which had grown and developed over the previous 150 years, refused to adhere to fashion dictates.

Nonetheless the decorative arts fad was so strong that by the late 1870s the quilt had begun to adapt to popular aesthetics.

A few years later, a number of magazines noted this growing trend. *Harper's Bazaar* wrote: 'We have discarded in our modern quilts the regular geometric design once so popular, and substituted what are more like the changing figures of the kaleidoscope, or the beauty and infinite variety of oriental mosaics.'[9]

The Crazy Quilt, which combined the Oriental notion of asymmetry with decorative arts embroidery techniques and concepts of individuality, quickly became the darling of the fashion world. These new-style silk quilts, made for decoration, were as well suited to the parlor as to the bedroom. This trend was encouraged and indeed strongly supported by a host of important women's magazines.

Harper's wrote that the Crazy Quilt 'deserves to be handed down as an heirloom'. *Dorcas* magazine explained, 'Of all the "crazes" which have swept over and fairly engulfed us, there is none which has taken a deeper hold upon the fair women of our land than this one of the crazy patchwork . . . Many a woman with strong artistic taste finds no other outlet for it than in work such as this.'[10]

This national passion for Crazy Quilts was shortlived, however, and they seemed to fall out of favor in fashionable circles by the mid-1880s. Magazines were quick to dismiss them as being ugly, awful and, indeed, crazy. Nonetheless, the stylistic concept of the Crazy Quilt continued well after the turn of the century, only it was then applied to more ordinary fabrics such as dark woolens and heavy suiting materials. The Patriotic Crazy Quilt made out of black wool, pictured on page 74, illustrates how this fashion didn't entirely die out for many years. The forty-eight silk stars on the flags indicate that this quilt might have been made at any time from 1912, when Arizona entered the Union as the 48th state, to 1959, when Alaska became the 49th state.

As the Gilded Age wore thin and a more progressive America prepared to meet the twentieth century, a new national sentiment arose which sought to revive the spirit of America's Colonial past. With it came a renewed passion for the

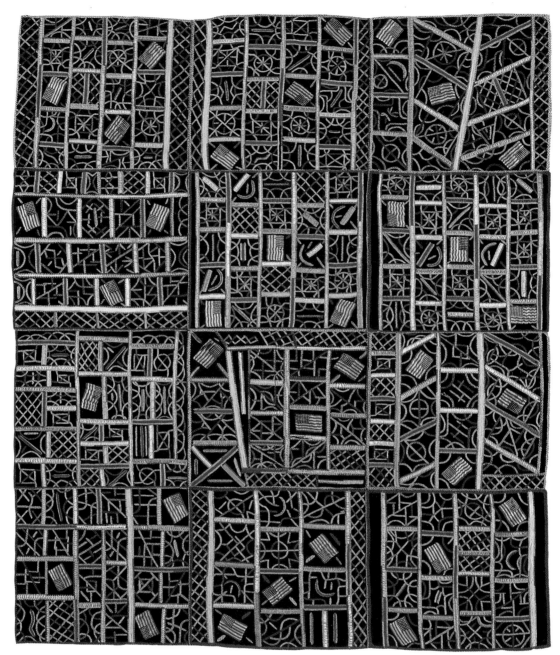

Size: 68 × 56″ / 172.7 × 142 cm

calico quilt as American women reconsidered their own heritage. Probably the clearest pronouncement of this came from an article in the *Ladies Home Journal* in 1894 entitled 'The Revival of the Patchwork Quilt':

The vagaries of fashion are unaccountable and no one can tell in what direction they will lead next. Of late months everything which could be recognized as old fashioned is the new fashion . . . The decree has gone forth that a revival of patchwork quilts is at hand and

PATRIOTIC CRAZY QUILT
This quilt grows more fascinating with close inspection. There is an interesting juxtaposition between the embroidered curvilinear topstitching and the well-defined basic block shape. Another contrast is created by the rather florid embroidery which is regulated by bands of silk ribbon placed in straight lines. A final contradiction is achieved by the use of shiny colored thread against a dull, black wool background. This quilt was made between 1912 and 1948.

dainty fingers whose owners have known only patches and patchwork from family descriptions are busy placing the blocks together in new and artistic patterns, as well as in the real old time order.[11]

By 1900, the overall range of designs and patterns used in quilts, inspired by all aspects of domestic, religious, political and social life, had reached astonishing proportions.

Quilt Patterns

There were literally thousands of named quilt designs which, by the end of the century, were known to a wide range of women in states and territories across the country. Many of these patterns had developed from basic designs through individual variation or by unaccounted-for changes as a pattern passed from region to region and from state to state. Before the widespread publication of quilt patterns in the early twentieth century, many designs were reproduced from memory by an increasingly transient society, which perhaps accounts for some of the variations. What was known as Flying Dutchman in one area became Indian Trail in another and Weathervane in yet another. The Bear's Paw in Ohio or Kentucky became Duck's Foot in the Mud in Long Island and Hand of Friendship in Philadelphia.

While many quilt names were rooted in factual events like Whigs' Defeat or Burgoyne's Surrender, others such as Glorified Nine-Patch, Dove in the Window, or Fish in a Dish conveyed a sense of romantic whimsy. The personal name which might have been given to a pattern developed by an otherwise anonymous maker became almost legendary when passed down through her family, or circulated among her neighbors. This can be observed in patterns such as Aunt Sukey's Choice, Aunt Vinah's Favorite or Flo's Fan. Many patterns, such as Candlelight or Tangled Briar, have been lost to history, while others have been carefully researched by catalogue companies. Some were renamed specifically for twentieth-century consumption, like the old English-style Hexagon or Mosaic which became Grandma's Flower Garden. According to quilt historians Patsy and Myron Orlofsky, certain names

changed over the years depending upon the issues of concern to quilters at any one time. Job's Tears, originally a religious name in the first quarter of the nineteenth century, changed to Slave Chain by 1825 when the issue of slavery was on people's minds. When Texas was annexed in 1840 the same pattern became Texas Tears, and after 1865 it was known as Rocky Road to Kansas or Kansas Troubles. Finally, during the third quarter of the century it was called Endless Chain.[12]

One of the most well-loved and handsome patterns was based on the lily. Often composed with

Detail of a North Carolina Lily Quilt. Note the diamond shape of the Lily itself.

diamond blocks, it was an extremely popular pattern that migrated across the continent bearing a variety of names to suit new locales. In northern New England the pattern was called Wood Lily, in southern New England Meadow Lily, in Pennsylvania Tiger Lily. It was called North Carolina Lily all through the South, except in Kentucky and Tennessee where it was known as Mountain Lily. It was named for the Fire Lily in Ohio, Indiana and Illinois, the Prairie Lily west of the Mississippi and the Mariposa Lily beyond the Rocky Mountains.[13] Tulip Quilts are similar to the diamond lily designs, but are generally less delicate and made with larger blocks.

THE ELEMENTS OF QUILT CONSTRUCTION

One approach to classifying patterns is according to the components of construction. All pieced, straight-edged patterns are based on variations of geometric shapes, most important of which is the square, which divides evenly along the bias into triangles. Curved shapes tended not to be used so often since they necessitated a higher degree of wastage and were not therefore a thrifty way of using fabric.

The particular arrangement of the units of geometric pieces of squares, diamonds and triangles, the proportion of those pieces and their dimensions made up a library of thousands of quilt names, from single-patch quilts like Hit and Miss or Brick Wall to patterns made from four- or nine-patch constructions. Simple nine-patch quilts might include The Shoo Fly, Double Monkey Wrench, or the Nine-Patch on page 21. Among the more complex nine-patch variations is The Young Man's Fancy Quilt pictured below. Made in New England sometime around the turn of the century, this handsome, somewhat patriotic, quilt is typical of the American penchant for fanciful names. This particular name may have had its origin in the tradition whereby a young man was presented with a quilt when he turned twenty-one. A pattern for this quilt appears on pages 214–17.

Diamonds are used to create both geometric and floral patterns. Geometric configurations of diamond patches translate into a host of star patterns based on the older LeMoyne Star. Sometimes called the Lemon Star, this pattern was named for the LeMoyne Brothers who founded New Orleans in 1718. The many star pattern variations include stars with five, six or eight points which fill up the entire quilt top, as in the Star of Bethlehem, the Lone Star and the Blazing Star. Other star patterns are worked in arrangements of multiple blocks and include simple patterns such as the Rolling Star, Chained Star, Ohio Star (see page 209) and the ingenious Falling Star. One of the most exciting star quilts is shown on page 38. This quilt was made in Texas in 1855 and a detail from it is shown below (right). The flowing, white on white embroidered initials and date (1855), both placed firmly in the central portion of the quilt, indicate the value which the maker placed on her handiwork.

Triangles are commonly used in such diverse patterns as Flying Geese, Baskets (see page 53), Pine Trees and Ocean Waves (see page 200), while the Double Wedding Ring, Snail Trail (see page 222), Hearts and Gizzards (see page 97), and Fan patterns are cut out of a variety of curved patches.

Size: 70 × 88"/178 × 223.5 cm

Individual Significance

Quilt names endowed a hand-crafted piece of needlework with personal meaning and were inspired by a wide range of experiences. Religion, domestic life, the community, nature, work, politics and literature were all reflected in thousands of expressive and often lyrical pattern names. Religious names included Cross and Crown, Jacob's Ladder, Coronation, Wonder of the World, and David and Goliath. Common or domestic objects such as the Monkey Wrench, Churndash and Carpenter's Wheel were all part of the quilt vocabulary. The Cake Stand and Cherry Basket Quilts pictured on pages 150 and 146 are two of the more popular of this type. Games and puzzles such as Yankee Puzzle, Merry-Go-Round and Leapfrog, community events like a Barn Raising, and particular square dance calls like Virginia Reel, Swing-in-the-Corner or Hands All Around were memorialized in graphically descriptive names. Significant buildings such as churches, schoolhouses and log cabins were stitched into a host of figurative patterns. The Schoolhouse Quilt shown on page 129 was a popular motif well into the twentieth century.

Traditional design motifs based on natural elements continued to inspire America's quilters. Flowers such as the rose formed a complete genre of pattern names including Whig Rose, Harrison Rose, Democratic Rose, Rose Wreath, Rosebud, Rosedream, Rose of Sharon and Ohio Rose among others. Love Apple, Kentucky Flower Pot, Hickory Leaf, Morning Glory, Indian Plum, Grapes and Vines, Iris, Tea Leaf, Dogwood, Corn and Beans, and Field of Daisies, are only a few of the multitude of botanical names which were translated into quilt patterns. Birds, animals and insects were well represented too, with myriad designs such as Spider's Web, Snake's Trail, Flying Geese, Swarm of Bees, Turkey Tracks, Bunnies, and Swallows' Flight. The Bluebird Appliqué, Snail Trail and Bear's Paw Quilts on pages 134, 159 and 222 are well-loved designs created by thousands of women over the years.

The movement of the sun, moon and stars was captured in titles like Moon and Stars, Rolling Star, Starburst, Falling Star, Half Moon Rising, Twinkling Star, Big Dipper and Rising Sun.

Symbolism

Many designs, whether geometric, figurative or abstract, conveyed a host of associated and symbolic meanings which were understood through custom. Pineapples stitched into a quilt (or carved on a gatepost) stood for hospitality, while a pomegranate meant abundance. Rings and hearts were clearly to do with love and courtship. Trees have long been associated with Christianity and the Pine Tree pattern in particular was alternately referred to as the Tree of Plenty and the Tree Everlasting. In times of pioneer settlement in the sometimes inhospitable West, it came to represent the pine forests of New England; many settlers, after building their sod hut or log cabin, would plant a pine tree to be reminded of home.

The Log Cabin quilt was made from the middle of the nineteenth century in any one of six different designs: Barn Raising, Straight Furrow, Courthouse Steps, Streak of Lightning, Light and Dark and Pineapple or Windmill (see page 70). The names in this instance relate to a visual

---

PINEAPPLE LOG CABIN
Stitched completely out of the everyday clothing from a Kentucky family during the last quarter of the nineteenth century, this remarkably energetic and graphic Log Cabin Quilt looks like a piece of sophisticated twentieth-century art.

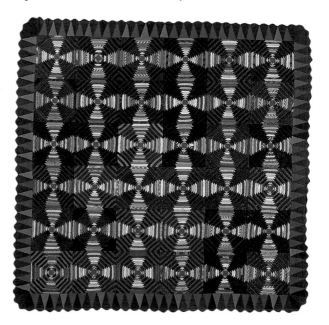

Size: 70 × 70″/178 × 178 cm

ALDEN QUILT

Size: 84 × 76"/213 × 193 cm

This splendid English-style hexagon quilt is beautifully stitched in the traditional template method. It is one of a pair made by Mary Hathaway Alden in the mid-nineteenth century.

Here is how Mary Alden probably assembled her quilt:

1. She made a cardboard template of the hexagon and, using this cardboard template, she cut paper templates.
2. She cut her fabric using the cardboard template, and tacked the fabric pieces around the paper templates.
3. The fabric hexagons were then arranged in a pattern, probably on the floor.
4. She oversewed the hexagons together with the paper still in them (as seen in the quilt pictured on page 39). She would then have ironed the whole piece.
5. Next, all the tacking stitches were taken out.
6. Finally, she would have held up the quilt and shaken it until there was a shower of paper falling to the floor. If she was lucky, all the paper templates came out.

The Alden family Bible, which has been passed down through the generations, and records the family's births, marriages and deaths.

Mary was born in 1833, and on 23 June 1859 married Martin Alden, an eighth generation direct descendant of the well-known Pilgrim leader John Alden, whose name was immortalized in Henry Longfellow's epic poem, *The Courtship of Miles Standish* (1863). Mary lived well into her nineties and died on 7 August 1924.

Martin Alden.

Mary Alden.

metaphor, with the choice of scale, color and fabric completely altering the final effect. The Pineapple Log Cabin (see page 77), made in rich, dark woolens, and the Light and Dark variation (see front cover) in brilliant pastels are as different as night and day. The Log Cabin Quilt was strongly associated with Abraham Lincoln's 'log cabin' campaign, in which he stood for rural, honest, pioneer ideas, while the traditional red center symbolized the domestic hearth.

Names relating to social rituals like love and marriage come down to us in a legacy of patterns such as Young Man's Fancy, Double Wedding Ring, Bridal Stairway, Lover's Knot, Old Man's Ramble, Wedding Knot and Widower's Choice. Other names related to politics, such as Washington's Plumes, Union Quilt, Clay's Choice and President's Wreath; or literature, for example Delectable Mountains (from John Bunyan's *Pilgrim's Progress*) and Lady of the Lake (from Sir Walter Scott's poem). It would seem that although a woman might have remained at home, her sensibilities and concerns embraced a wider world.

While most quilts reflected American concerns, others, such as the Pieced Mosaic or Hexagon, continued to follow English designs. The remarkable and finely stitched quilt pictured on page 78, made by overstitching in the English template style, is one of a pair made by Mary Hathaway Alden in the mid-nineteenth century.

Ethnic Communities

There were also a number of characteristic quilts produced by particular regional or ethnic groups, in addition to the Amish and European sects (see page 81). While these quilts often share features with mainstream quilts, they do reflect the special concerns, beliefs or aspirations of the communities which made them.

Hawaiian quilts are characterized by their central medallion format and highly contrasting appliquéd patterns made from folded cut-paper designs, often based on native plants, flags and symbols of royalty. A combination of native art motifs and missionary-inspired traditional cotton quilting techniques gave rise to these uniquely crafted quilts.

The German settlers who emigrated to Penn-

sylvania learned the tradition of quilting from their neighbors from the British Isles. They tended to create quilts mostly out of red and green on a white background; when a third color was added it was either yellow or orange or possibly pink. Popular motifs included tulips, birds and hearts, and appliqué flower patterns such as Rose Wreath, Cockscomb and Currant and Peony among others. Often these would be arranged in quarters or smaller blocks. There are few Pennsylvania German quilts which can be documented before 1850, since until this period families in the communities preferred the German-style feather beds and comforters to quilts.

Afro-American quilts reflect both an American and an African heritage. Popular perceptions of these quilts, however, often end up as stereotypes which are not accurate. Black people have been in America for many generations; they fought in the Revolutionary and Civil Wars, helped to settle the frontier, and formed stable communities throughout the country, and many black quilt designs reflect this American heritage. Nevertheless, a segment of documented black quilts also reflects African influences, including the use of vivid color combinations, irregular piecing, big stitches and multiple patterns.

To date there is insufficient research and documentation of black-American quilts. However, what is evident is that there is no single identifiable quilt which can be called typical of black-American quilts.

Probably the best-known of those quilts created by black American women which have been documented is one made by the former slave Harriet Powers, in Georgia in 1895. Called 'Creation of the Animals', it contains a series of fifteen appliquéd blocks depicting a narrative based on biblical motifs. This remarkable quilt, now in the Museum of Fine Arts in Boston, is said to be reminiscent of traditional appliquéd textiles from Dahomey in West Africa.

Oral interviews with ex-slaves and their descendants, conducted in the 1930s as part of a study, indicate that quilts were primarily made to supply much-needed bedding for the slave quarters, as well as for the main house. The quilts were patched together out of worn clothing and scraps and filled with cotton bits left on the ground, or with sheep's wool that clung onto fences or plants. Sometimes women could buy new material with occasional money they earned by selling produce. Or they might be given left-over material from the big house. The so-called 'sewing slaves' would have made quilts among other items for the mistress. According to the authors of *Hearts and Hands*, quilting, even during the period of slavery, prior to the Civil War, was an important social activity in the South, reinforcing a sense of community and family.[14]

Amish Quilts

The Amish and Mennonite Sects created one of the best known and most distinctive bodies of American quilts. Amish quilts are noted for the quality of their craftsmanship and their heightened use of color and design, expressive of a history and culture particular to the Amish people.

The Amish, or 'Plain People', are an Anabaptist sect that broke from the Swiss Mennonite movement in the 1690s. Determined to hold them-

selves aloof from the vanities of the outside world and to model themselves on the early pure Christians, they emigrated from southern Germany to America during the nineteenth century at the invitation of William Penn. Like many other religious groups they settled in Pennsylvania, but unlike any other Pennsylvania Dutch immigrants the Amish managed to maintain a strong sense of faith and community spirit over successive generations.

The rules of the Amish social order are provided by the *Ordnung* (pronounced ott-ning),

---

CROWN OF THORNS
This finely stitched Ohio Amish quilt, made in the 1920s, illustrates the color palette most often favored by the Amish women of this area. The sixteen pattern blocks within the handsome purple interior border are framed by eight rows of fine rope quilting. The binding is, as usual, machine stitched and the backing is made of simple, hand-dyed green muslin.

Size: 75 × 64″/190.5 × 162.5 cm

are still followed to a greater or lesser degree by all members. Basic rules concerning dress and the use of decoration in the home are set out in the first part of the *Ordnung*. For example:

Decided that there shall be no display in houses, namely when the houses are built or painted, with various colors or filled with showy furniture . . . not to make such proud kinds of furniture and not to decorate them with such loud or gay colors . . . No ornamental, bright, showy, form fitting, immodest or silk like clothing . . . dress coats . . . to be black only . . . dress socks to be black . . . hats to be black . . . no pressed trousers . . . women to wear shawls, bonnets or caps in public . . .[15]

The second part of the *Ordnung* is the set of understood customs and traditions governing all aspects of daily life; these vary among sects and regions.

By the second half of the nineteenth century, the Amish had begun to form communities throughout the Midwest, and by the 1860s they began to acquire the American penchant for quiltmaking, as part of a general exchange of ideas, goods and practices between themselves and their 'English' (as anyone who is not Amish is called) neighbors. Different communities evolved different sets of traditions and these were applied equally to their needlework. For example, women from Lancaster County, Pennsylvania, when making quilts, relied on one set of colors such as rich blues, purples and greens, and favored large geometric designs, while Amish women from an Ohio church would have employed colors and designs from a brighter palette, including yellows, pinks and greens against a navy, black or blue background. There were no written rules for these choices; rather it was a matter of custom within a particular community. Midwestern Amish quilts are in general much freer in their designs, vary widely in patterns and are less easily identifiable than their Eastern counterparts. The beautifully made purple and black 1920s Crown of Thorns Quilt on page 81, and the vibrant 1940s Broken Star Quilt on page 83 are typical of vibrant Ohio Amish work.

It was the custom for an Amish woman to do most of the piecing of the quilt at home. Fre-quently it was the older Amish women – the grandmothers and the great-aunts – who did this cutting and piecing. Most of the pieces in the tops were cut from straight-edged abstract shapes such as squares, triangles and diamonds, which were then sewn together with a treadle sewing machine. The tops were lined with soft wool and quilted, starting from the center and working outward, by a group of women at a frolic or bee.

Shunning what they felt to be frivolous, the Amish generally avoided appliqué on their quilts and printed fabrics, if used, were restricted to the backing material. Yet they used elaborate quilting patterns that kept the filling in place, an addition both decorative and functional. These quilting designs – from the loose feather to the basket and the multi-pointed star – deliberately play off against the patterns of the colors. There is some evidence that the ornamental stitching patterns used by the Amish were influenced by the gay appliquéd motifs of the quilts created by their Pennsylvanian German, non-Amish neighbors, but without their reds and yellows.

Until the end of the nineteenth century most Amish women continued to make and dye their cloth and clothing by hand, and quilts were mostly made out of carefully salvaged remnants. The earliest Amish quilts, which were of the wholecloth style in the mid-nineteenth century and medallion design by the late nineteenth century, seem to have been deliberately chosen by Amish women because they were out of fashion with the 'English' community. By the twentieth century, however, Amish styles became more widely diversified as stable and prosperous communities developed, and less restrictive practices encouraged Amish women to experiment more freely with color and design.

Quilts and the Women's Christian Temperance Union

While Amish quilts reflect a unique chapter in quiltmaking by American women from a cohesive community, other American women during the last years of the nineteenth century were beginning to address themselves to issues outside their own communities. Quiltmaking, which had become an activity to help raise money for

Size: 76 × 76″ / 193 × 193 cm

AMISH BROKEN STAR
The star is one of the earliest quilt motifs and there are countless
variations on the same theme. Stars feature strongly in Amish quilts
and this particular piece was made in Ohio in the early 1940s, its
strong pastel colors being unique to the Midwest Amish sects. It is
beautifully pieced and quilted.

Size: 80 × 74″/203 × 188 cm

the worthy causes in the mid-nineteenth century, continued to be strongly associated with reform, and in particular with the growing temperance and suffrage movements.

The Industrial Revolution had created a class of women with leisure who were receptive to new ideas and activities. Simultaneously it created a society with glaring evils to which women who had the time to see and investigate responded by urging reform.[16]

After the Civil War, women who were determined to create a suitable domestic setting in which to raise their families carried on the tradition of temperance crusading in an effort to stop widespread alcoholism among men. Following the loosely organized temperance 'crusades' of the 1870s in which Ohio women literally smashed up saloons and bars with axes, a new, more organized group, the Women's Christian Temperance Union, was formed in 1874 to uphold religious and moral standards. The achievements of the Ohio women were recognized by the WCTU when in 1876 the new membership of hundreds of women each paid a dime to have their name embroidered on what was known as the 'Crusader Quilt'.[17]

The WCTU grew into an organization of and for women, one in which women could gain self-confidence through public activities, and internal leadership and support in far-reaching bonds with other women. It sought to transform women's religious enthusiasm into an explicitly political set of concerns, centered around, but by

no means limited to, the issue of alcohol and its indirect effect upon women in the home. Emma Willard, the president of the WCTU from 1879 until her death in 1898, played a major role in linking temperance to the wider issue of women's suffrage. She argued that only the vote could give women the power necessary to eradicate alcoholism.[18]

Quilts made in support of the WCTU relied heavily on symbolism, and the Drunkard's Path pattern was strongly associated with the movement. The Drunkard's Path Quilt pictured on page 84 is unusual since it departs from the traditional blue and white colors normally used by the WCTU for the design.

The WCTU remained an important and indeed crucial organization during the early part of the twentieth century in the run up to full female suffrage. And while vigorously crusading for reform, its mostly 'respectable' membership continued to reflect the conservative opinions and outlook of the native-born Protestant and Methodist women of the Northeast and Midwest. Indeed, many of these women endorsed the growing fashion that encouraged the glorification of America's Colonial past and, paradoxically, women's second-class status. The Colonial Revival Movement, which had become the new national fad by the turn of the century, ironically celebrated a past which had tied women to a dependent role within a domestic setting. Despite this, the twentieth century was to produce a remarkable body of quilts which continued to reflect women's concerns with both personal and public events.

DRUNKARD'S PATH

This early-nineteenth-century pattern illustrates the wide diversity of names given to a single design. Other names for this particular pattern include Solomon's Puzzle, Rocky Road to Dublin, Rocky Road to California, Country Cousin, and Robbing Peter to Pay Paul. Technically, the pattern itself is simple, but the particular arrangement of blocks with curved seams makes its construction rather complex. The lovely beige and red colors in this example, as well as the pieced border treatment, create an overall satisfying and harmonious quilt. This quilt was made in Ohio in the 1880s. A pattern for it appears on pages 162–4.

—5—
The Twentieth Century

The cotton quilt, which had suffered from the vagaries of fashion in the 1870s and 1880s, was now widely embraced as part of the sentiment connected to the Colonial Revival Movement. This national revival celebrated pioneer life and presented a romantic image of the Colonial past with stable social relationships and ethnic and cultural homogeneity.

By the turn of the century, the country was ablaze with patriotic fervor and the 'simple' life of the early settlers – from the Pilgrims through to Thomas Jefferson – was represented as wholesome, pure and commendable. A *Harper's Bazaar* article in 1905 noted that the American woman had 'made herself acquainted with the lives of her Colonial and Revolutionary ancestors'.[1]

At the same time, however, in stark contrast to the fife and drums of the Revolutionary past, a modern consumer ethic was developing for, by the early twentieth century, American industry had flooded the market with a host of consumer delights. From clothing to appliances to toothpaste and socks, Americans were buying and using a heretofore unheard-of number of goods. By 1928 almost two out of every three families owned an automobile and one out of three had a radio. National and state expenditures on education, the arts, medical and scientific research, and social charities reached record levels.[2] The advertising industry successfully sold the plentiful products of this new large-scale mass production to the public.

The Colonial Revival, with its emphasis on the 'simple life of yesteryear', came as a national palliative to the headiness of such widespread materialism. Much of the popular literature of the day, for example, played to the nostalgic sentiments of the urban reading public for whom rural life was synonymous with virtue.

OPPOSITE: *SAILORS*
This quilt was probably made during the early 1940s for a loved one going to serve in the United States Navy. The fanciful sailor figures are appliquéd onto the centers of the diamond blocks and are surrounded by a colorful purple and black grid. Perhaps the most charming feature of the quilt is the expressive character of each sailor, created by the asymmetry and uneven cutting and stitching. The four anchors which complete the border triangles frame the quilt, while the unique neckties on each sailor add a decorative note.

Size: 84 × 66"/213 × 167 cm

This idealization of the past, of home and hearth, simple times and rural pleasures, characterized liberal thinking in early twentieth-century America. An article in *The Designer*, from 1915, illustrates the domestic interpretation of these ideas:

There is, at the present time, a great rage for interior decoration that represents a distinct period of life. And perhaps, among Americans, there is no more popular style of furnishings than that which reproduces in every minutest detail the house of the first inhabitants of the United States. Picturesque, indeed, is the atmosphere of legend and story which surrounds the home of those early settlers. Simplicity is the keynote – and good taste in every particular carried out in the colonial scheme.[3]

A consequence of this 'Revival' was a widespread interest in folk art and handicrafts. For the first time folk art assumed a national prominence and during the 1920s and 1930s important exhibitions were held in major American museums. This focus on images of the American past and 'folk' traditions led to the creation of many new institutions such as Colonial Williamsburg (1926), the American Wing of the Metropolitan Museum of Art (1928), and Henry Ford's Greenfield Village (1929). The prototype for these 'living' exhibitions may well have been the early 'New England Kitchens' which were so well attended at the great Sanitary Fairs held during the Civil War.[4] Central to many of these 'kitchens' had been the quilting frame at which whitecapped and aproned 'Colonial' dames sat, busy stitching a hand-made quilt.

Another active trend at this time was the Arts and Crafts Movement, a popular manifestation among the working and middle classes of the Decorative Arts Movement, which emphasized a return to the pre-industrial standards of workmanship, craft and aesthetics. By the early 1900s, there were many locally organized Arts and Crafts societies which encouraged the creation of objects defined by a style of 'artful simplicity'. There were also a number of rural Arts and Crafts colonies scattered across the country.

New styles of art and architecture, many rooted in the decorative art tradition, also strongly influenced quilt designs. Both the 'Art-Nouveau' style of the 1900s and the 'Art-Deco' style of the 1920s and 1930s adapted easily to pieced and appliquéd quilt patterns. The New York Beauty Quilt pictured on page 89 features a design originally known as Rocky Mountain Road or Crown of Thorns in the previous century. However, commercial forces insisted that it be renamed in the twentieth century. The scalloped edges were an addition inspired by the Art-Deco style.

Thus, the influence of these social and economic trends stimulated twentieth-century quiltmaking practices. The quilt had now become both a symbol of a rich Colonial heritage and a testament to a woman's ability to create an artistic personal statement. As the national fashion for quiltmaking grew, the quilt came to be part of a larger commercial network.

The Quilt Industry and the Media

At the turn of the century, for the first time quilt designs became popularized on a commercial basis. In 1898 new catalogue companies, such as the St Louis, Missouri-based Ladies' Art Company, had begun publication of inexpensive books of quilt patterns and instructions. Researchers in these companies worked to rediscover, document and publish traditional patterns.

Women artists and designers, many professionally trained, developed a multitude of new patterns which both adapted older designs to the popular Art-Deco fashion and created entirely original patterns in a range of sparkling new textiles. The older dark fabrics of the turn of the century, which bore sober little geometrics and sprig-like prints, were replaced by the mid-1920s with jazzy-looking, large floral motifs, Art-Deco designs, and pastels in new sherbet shades of lilac, raspberry, turquoise and green.

Companies which manufactured products associated with quiltmaking – cotton, thread, batting, etc. – advertised heavily in publications targeted for a female readership. These magazines, journals and, later, newspapers promoted a multitude of new patterns in numerous articles and features.

Crib and children's quilts were produced which featured for the first time motifs such as fairy tale and nursery rhyme characters, toys,

Size: 96 × 80″ / 244 × 203 cm

NEW YORK BEAUTY
This elegant, traditional pattern was taken to new heights in the
1920s when the design treatment echoed the art and architecture
of the Art-Deco period. A pattern for this quilt appears on
pages 165–71

FEED SACKS

During the Depression years of the 1930s, manufacturers of feed, flour, salt and sugar bags began using cheap, printed fabrics for their sacks. Bags were manufactured by companies such as the Bemis Bag Company in St Louis and were made out of colorful geometric and floral patterns as well as solid pastel shades. These sacks, cleverly designed with the consumer in mind, were sold in paper wrappers which could be easily slipped off by the purchaser.

Many families took advantage of this and used the feed sacks to make clothes and household goods. Ray Beckmann, who lives in St Charles, Missouri, remembers his grandmother sending his grandfather off to the store to buy some feed, reminding him to make sure the bags 'matched'. An entire sack was evidently only good for making one small shirt and anything bigger, a dress or curtains for example, certainly required a careful matching of sacks. To encourage the continued interest in cotton sacks, some companies actually designed them to become particular sewing projects. For example, sacks intended to become pillowcases were imprinted with floral embroidery motifs. Others were made with quilt blocks printed on them, while some bore patterns for hand puppets or stuffed animals.[5]

Courtesy: Ray Beckmann

animals and alphabets. One of the best known, specifically twentieth-century designs is the childlike Sunbonnet Sue.

Several designs of this period were created to suit the sentimental temperament of the twentieth-century woman. These included the popular Double Wedding Ring pattern, the Dresden Plate and Grandma's Fan. The Grandmother's Flower Garden Quilt pictured on page 92 is an ingenious three-dimensional reinterpretation of the traditional English Hexagon coupled with the Tumbling Blocks pattern.

The *Ladies Home Journal* was one of the most important of the women's magazines and by 1910 it had reached a circulation of nearly 2 million readers. Edward Bok, its influential editor, advocated a return to the traditions of simplicity and domesticity for women. For him a woman's place was still in the home. 'My idea,' he wrote, 'is to keep women at home, especially as there are enough writers who are trying to take her out of it.'[6]

Bok instituted a department called 'How Much Can be Done with Little' in an effort to provide practical tips for simple living. Features such as 'How We Can Live a Simple Life, by an American Mother', 'How to Live Cheaply' and 'A Lesson in Plain Sewing' were all intended to distance women from decades of ornate Victoriana. 'The curse of the American woman today is useless

Mrs Clarence N. Pace with her children and her mother-in-law, in Transylvania, Louisiana, working on a Double Wedding Ring Quilt in June 1940.

Courtesy: The Library of Congress

bric-a-brac,' wrote Bok in 1900. Like other editors, he strongly supported the Arts and Crafts Movement and observed in 1901 that a 'William Morris craze has been developing, and it is a fad we cannot push with too much vigor.'[7]

Marie Webster, the prominent needlework editor of the *Ladies Home Journal* from 1911 to 1917, who in 1915 wrote the first substantial book about quilts, entitled *Quilts, Their Story and How to Make Them*, not only pointed to the value of the hand-made over the machine-manufactured,[8] but went on to equate quilt-making with patriotism.

In its suitability for manufacture within the home, the quilt possesses a peculiar merit. Although exposed for a full century to the competition of machinery, under the depressing influence of which most of the fireside crafts have all but vanished, the making of quilts as a home industry never languished. Its hold on the affections of womanhood has never been stronger than it is today . . . There are more quilts being made at the present time – in the great cities as well as in the rural communities – than ever before, and their construction as a household occupation – and recreation – is steadily increasing in popularity. This should be a source of much satisfaction to all patriotic Americans who believe that the true source of our nation's strength lies in keeping the hearth flame bright.[9]

The Quilt as a Colonial Symbol

Extensive research into the popular media of this period by Jeannette Lasansky and other historians has unearthed a remarkable body of literature dedicated to the presentation of the

GRANDMOTHER'S FLOWER GARDEN
WITH GARDEN PATH

Size: 72 x 96"/
183 x 244 cm

This astonishing quilt was made by Dena Williams of Wright City, Missouri, in the 1930s. The hexagonal blocks are beautifully organized, radiating out from the central six-pointed star. An intricately pieced, green grid separates the successive rings of color-coordinated layers, which are bonded by eye-catching yellow centers. The entire quilt is orchestrated into a subtle optical triumph by the careful placing of light and dark blocks.

FAITHFUL AND TRUE

A Comment on the Institution of Marriage

Nationally known artist Betsy Nimock, of St Louis, Missouri, composed this marvelous collage primarily out of nineteenth-century wedding photos and old quilts. The bottom right-hand photograph is of Dena Josephine Bruning and Arthur Williams on their wedding day.

ABOVE: Dena pictured in 1967 with her church quilting group. She is standing on the left.

TOP LEFT: Dena Williams was born on 29 November, 1889, in this farmhouse. She was the eighth of twelve children, and died in Wright City on 5 March, 1984.

LEFT: Dena and Arthur in 1980.

Even during the early part of the twentieth century, when cities like Chicago and New York were bustling metropolitan centers, many women on the prairies and plains still lived in stark pioneer conditions. Like their mothers before them, these women took great pride in ownership of a sewing machine.

Courtesy: Nebraska State Historical Society

hand-made quilt as an important symbol of Colonial life, family ideals and women's artistic spirit. Articles with titles such as 'Patchwork Romance: Century-Old Quilts Found in Small Weather-beaten Log Cabins in Tennessee' (*House Beautiful*, 1919), 'A Story of Patchwork, Old and New' (*Needlecraft Magazine*, 1929) and 'The Bed Of Yesterday In The House Of Today' (*Good Housekeeping*, 1933) all contributed to the spread of quilt lore.[10] In a fascinating article about the Colonial Revival Movement, Mrs Lasansky quotes an advertisement from the April 1928 edition of *Good Housekeeping* by the Louisville Bedding Company of Kentucky which indicates the way in which commercial enterprises capitalized on the sentiment attached to the word 'Colonial':

Day by day, the magic and beauty of Colonial America is making its way into the modern house. Olde Kentucky Quilts are a delightful result of this desire to recapture the charm of Early American house furnishings. No quest for antiques is more eagerly pursued today than the quest for quilts – the uniquely patterned and brightly colored bed coverings that were the pride of our grandmothers. Unfortunately few of the old quilts remain . . . fortunately, now at a very

modest cost, every room in your house may be fitted with its own particular pattern and color. Olde Kentucky Quilts are rich in tradition and true to their noble ancestry. Each design is faithfully copied from an antique quilt.[11]

The aesthetic impulse calling for simplicity and individual craftsmanship, and the renewed interest in a Colonial past, were also the social and cultural antidotes to political activities which were seen as potentially threatening to national stability. Early twentieth-century America was punctuated by a series of reform movements collectively called Progressivism which sought to bring the nation back to commonsense values.

The Progressive Era

The scandals, public corruption and general immorality of the 'gilded' last years of the previous century were publicly condemned at the highest levels. President Theodore Roosevelt, writing in his autobiography in 1913, noted that the industrial and financial revolutions had provoked a 'riot of individual materialism, under which complete freedom for the individual . . . turned out in practice to mean perfect freedom for the strong to wrong the weak'.[12] Indeed, farmers, shopkeepers, factory workers and prohibitionists formed a number of separate political parties which demonstrated against the rule of big business and the banks.

By the end of the nineteenth century America had experienced violent scenes of labor unrest and with it the growing influence of socialist and anarchist groups. Even Emma Willard, the leader of the WCTU and one of the leaders of the suffrage movement, joined the editorial board of a Christian Socialist magazine. Roosevelt and other reformers were forced to recognize that slums, sweatshops, child labor and giant trusts had become a blight on American society that needed to be severely controlled.

The sense of civic virtue that encouraged the formation of settlement houses, which helped educate and assist the urban poor, and consumer protection agencies was the social gospel that went hand in hand with the revival of personal ethics associated with uncluttered living, aesthetic simplicity (including an emphasis on handicrafts and especially quilts) and renewed contact with nature. The emphasis on nature, which corresponded to a general 'back to the land movement', was a widely espoused popular sentiment, supported by many books and magazines. These included the *Ladies Home Journal*, which actively promoted the invigorating effects of nature, especially for women and children. The widespread effects of these ideas may well have contributed to the cultural environment surrounding interior design in the 1920s, which strongly featured natural motifs.

The cultural nationalism that was expressed by the Colonial Revival Movement carried on in force for most of the first half of the twentieth century and the fashion for Colonial decoration and, in particular, for the hand-made quilt continued unabated. There were many reasons why this movement was so deeply rooted, why it didn't fade away or shift out of fashion like previous styles. One reason was that America needed an embracing set of ideas to temper the excesses of industrial expansion and radicalism. Another was to assure middle-class, white America that the tremendous influx of immigrants wouldn't interfere with the dominant American culture. The First

Rural women and city women alike continued to make calico quilts well into the 1940s. The eloquent piecework on this unnamed pattern belies the simple setting in which the quilt is being assembled.

Courtesy: The Library of Congress

World War created the backdrop for a renewed national identity and need for patriotism, while the onset of the Depression years gave rise to the widespread and reassuring imagery connected to traditional home values and rural America. The advertising industry articulated the national tendency to resurrect folk culture. A host of trade cards and advertisements which evoked rural life was part of a wider trend to sanctify familiar domestic ideals and to resurrect the home as a refuge from the economic ravages of the day.[13] By the Depression years of the 1930s President Franklin D. Roosevelt had instituted a host of grassroots projects as part of the 'New Deal' which attempted to systematically document American folk and art traditions. One of these, the Index of

American Design, lent aesthetic credibility to folk art.[14] These traditions were subject, like the rest of American life, to changes which reflected the twentieth-century experience.

Published Quilt Patterns and Exhibitions

Despite all the popular pressures and influences upon quilters, older established traditions remained unchanged. Women continued, as their mothers and grandmothers before them, to go to church guilds and other organizations and quilt together. Many other women, heedless of fashion, carried on individually making quilts in a variety of calico prints and designs.

The Hearts and Gizzards Quilt on page 97 was made by Mrs Kunze of Illinois sometime around the early part of the century. It may have been quilted jointly by members of her church sewing guild. The old custom of local women getting together to quilt was in fact reinforced by all of the quilting information in the media. Farm journals such as *The Progressive Farmer*, *The National Stockman* and *Farm and Fireside*, as well as home decorating and fashion publications like *Good Housekeeping*, *Hearth and Home* and *Better Homes and Gardens* had all, by the 1920s, begun the widespread publication of printed patterns and instructions. Many of these were taken up by local groups.

The idea of printing patterns certainly was not a new one. English magazines of the nineteenth century such as *The Family Friend*, and books such as *Treasures in Needlework* had published a number of patterns and instructions which were promptly copied by the American magazine *Godey's* and later by both *Graham's* and *Peterson's* magazines. In the 'Crazy Quilt' years, magazines and journals such as *Art Amateur* published detailed descriptions of how to make a Crazy Quilt. What was new, however, was the commercialization of the quilt pattern industry.

These early published patterns were produced by providing quilters with large sheets of paper with the actual design printed on them. This was then traced and transferred onto a piece of heavy paper which was used as a template. Advances in techniques soon led, in the early 1900s, to methods where a pattern could be transferred onto fabric simply by running a hot iron over it. The commercialization of quilting led companies to an ongoing search for new products and new designs. An advertisement from a 1933 edition of the *Knoxville News Sentinel* exclaims about a new cold-transfer method called 'The Wonder Package', which offered readers: 'No more hot irons – no more waste!' Sears, Roebuck and Company offered perforated quilting patterns and stamping wax: 'No more tiresome marking of quilts in the old-fashioned way.'[15]

The Ladies' Art Company, as mentioned earlier, was the first company to publish an inexpensive catalogue, entitled *Diagrams of Quilt, Sofa and Pin Cushion Patterns*. Their method was to cut out paper pattern pieces by hand, which were then hand-painted in watercolor, numbered, folded and tucked into an envelope.[16] The Ladies' Art Company advertisement admonished: 'Every quilter should have our book of 400 designs, containing the prettiest, queerest, scarcest, most grotesque patterns from the old log cabin to star and puzzle designs.'[17]

Other early companies and individuals included Clara Stone's *Practical Needlework Patterns* and Marie Webster's home business in Indiana. Prominent publishers included Rose Kretsinger, and Anne Orr, the Art-Needlework editor of *Good Housekeeping* from 1919 until 1940, who directed a remarkably brisk pattern business from Nashville, Tennessee.

Pattern Designers

A new development in twentieth-century quilting which followed from the publication of commercial patterns was the promotion of a number of women artists who created individual and distinct designs. The names are associated with their companies: Marie Webster, Anne Orr, Rose Kretsinger and Ruby Short McKim, among others. The designs were not only published by the artists themselves, but were also used by various syndication companies and the batting (wadding) manufacturers.

Marie Webster's designs were very much influenced by Art-Nouveau ideas. She tended to create floral motifs in a more linear flowing style coupled with new pastel shades. Her well-known

HEARTS AND GIZZARDS

Size: 80 × 82"/203 × 208 cm

Instructions on how to make this quilt are on page 143.

This evocatively named quilt was made in Illinois around the turn of the century by Mrs Lena Kunze. The tiny prints on both shades of the red and blue fabrics were typical of the millions of yards of inexpensive calico which was printed in US textile mills every year during this period.

Lena Kunze, née Kertz, was born in Millstadt, Illinois in 1880, one of six children of John and Elizabeth (Mueller) Kertz. She is pictured, right, with her husband, Ferdinand Kunze, a widower, whose three children she raised as her own. Lena was involved in many church activities, including the Quilting Guild, and a completed quilt was a happy occasion for the ladies of her Guild.

Her birthdays were always spent with the entire family, and on her 88th birthday, Lena's family and friends gathered once more to celebrate her life as she was laid to rest.

PATTERN BOOKS

A selection of quilt catalogues from the early twentieth century, kindly loaned by Doris Beckham.

Early twentieth-century pattern books bore titles such as *Grandmother Clark's Quilting Designs*, *The Farmer's Wife New Book of Quilts* and *Grandma Dexter's Appliqué and Patchwork Quilt Designs*. The names were very much bound up with popular, old-fashioned, rural nostalgia. Companies outdid themselves in an effort to appeal to the sentiments of their growing readership.

The introduction to Grandma Dexter's book (Dexter's was, incidentally, a major manufacturer of sewing cotton), published by the Virginia Snow Studios in Elgin, Illinois, reads:

In the colonial homes of our grandmothers the patchwork quilt held a high place in the esteem of all women. Our resourceful ancestors saved every scrap of material available and worked out many original, odd and beautiful designs for the pieced quilt. Many of these patterns have been handed down from one generation to another for years and are highly prized for their decorative value.[18]

Grandma Clark's book was no different:

In the pioneer days of our grandmothers, every home, even to the little log cabin, had its share of patchwork quilts. There was calm and contentment in sewing the tiny pieces together until they gradually took on the semblance of flowers, stars, rings or fanciful figures . . .[19]

patterns included Sunflowers, Dogwood, Grapes and Vines, Indiana Wreath, Irises, Poppies and the intricate Tree of Life.

The quilts favored by Anne Orr were mainly floral appliqués of soft pastel fabrics stitched onto light backgrounds. Often these would be in the central medallion style reminiscent of the Colonial period and finished with a scalloped edge. Designs included The Jonquil, Nosegay and Poppy. Anne Orr was also well known for a series of intricate, pieced floral and basket patterns which resembled cross-stitched embroidery. The French Wreath and Heirloom Basket were two of her most popular patterns.

Ruby Short McKim, Art-Needlework editor for *Better Homes and Gardens*, published a number of inspired designs from her studio in Independence, Missouri. One of the most well known of her patterns, which tended to be done in blocks, was the Iris pictured on page 99.

By the 1920s, newspapers began to feature quilt columns in their Saturday and Sunday editions. These features were either locally produced or part of a national syndication network, and by 1934 more than 400 newspapers included such columns.[20] *The Chicago Tribune*, *The Kansas City Star* and *The Rural New Yorker* were among those papers which published hundreds of patterns over the years. Many of these appeared under 'apple pie' names like Aunt

Size: 96 × 78″/244 × 198 cm

Size: 86 × 66″/218 × 167 cm

IRIS QUILT
The six-sided, lozenge-shaped background of each block of this quilt creates a compelling setting for these colorful irises. Although the designer, Ruby Short McKim, suggested a general approach to the design, it was the maker's personal interpretation to add the charming inner green border that gracefully follows the block contour. The design is further individualized by the decorative top-stitching on the Deco-inspired petals and stems. The outer border frames of green and white are simple and crisp.

ROUND-UP TIME
Possibly derived from a 1940s quilt kit, this design has been painstakingly personalized with detailed and elaborate embroidery. Distinctive quilting radiates in a sunburst pattern from the center, and there is a fine feathered border around the beautifully scalloped edge. The rather inspired central motif bears a strong resemblance to earlier central medallion styles, the colors of the appliquéd figures having been carefully chosen to give depth and a three-dimensional quality to the scene.

Martha or Grandmother Clark. The most well known of the designers who produced patterns for newspapers was Laura Wheeler, whose designs were syndicated through the Old Chelsea Station Needlecraft Service of New York. Her patterns were popular because often they were pieced, which encouraged women to use up old scraps.[21]

National batting companies, such as Stearns & Foster's Mountain Mist, Rock River Cotton Company and Lockport took the mantle for popularizing quilt patterns when they began to include free patterns in or printed on their packaging.

Quilt kits were introduced during the 1920s and 1930s, by a number of firms, including the Ladies' Art Company in 1922. The more expensive kits would include a cotton sheet with the appropriate design stamped on it as well as the quilting lines, and pieces of pre-cut, color-sorted fabric were also included. For example, a Pansy appliqué kit available from *Needlecraft Magazine* included a piece of cotton sheet stamped with appliqué placements and quilting lines.[22] The Western motif which inspired the Round-Up Time Quilt pictured above may very well have been the result of a purchased kit pattern. The

MAMMY QUILTS

In the early part of the twentieth century, a type of quilt which found a limited audience was that made by white women depicting their interpretation of black characters. These quilts were for the most part inspired by the deeply ingrained racist attitudes which dominated American society at all levels, particularly around the turn of the century.

The vintage photograph below shows a black

Courtesy: Missouri Historical Society

nurse caring for a white child; these women were popularly cast in America as 'Mammy' figures, and by 1890 this had become one of the most well-known black folk images. Although Mammy had existed since well before the Emancipation Proclamation of 1862, this symbol of the southern black character, associated with benevolence and nurturing, still endures, nearly 130 years after.

Stereotypical black characters, which included the black mammy, were part of the dominant American culture in the early years of the twentieth century. References to this character were well known as advertising symbols, as early as 1890, for maple syrup and pancakes, among other products. It is not surprising to find Mammy turning up in both published quilt patterns and folk designs. A number of specific patterns, including Black Boy, Little Brown KoKo, Sugar Pie, Kinky and Aunt Jemima, were published by the Capper Publishing Company of Topeka, Kansas, the Ruby McKim Studios, and the Aunt Martha Studios, Kansas City, Missouri.[23]

The Mammy (Aunt Jemima) Quilt pictured opposite has an unusual history. Purchased at an auction in the South, it was said to have been made by a sharecropper who, in the auctioneer's words, 'really used it'. It is signed and dated on the back in indelible ink: 'Lola 1902'. The colorful calico prints on the figurative portion of this quilt may have come from cotton feedsacks or perhaps from cotton housecoats worn by members of Lola's family. The appliquéd portions have been tacked first by hand, then machined onto the block in a variety of thread colors. The pink sashings with blue posts separate the blocks and complement the scrap-like quality of the prints. The quilt is tied, rather than quilted, and is said to have a summer quilt stitched inside as its lining.

Despite the inscribed date, however, the fabrics are definitely of 1920s vintage. Perhaps the puzzlement might be resolved if 1902 were, as suggested by one historian, Lola's year of birth. However, many of the stories which accompany quilts are sometimes apocryphal, despite good intentions.

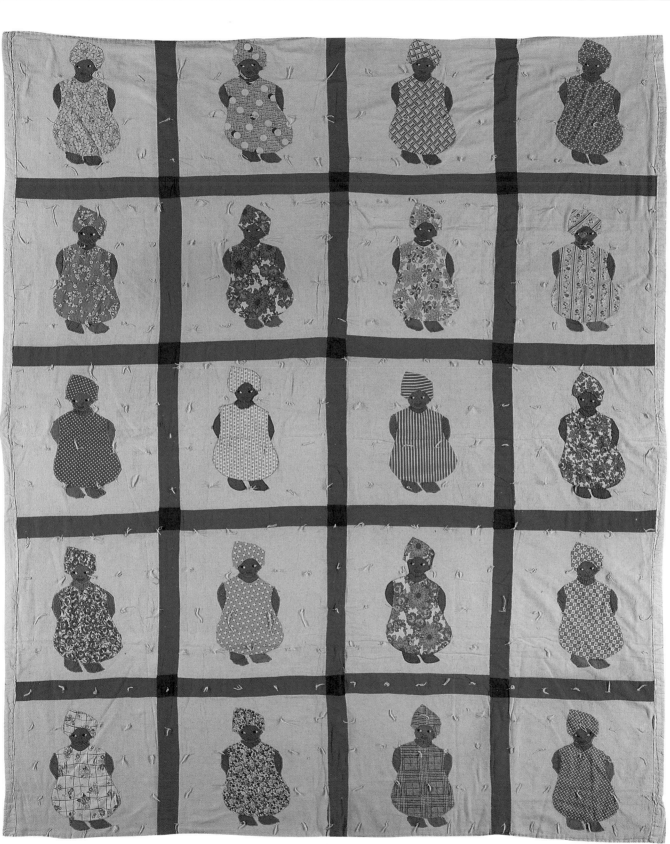

Size: 86 × 72″/218 × 183 cm

detailed appliqué work and the subtle coloring artfully contrived to produce the effect of shadows strongly suggest either the hand of an expert needlewoman, or a kit.

Published patterns, quilt kits and successful quilt designers all represented a new era in quiltmaking where patterns became associated with artists rather than evolving through processes of historical anonymity.

However, there were many other patterns popular during the twentieth century which are unattributable. Many of these designs were interpretations of everyday items, such as had been the practice in the nineteenth century. However, instead of churndashes and cakestands, there were umbrellas and coffee cups; popular and somewhat obscure animal motifs included turtles, birds and Scottie dogs, as well as purely graphic designs. One of the most interesting genre of twentieth-century quilts was that related to national events and people. The charming folklike Sailors Quilt pictured on page 87 illustrates the relentless desire to symbolize important events, and this quilt may well have been made for a relative going off to the navy. The historic solo flight of Charles Lindbergh occasioned the Lone Eagle quilt, Charles Lindbergh Commemorative, pictured on page 204. There was also a strong relationship between quilts and new comic book characters and many charming quilts of this period feature popular comic heroes.

Exhibitions and Contests

By the twentieth century quilts, as well as other forms of American folk art, were also beginning to be shown at exhibitions and taken more seriously as cultural artefacts. The Newark Museum featured quilts in a show in 1914, followed by one at the University of Kansas in 1920.[24] Quilts also continued to be presented in contests in both agricultural and county fairs. Stearns and Foster, along with department stores and other commercial enterprises directly connected to sewing, sponsored enormously popular quilt contests during the 1930s. The commercialization of quiltmaking encouraged a huge audience of quilt enthusiasts and, for the first time, a major contest was held at a national level. This most spectacular quilt display was one of the main features of the Chicago Exposition in 1933 which was entitled the Century of Progress. A rather brilliant marketing strategy was conceived by Sears, Roebuck and Company who initiated a nationwide quilt contest six months before the fair, offering prize money of $7,500. Over 25,000 women entered their quilts at regional Sears branches.

These quilts were then judged by regional panels of local quilt and art authorities, and thirty of the winning quilts were put on display at the magnificent Sears Building exhibit just inside the fair grounds. The prize for the winning quilt, an Eight-Point Combination Feathered Star made by Margaret Rogers Caden, was handed out by no less a luminary than First Lady Eleanor Roosevelt. Naturally this generated unprecedented publicity and business for Sears and inspired other manufacturers to sponsor similar events on a mostly local level through department stores. Quilts had become part of America's big-time business. But as the war years drew closer, women's interests turned to other more pressing considerations.

By the 1940s, the fad for quilting began to diminish. With America's involvement in the Second World War, women were called upon in large numbers to join the workforce, and as both time and fabric became scarce there seemed to be less and less reason to make quilts. Although quilting certainly continued locally among women all over America, it wasn't until thirty years later, in the early 1970s, that quilts were once more to gain national attention when new, aesthetic considerations previously applied to paintings were now directed to quilts.

Conclusion

By the twentieth century, quiltmaking had come to acquire a grass-roots force of its own. It had evolved its own folklore, its own symbols and its own traditions which were passed down verbally, or by example, through families and exchanged among communities. American life as experienced by women – personal and social, material and spiritual, everyday and artistic – had been stitched into a remarkable legacy. And whether pieced, embroidered or appliquéd, quilts came to reflect the enduring spirit of women. With their profusion of colors, fabrics and detailed stitchery, quilts can be read as a kind of textile journal.

Quiltmaking in America has been subject to many influences over the years. Economics, politics, religion and technology as well as cultural ideas have all played a role in defining the history of the American quilt. But while these trends were certainly a part of a woman's daily experience, the greater or lesser individual act of creativity, out of which every quilt was fashioned, came from the same timeless impulse that informs any work of art.

From the delicate chintz and flowered quilts of the eighteenth century, the heavy woolen Log Cabins of the 1860s and silk and velvet embroidered Crazies of the 1880s, to the airplanes and sailors of the twentieth century, quilts imbue American history with both a social and visual dimension.

Nowhere else do quilted bedcoverings show the degree of skill and originality seen in American quilts. For indeed quilts are more than decorative covers, they are genuine documents that illustrate the generosity of spirit, the strength and creativity of generations of American women.

Notes to Text

CHAPTER 1

1 William Bradford, quoted in Daniel J. Boorstin. *The Americans: The Colonial Experience*, p.1.
2 Sally Garoutte. 'Early Colonial Quilts in a Bedding Context'. Garoutte and Horton (Eds.). *Uncoverings*. Vol. 1, 1980, pp.18–25.
3 The Museum of American Folk Art. *The Fabric of the State*. New York, 1972. Unpaginated.
4 Frances Little. *Early American Textiles*, p.223.
5 Marie D. Webster. *Quilts: Their Story and How to Make Them*, p.70.
6 George Francis Dow. 'The Arts and Crafts of New England 1704–1775', quoted in Patsy and Myron Orlofsky. *Quilts in America*, p.33.
7 Barbara Brackman. *Clues in the Calico*, p.16.
8 Patsy and Myron Orlofsky. *Quilts in America*, p.216.
9 Patricia Wardle. *Guide to English Embroidery*. Victoria & Albert Museum, HMSO, London, 1970, p.9.
10 Averil Colby. *Patchwork*, p.26.
11 Lacy Folmar Bullard and Betty Jo Shiell. *Chintz Quilts: Unfading Glory*, p.14.
12 Judy Wentworth. 'English Patchwork Covers'. *Antique Collecting*, pp.27–30.
13 'Nineteenth-Century Appliqué Quilts'. Dilys Blum and Jack Lindsey (Eds.). *Philadelphia Museum of Art Bulletin: Quilts*, p.20.
page 11: 'Scenic Farmyard' from Goodrich, S. G. *A Pictorial Geography of the World*.
page 13: John Hewson Coverlet given by Miss Ella Hodgson to the Philadelphia Museum of Art.

CHAPTER 2

1 Jack Larkin. *The Reshaping of Everyday Life 1790–1840*, p.4.
2 *Ibid.* p.16.
3 *Ibid.* p.268.
4 Orlofsky. *Quilts in America*, p.45.
5 Lucy Larcom. *A New England Girlhood*, pp.27–9, 122.
6 J.G.M. Ramsey. 'The Annals of Tennessee', quoted in Orlofsky. *Quilts in America*, p.45.
7 Francis Underwood. 'Quabbin: The Story of a Small Town with Outlooks on Puritan Life', quoted in Larkin. *The Reshaping of Everyday Life*, p.26.
8 'The Female World of Love and Ritual: Relations between Women in Nineteenth-Century America'. Linda K. Kerber and Jane De Hart Mathews (Eds.). *Women's America: Refocusing the Past*, pp.167–82.
9 Francis Lichten. 'Folk Art of Rural Pennsylvania', quoted in Orlofsky. *Quilts in America*, p.49.
10 Adolph B. Benson (Ed.). *America of the Fifties: Letters of Frederika Bremer*, p.54.
11 Larkin. *The Reshaping of Everyday Life*, p.122.
12 Frederick Marryat. 'A Diary in America with Remarks on its Institutions', quoted in Larkin. *The Reshaping of Everyday Life*, p.2.
13 Barbara Brackman. *Clues in the Calico*, p.17.
14 Jonathan Holstein. 'The American Block Quilt'. Jeannette Lasansky (Ed.). *In The Heart of Pennsylvania: Symposium Papers*, p.21.
15 Blum and Lindsey (Eds.). *Philadelphia Museum of Art Bulletin: Quilts*, p.18.
16 Judy Wentworth. *English Patchwork Covers*, p.27.
17 Blum and Lindsey (Eds.). *Philadelphia Museum of Art Bulletin: Quilts*, p.26.
18 Daniel J. Boorstin. *The Americans: The National Experience*, p.27.

19 Caroline Howard King. 'When I Lived in Salem 1822–66', quoted in Judith Reiter Weissman and Wendy Lavitt. *Labors of Love: America's Textiles and Needlework 1650–1930*, p.73.
20 Larkin. *The Reshaping of Everyday Life*, p.50.
21 Lydia Sigorney. 'Letters to Mother', quoted in David E. Shi. *The Simple Life*, p.113.
22 Nancy F. Cott. *The Bonds of Womanhood*, p.158.
23 Kerber and Mathews (Eds.). Essay 'The Republican Mother'. *Women's America: Refocusing the Past*, p.85.
24 Lydia Maria Child. *The American Frugal Housewife*. S. & W. Wood, New York, 1845, p.1.
25 Catherine Beecher. *A Treatise on Domestic Economy*. Boston, 1841, p.298.
26 Harriet Beecher Stowe. *The Minister's Wooing*, W.B. Conkey, Chicago, p.287.
27 Barbara Welter. 'The Cult of True Womanhood: 1820–1860'. *American Quarterly*, pp.151–74.
28 John A. Garraty and Robert McGaughey. *The American Nation*, p.290.
29 Charles Dickens. 'American Notes for Circulation', quoted in Garraty and McGaughey. *The American Nation*, p.290.
30 Edith Abbott. 'Women in Industry'. New York, 1910. *Encyclopaedia Britannica*. 14th Edn., Vol. 14, 1929, p.443.
31 *Voice of Industry*, 7 May, 1847 quoted in Hélen C. Sumner. *History of Women in Industry in the United States*. Govt. Printing Office, Washington D.C., 1910, p.102.
32 Pat Ferrero, Elaine Hedges and Julie Silber. *Hearts and Hands: The Influence of Women & Quilts on American Society*, p.33.
page 23: 'Quilting Bee' from *Anonymous was a Woman*, p.63.
page 24: 'Framing a Building' from *Stories of Henry and Frank*, Part II, New York, p.6.
page 32: 'Attributes of True Womanhood'. Illustration from *Anonymous was a Woman*, p.87.

CHAPTER 3

1 Kerber and Mathews (Eds.). *Women's America*, p.172.
2 Dena Katzenberg, quoted in Dennis Duke and Deborah Harding (Eds.). *America's Glorious Quilts*. Park Lane, New York, 1987, p.22.
3 Ricky Clark. 'Mid-19th-Century Album and Friendship Quilts: 1860–1920'. Jeannette Lasansky (Ed.). *Pieced by Mother: Symposium Papers*, pp.77–85.
4 Barbara Brackman. 'Signature Quilts'. Garoutte and Horton (Eds.). *Uncoverings*. Vol. 10, 1989, pp.25–37.
5 Ferrero, Hedges and Silber. *Hearts and Hands*, p.54.
6 Lillian Schlissel. *Women's Diaries of the Westward Journey*, p.58.
7 Elizabeth Weyhrauch Shea and Patricia Cox Crews. 'Nebraska Quiltmakers: 1870–1940'. Garoutte and Horton (Eds.). *Uncoverings*. Vol. 10, 1989, p.59.
8 Glenda Riley. *The Female Frontier*, p.88.
9 *Ibid.* p.26.
10 *Ibid.* p.27.
11 Schlissel. *Women's Diaries of the Westward Journey*, p.136.
12 *Ibid.* p.138.
13 Eliza Calvert Hall. *Aunt Jane of Kentucky*, p.76.
14 Joanna L. Stratton. *Pioneer Women: Voices from the Kansas Frontier*, p.69.
15 Carol Pinney Crabb. 'The Evolution of Quilt Shows at Nineteenth-Century Missouri Fairs'. *Missouri Folklore Society Journal*. Vol. V, 1983, pp.1–15.
16 Schlissel. *Women's Diaries of the Westward Journey*, p.147.
17 Kerber and Mathews (Eds.). *Women's America*, p.123.

18 Stratton. *Pioneer Women*, p.68.
19 Lillian Schlissel, Byrd Gibbens, & Elizabeth Hampsten. *Far From Home*, p.23.
20 Garraty and McGaughey. *The American Nation*, p.294.
21 Shi. *The Simple Life*, p.105.
22 Brackman. *Clues in the Calico*, p.165.
23 Suellen Meyer. 'Visible Machine Stitching'. Garoutte and Horton (Eds.). *Uncoverings*. Vol. 10, 1989, pp.38–53.
24 *Ibid.*
25 Virginia Gunn. 'Quilts for Union Soldiers in the Civil War'. Garoutte and Horton (Eds.). *Uncoverings.* Vol. 6, 1985, pp.95–117.
26 *Ibid.*
27 Riley. *The Female Frontier*, p.161.
28 Gunn. 'Quilts for Union Soldiers in the Civil War'. Garoutte and Horton (Eds.). *Uncoverings*, Vol. 6, 1985, p.114.
29 Laurel Horton. 'South Carolina Quilts and the Civil War'. Garoutte and Horton (Eds.). *Uncoverings.* Vol. 6, 1985, pp.53–69.
30 Ferrero, Hedges and Silber. *Hearts and Hands*, p.81.
31 *Ibid.* p.77.
32 Gunn. 'Quilts for Union Soldiers in the Civil War'. Garoutte and Horton (Eds.). *Uncoverings*, Vol. 6, 1985, p.106.
33 Riley. *The Female Frontier*, p.163.
34 Daniel J. Boorstin. *The Americans: The Democratic Experience*, p.97.
page 44: 'Madonna of the Prairie', 1921 Oil on canvas by W.H.D. Koerner (1878–1938).

CHAPTER 4

1 Virginia Gunn. 'Dress Fabrics of the Late 19th Century'. Jeannette Lasansky (Ed.). *Bits and Pieces: Textile Traditions*, pp.4–15.
2 Ruth Bordin. *Women and Temperance*, p.11.
3 Mark Twain quoted in Shi. *The Simple Life*, p.155.
4 Jeannette Lasansky. 'The Role of the Haps in Central Pennsylvania's 19th and 20th Century Quiltmaking Traditions'. Garoutte and Horton (Eds.). *Uncoverings*, Vol. 6, 1985, p.88.
5 William Morris quoted in E.P. Thompson. *William Morris: Romantic to Revolutionary*, p.106.
6 Virginia Gunn. 'Crazy Quilts and Outline Quilts: Popular Responses to the Decorative Art/Art Needlework Movement 1876–1893'. Garoutte and Horton (Eds.). *Uncoverings*, Vol. 5, 1984, p.135.
7 *Ibid.* p.136.
8 *Ibid.* p.132.
9 Gunn. 'Crazy Quilts and Outline Quilts'. Garoutte and Horton (Eds.). *Uncoverings*, Vol. 5, 1984, p.142.
10 *Dorcas Magazine* quoted in Virginia Gunn. 'Crazy Quilts and Outline Quilts'. Garoutte and Horton (Eds.). *Uncoverings*, Vol. 5, 1984, p.145.
11 Jeannette Lasansky. 'The Colonial Revival and Quilts 1864–1976'. Jeannette Lasansky (Ed.). *Pieced by Mother: Symposium Papers*, pp.97–105.
12 Orlofsky. *Quilts in America*, p.247.
13 Ruth Finley. *Old Patchwork Quilts and the Women Who Made Them*, p.90.

14 Ferrero, Hedges and Silber. *Hearts and Hands*, p.45.
15 Eve Wheatcroft Granick. *The Amish Quilt*, p.15.
16 Bordin. *Women and Temperance*, p.12.
17 Jeannette Lasansky (Ed.). *Pieced by Mother: Symposium Papers*, p.88.
18 Barbara L. Epstein. *The Politics of Domesticity*, p.116.
19 *Ibid.*

CHAPTER 5

1 Virginia Gunn. 'Quilts for Milady's Boudoir. Garoutte and Horton (Eds.). *Uncoverings*. Vol. 10, 1989, p.82.
2 Shi. *The Simple Life*, p.221.
3 Jeannette Lasansky (Ed.). *Pieced by Mother: Symposium Papers*, p.102.
4 Jeannette Lasansky (Ed.) *Pieced by Mother: Over 100 Years of Quiltmaking Traditions*, p. 105.
5 Merikay Waldvogel. *Soft Covers for Hard Times*, p.67.
6 Edward Bok. 'Is It Worthwhile?'. *Ladies Home Journal*. Vol. 17, November 1900, p.8.
7 Edward Bok quoted in Shi. *The Simple Life*, p.190.
8 Waldvogel. *Soft Covers for Hard Times*, p.2.
9 Marie D. Webster. *Quilts: Their Story and How to Make Them*, p.xvi.
10 Jeannette Lasansky (Ed.). *Pieced by Mother: Symposium Papers*, p.102.
11 Jeannette Lasansky (Ed.). *Pieced by Mother: Over 100 Years of Quiltmaking Traditions*, p.106.
12 Theodore Roosevelt. *An Autobiography*. New York, 1913, pp.460–3.
13 Jackson Lears. From an essay in Jane S. Becker and Barbara Franco. *Folk Roots, New Roots*, p.124.
14 Waldvogel. *Soft Covers for Hard Times*, p.xii.
15 *Ibid.* p.12.
16 Thomas K. Woodard & Blanche Greenstein. *Twentieth-Century Quilts*, p.20.
17 Brackman. *Clues in the Calico*, p.28.
18 Grandma Dexter. *Appliqué and Patchwork Quilt Designs*. Book No. 36. Virginia Snow Studios, Elgin, Illinois.
19 Grandmother Clark. *Patchwork Quilt Designs*. Book No. 20. St Louis, Missouri. 1931.
20 Brackman. *Clues in the Calico*, p.31.
21 Waldvogel. *Soft Covers for Hard Times*, p.16.
22 *Ibid.* p.14.
23 Cuesta Benberry. 'White Perspectives of Blacks in Quilts and Related Media'. Garoutte and Horton (Eds.). *Uncoverings*. Vol. 4, 1983, p.67.
24 Jeannette Lasansky (Ed.). *Pieced by Mother: Over 100 Years of Quiltmaking Traditions*, p.107.
page 91: 'Double Wedding Ring Quilt'. Photograph taken for the Farm Security Association by Marion Post Wolcott. LC-USF 34-54023-D-100336.
page 95: 'Negro Woman Quilting'. Photograph taken for the Farm Security Association by Jack Delano, April 1941. LC-USF 34-43775-D.

Quiltmaking Techniques

Selecting a Quilt

The thirty quilts that follow have been divided into three groups: easy designs that a beginner can tackle with no difficulty, intermediate patterns for those with a bit of experience, and advanced projects for accomplished quilters who are not afraid of a challenge. The instructions for each quilt include the size of both a single block (if applicable) and the finished quilt, a complete list of materials, and easy-to-follow, step-by-step instructions accompanied by clear diagrams to guide you every step of the way.

While instructions are only given for constructing the quilts shown in the color photographs, you need not feel limited to making a full-size quilt. You can use the designs in this book as a springboard to create your own unique projects.

Any of the patterns can be easily adapted to make a wallhanging, child's quilt, table runner, cushion cover and many other projects.

ENLARGING AND REDUCING QUILT SIZES

The sizes of the quilts in this book vary, so you must first decide how big you want your quilt to be. Study the conversion table below to see which size quilt would be right for your bed, then compare this measurement with the size of the quilt you have chosen to make. If the quilt in this book is smaller or larger, there are various ways that you can adapt the design in order to create a quilt that's just right for your needs.

The first, and most obvious way, is to make more or less blocks. Add or subtract the size of a single block to the length and width of the quilt. If

Conversion Chart

STANDARD BED SIZES			SIZE OF QUILT	
Type	Width	Length	Width	Length
crib (cot)	27–28″/69–71 cm	50–52″/127–132 cm	37″/94 cm	52–56″/132–142 cm
single	30″/76 cm	75″/190 cm	66″/168 cm	90–96″/229–244 cm
twin	39″/99 cm	75″/190 cm	66″/168 cm	90–96″/229–244 cm
double (queen)	54″/137 cm	75″/190 cm	80″/203 cm	90–96″/229–244 cm
queen (king)	60″/152 cm	80″/203 cm	90″/229 cm	96–100″/244–254 cm
king	72–79/183–200 cm	80–84″/203–213 cm	104″/264 cm	96–100″/244–254 cm

Color Values

Value is the degree of lightness or darkness of a color – for instance: light pink, medium pink and dark pink (see the Color Diagram).

Most of the quilt designs in this book are not monochromatic, so you may be selecting a light value of one color to be set against a medium value of another. How do you go about determining the difference between color values?

When you look at a quilt, there will be a number of fabrics that really stand out among the rest. In a highly contrasting quilt, these will usually be light and dark fabrics. In quilts with more colors, a medium fabric will be used to bridge the gap between the light and dark fabrics. These three values, light, medium and dark, are the 'major' fabrics that you need to select first. You can then choose additional 'minor' fabrics to work with them. When following the list of color values given with each set of quilt instructions, refer to the list below to understand how the values have been used.

White is a neutral color – it is not actually a value at all. A reference to white will only be included on the list to differentiate it from a light color or when it is a very important part of the color scheme – as in a white, red and green quilt. Otherwise, white will be referred to as 'light'.

Light is the term used for the major fabric with the least amount of color saturation.

Pale is used to describe a minor fabric that is lighter in value than the major light fabric; usually you will not need much pale fabric in a quilt – it is more of a blending fabric.

Medium is the term for the major fabric that holds the color scheme together, acting as a bridge between light and dark.

Dark describes the major fabric with the most saturated amount of color.

Bright fabric is used as an accent color; it may match or highly contrast with the light, medium and dark fabrics.

Remember that the values in the list of colors given with each of the quilt designs is individual to that particular quilt. So, what would be medium in one quilt may be termed light or bright in another. For quilts with a great many colors, or with a color scheme that might be confusing, the colors are listed as they appear on the quilt.

a single block isn't enough, keep trying until your measurements come close enough.

Another way to adapt the size of a quilt is to add or subtract sashing and borders. If a quilt is too large and has sashing in between the blocks, either remove the sashing altogether (which will result in a very different look to the quilt) or make the sashing narrower. If a quilt is too small, make the sashing or the borders wider, or add extra borders in coordinating colors.

Experiment on graph paper with your various options until you have come up with a size as near to your requirements as possible. If the size of a quilt is off by a few inches/centimeters either way it doesn't really matter, although as a rule it would be better to have a quilt that is too large than too small.

Fabrics

Each project includes a materials list with the fabric requirements for making the quilt shown in the photograph. While you can exactly duplicate the antique quilt shown, you have been given the leeway to create your own individual color scheme, should you wish to do so – the different fabrics that are required are listed in color **values** (the degree of light or dark) so as not to sway your color choices. The box above will assist you in selecting your fabrics.

Try to choose highly contrasting fabrics; if your colors blend beautifully in the fabric shop, you may end up with a rather bland quilt. Be daring! You'll see that many of the quilts shown here are in rather unorthodox color combinations which work beautifully as a finished quilt.

You may find that modern fabric colors seem brash compared with those of the antique quilts you'll see in this book. If it proves impossible to find exactly what you want, try soaking your fabric overnight in a bowl filled with strong dark tea; rinse the fabric thoroughly in the morning before drying and ironing it. You could also leave a brightly colored fabric in the sun to bleach naturally to a more muted shade.

The yardage requirements assume that you are very accurate at laying out and cutting your pieces. If you are a beginner or feel that you would like a bit of leeway, buy slightly more yardage than is required. If you have leftover fabric, you can always use it in some future project.

CHOICE OF FABRIC

The old quilts shown in this book are all made with fabrics woven from natural fibers like cotton and wool. You would be very fortunate indeed if you were able to use old fabrics to reproduce these quilts. But since old fabrics are not an option for most quilters, how do you go about selecting your fabrics from those available in stores today?

First, decide how you are going to use your quilt. If it is to be hung on a wall, you have only to think of the aesthetic values of the materials you choose. But if the quilt is going to be used on a bed, it will have to stand up to continual wear and fairly regular washing. In this case, it is important to make sure that all the fabrics are of the same weight (a heavy fabric joined to a light fabric would pull at the seams and cause uneven wear). The fabrics should also have the same laundry requirements – silks and cottons side by side would cause problems.

Very sheer fabrics and stretch fabrics are unsuitable for quiltmaking, and heavy, or too closely woven fabrics are difficult to sew and quilt. The safest choice is dress weight, 100 percent cotton. This washes and wears well and is easy to sew and quilt, either by hand or by machine. It also presses more crisply than polyester-cotton blends, making it easier to achieve precise corners. After you have made your fabric selection, choose a sewing thread that will blend unobtrusively with all your fabrics – white, ecru or gray are safe choices.

PREPARATION OF FABRIC

When you have chosen your fabrics you would be well advised to wash them before you start work. Clip into the selvages (finished edges) to prevent uneven shrinkage, then wash all the fabrics of a similar color in very hot water – it is not necessary to use soap, although you may wish to use a little fabric softener. Washing will test for color fastness and shrinkage and it will also remove any excess sizing. If the fabric shows any sign of 'bleeding', add three parts cold water to one part white vinegar to the water, then rinse until the water runs clear. To make quite sure, wash again with a piece of white fabric. If the white fabric stays white, you are safe.

After washing your material, hang the fabrics to dry, then iron them while still slightly damp. (It is inadvisable to dry the material in a tumble dryer as this may pull the fabric off-grain.) Trim away any frayed edges. After ironing, check that the grain of the fabric is straight. You will be able to tell by looking to see if the horizontal and vertical threads are perpendicular to one another. If they aren't, ask a friend to help you straighten the grain. Grasp the four corners of the fabric and pull from opposite corners diagonally, alternating from side to side until the grain is straight.

Making Templates

Using tracing paper, a pencil and ruler, trace all the full-size templates given with the quilt you have chosen to make. Using a pencil and ruler, add a ¼ inch/6 mm seam allowance all around each patchwork template. Do not add seam allowances at this time to appliqué templates. (Details on how to mark and cut appliqué pieces appear later on page 112.)

Templates too large to fit into this book have been dealt with in two ways:

For simple templates, the sizes required are given at the end of the Materials list; in this case, draw these pieces to the required measurement on tracing paper. The sizes given include a seam allowance, so you need not add one.

Appliqué templates and quilting patterns will have to be **enlarged**. Each pattern that must be enlarged will have a pink grid of squares over it.

Each square on the grid is equal to 1 inch/2.54 cm or 2 inches/5 cm – a label on the pattern will inform you as to the size. To enlarge the pattern, count the number of squares crosswise and lengthwise and multiply by the size given (1 or 2 inches/2.54 or 5 cm) – you'll need a sheet of paper this width and length. Draw the same number of 1 or 2 inch/2.54 or 5 cm squares on this paper. Holding the drawing in this book next to your paper, copy each part of the design from the small squares into the corresponding large squares (see Diagram 1).

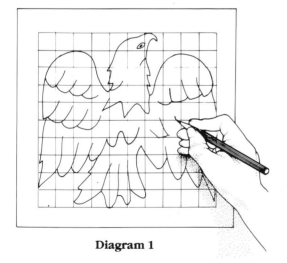

Diagram 1

Next, mark each template with the appropriate letter and the direction of the grain (if given). (**Note:** the letter 'I' is not used in this book.) Then glue each tracing paper template to medium-weight cardboard or plastic. (Leave at least ½ inch/13 mm between appliqué templates; for further instructions, see How to Appliqué on page 112.) Cut out each template using a utility knife or scissors. If you find that a template becomes distorted from use, make up another template as directed above.

Cutting the Pieces

To prepare your fabrics for cutting, straighten the uneven edges of the fabric with a pencil and ruler or a rotary cutter (see Diagram 2). It is best to cut the largest pieces first, so start with the pieces for

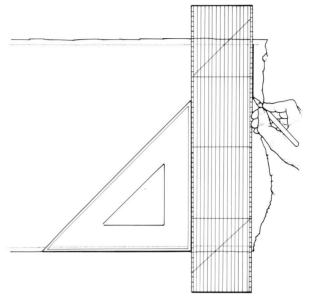

Diagram 2

the back of the quilt. Next cut the borders and sashing. Finally, cut out the patchwork or appliqué pieces from the fabric and strips that are left (see Diagram 3).

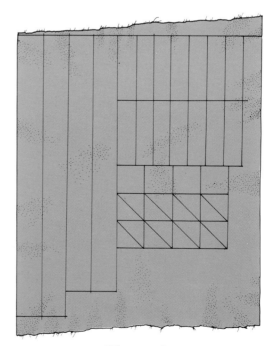

Diagram 3

The cutting list will tell you how many pieces you must cut to make the quilt shown in the color photograph. The number of pieces required for one block is given in parentheses, should you wish to alter the size of your quilt by making more or less blocks.

When marking patchwork templates on fabric, it is best to place them next to one another so that you need only make one cut to separate the pieces. This will save fabric as well. Always mark pieces on the wrong side of the fabric. To mark a template, place the longest edge of the template on the straight grain of fabric and mark around it with a sharp, hard-lead pencil, white dress-maker's pencil (for dark fabrics) or a fabric marker.

Asymmetrical pieces will need to be 'reversed' to complete a pattern; simply turn the template over and mark the required number of pieces on the fabric. When a template is asymmetrical and you are not instructed to reverse it, the template has been drawn in reverse for you.

After all the pieces have been marked, cut them out accurately using very sharp sewing shears. Accuracy is the key to successful quiltmaking. After cutting, be sure to organize your fabric pieces in separate envelopes or folders to avoid confusion when it comes time to sew them together.

Rotary cutting is a fast and easy way to cut out strips, squares, rectangles and triangles. With this method you can cut patchwork pieces, sashing and borders quickly and accurately. You will need a rotary cutter with a large blade, a rotary ruler and a self-healing cutting mat (all available from quilt suppliers). To prepare the fabric for cutting, fold it in half on the straight grain with the selvages or cut edges matching; steam-press. Fold in half again, matching the first fold with the selvages; steam-press again. Gently place the pressed and folded fabric on your cutting mat. Place the rotary ruler on the fabric, aligning one of the grid lines with the pressed folded edge as shown in Diagram 4. Then, pressing down firmly on the ruler with one hand, run the blade of the rotary cutter against the ruler to cut through the four layers of fabric. This will straighten the edge of your fabric. Always push the blade away from you when cutting fabrics.

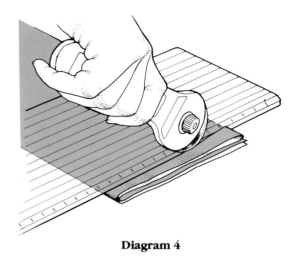

Diagram 4

To cut strips, turn your fabric around in the opposite direction. Measure the required width of the strip you wish to cut using the marked grid lines on your rotary ruler. Then, holding the ruler firmly in place, run the blade against the ruler to cut the strip.

To cut squares, trim one edge of the strip, then measure the required distance away from the cut end. Cut along this measurement for four perfect squares. To cut triangles, cut a square in half diagonally or into quarters.

Sewing Patchwork

Each quilt is accompanied by complete step-by-step instructions for sewing the pieces together to create a patchwork block or a whole patchwork quilt top. You can sew the patchwork by hand or machine. Machine-sewing is definitely the quickest way, although not as peaceful and portable as hand sewing. If you are sewing by machine, you can speed up your patchwork even more by **chain-sewing**, that is, by feeding subsequent pieces through the machine without cutting the thread (see Diagram 5). When sewing, place the pieces together with right sides facing

Diagram 5

and raw edges even, then sew the appropriate edges together following the individual instructions and making a ¼ inch/6 mm seam.

Always press the seam allowances of your patchwork to one side (toward the darker fabric) before sewing to other pieces. When sewing rows of pieces together, pin the pieces at crucial points, with matching seam allowances turned in opposite directions as shown in Diagram 6.

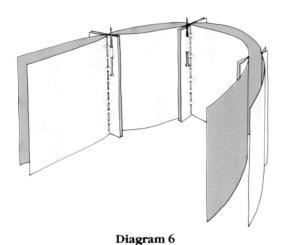

Diagram 6

Insetting is required for many patchwork designs. This is when a triangle or square is set into a corner formed by two other patchwork pieces (see Diagram 7) – the pieces will join

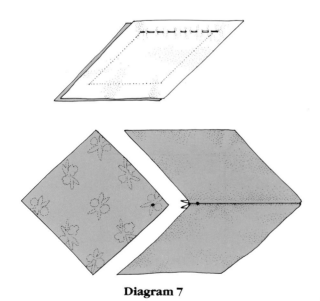

Diagram 7

exactly at the dots shown on the diagram. When sewing together the two pieces that form the

angle, end your stitching ¼ inch/6 mm away from the edge to be inset, backstitching or knotting the end. Pin the piece to be inset along one edge of the angle and stitch from the middle (seam) to the edge in the direction of the arrow (see Diagram 8). Swing the unsewn edge of the

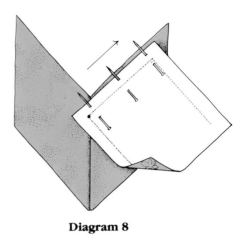

Diagram 8

piece to be inset over and stitch from the middle point to the outer edge (see Diagram 9). Open the fabrics and steam-press carefully to remove any puckers.

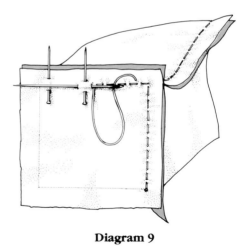

Diagram 9

Curved seams are time-consuming but relatively easy to execute. First, make sure that you cut your pieces with the curved edges on the bias (diagonal) of the fabric; this will happen automatically if you place the straight edges on the straight grain (see Diagram 10). Be sure to mark the notches from the templates onto the fabrics. Then, pin the pieces together with right sides facing, first matching the notches in the middle

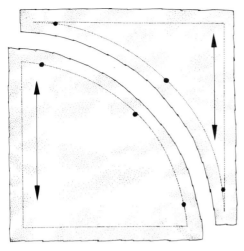

Diagram 10

and then at the side edges. Use as many pins as necessary to achieve a smooth fit (see Diagram 11). Sew together, removing the pins as you go.

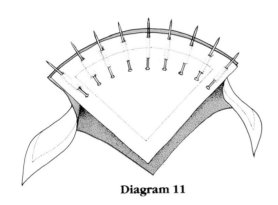

Diagram 11

How to Appliqué

It is very important to select 100 percent, medium-weight cotton fabrics for appliqué work. Use your templates to mark the appliqués on the wrong side of the fabric, leaving at least ½ inch/ 13 mm between the pieces. Add a ¼ inch/6 mm seam allowance to all the edges, then cut out the pieces. Clip into the seam allowance at the curved edges for ease in turning. Fold the seam allow-

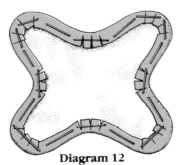

Diagram 12

ances to the wrong side of the appliqué, basting or steam-pressing in place as you go (see Diagram 12).

Lightly press the base fabric in half horizontally and vertically (or diagonally) to create guidelines that make placing the pieces easier. Place the appliqué pieces on the base fabric following the Assembly Diagram given with the quilt you have chosen to make. Baste the appliqués to the base fabric, overlapping the pieces as directed in the individual instructions. (**Note:** Read these instructions first, because where pieces overlap, you do not have to turn the seam allowance to the wrong side.) Then, using matching thread, slipstitch the appliqués to the base fabric making tiny invisible stitches. Gently steam-press the finished appliqué block to remove any puckers.

Borders

When sewing borders (and sashing) to create a quilt top, always press the seam allowances toward the borders (or sashing). Sew the borders to the quilt top in the order given in the individual instructions.

When the quilt has **mitered corners**, you must sew the borders to the quilt top with the ends extending evenly beyond each edge of the quilt top. Press with the ends of all the borders extending beyond the top. To miter a corner, fold one of the borders under at a 45° angle; press and pin in place (see Diagram 13). Then, using

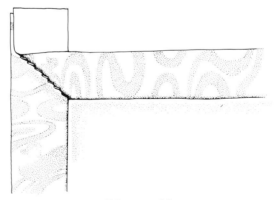

Diagram 13

matching thread, slipstitch the angled edge to the border beneath it, making tiny invisible stitches. Turn the corner over and trim the seam allowances to ½ inch/13 mm; trim the corners at the edges (see Diagram 14). Repeat for the other three corners of the quilt.

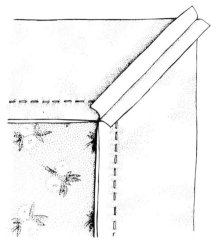

Diagram 14

Transferring a Quilting Design

If you are planning to use one of the many quilting designs given in this book, it is best to transfer the design to your fabric **before** assembling the quilt, although if you wish to transfer a design after the quilt is assembled you can do so (there may be some distortion, however). Trace or enlarge the quilting design of your choice and make a template (see page 108); you do not need to add a seam allowance. For quilting designs with interior design lines, use a utility knife to cut channels in the template wide enough to accommodate your marking pencil. Cut channels only for the major interior design lines; after marking the template, you can then sketch in the minor lines freehand. Place the template on the right side of your quilt top and, using a sharp, hard-lead pencil on light fabrics or a white

dressmaker's pencil on dark fabrics, trace around the template to transfer the quilting lines to the fabric (see Diagram 15). The marked lines will become virtually invisible after quilting.

Assembling the Quilt

A quilt is actually a sandwich made of three layers: the quilt top, the batting/wadding in the middle, and the quilt back. To assemble a quilt, you need a large, clean, flat surface. Thoroughly press the quilt back, then place it wrong side up on the flat surface. If you are working on a wood or linoleum surface, it might be helpful to tape the corners in place to prevent shifting. Next, place the batting/wadding on the quilt back. If the quilt has a self-binding, the back will be larger than the batting/wadding, in which case you must center this middle layer over the back.

Finally, very carefully press your quilt top, removing any loose threads from the wrong side. This is the last time your quilt top will be pressed, so do a thorough job. Then carefully lay the quilt top, right side up, on top of the batting/wadding. Using safety pins or bead-headed dressmaker's pins, pin the layers together, starting in the middle and working out to the sides, horizontally, vertically and diagonally. Then, baste the quilt as shown in Diagram 16, using a light color thread.

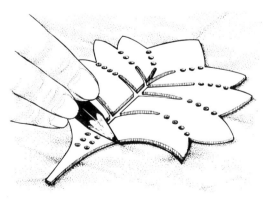

Diagram 15

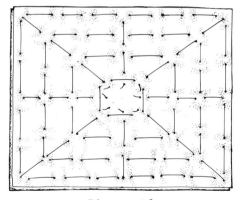

Diagram 16

This is a time-consuming but important step. Make sure that the quilt back does not pucker or shift as you work. Protect yourself by basting *more* than you think is necessary! Remove the pins and your project is ready for quilting.

113

Quilting

Hand quilting is the method used to quilt the majority of the quilts in this book. You'll need a quilting hoop or frame, a thimble, quilting thread and a 'between' needle (size 8 is standard).

Thread your needle with an 18 inch/46 cm length of quilting thread, knotted at one end. Starting somewhere in the middle of the quilt, insert the needle through the quilt top and the batting/wadding only, then pull through so that the knot pops beneath the surface of the quilt, burying itself in the batting/wadding. Work a series of small running stitches through all three layers of the quilt (see Diagram 17). With the eye

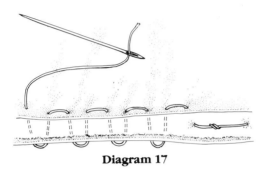

Diagram 17

of the needle resting against the thimble on top of the quilt, guide the needle through the layers until it makes contact with the finger beneath the quilt (you can use a thimble on this finger as well). Continue making a series of running stitches along the marked lines of the quilting design or following the seamlines – this is called **outline quilting**.

To end a line of hand quilting, wind the thread twice around the needle close to the fabric of the quilt top; then insert the needle through the quilt top and batting/wadding only. Run the needle beneath the surface of the quilt top about 1 inch/ 2.54 cm away from your last stitch. Give the thread a tug to pop the knot beneath the surface of the fabric; hold the thread taut and clip off the excess, close to the quilt top. Start your next length of thread close to where you ended the first to keep your quilting lines smooth and continuous.

If you are using a hoop, baste strips of fabric 6–12 inches/15–30 cm wide to the sides of the quilt so that you can quilt the outer edges. Remove the strips of fabric after quilting.

To **machine quilt**, use a size 14 (90) needle in your sewing machine, slightly loosen the thread tension and set the stitch length for 12 stitches per 1 inch/2.54 cm. Use a zigzag foot or quilting foot if you have one. Place the quilt beneath the foot, holding the layers taut to imitate the tension of a frame. Then begin to stitch slowly.

To prevent the top layer from shifting when machine stitching a long line, pin the three layers together directly over the marked quilting line, removing the pins before sewing over them. When you are machine-quilting a large quilt, you must roll the quilt tightly and evenly to fit it into the machine; work from the middle outward to prevent the layers from shifting unevenly.

When you begin and end a line of machine stitching, either backstitch to secure the ends of the threads, or pull the thread to the wrong side and knot. Insert both thread ends into a needle and run them through the quilt back and batting/ wadding, bringing the needle out some distance away. Pull gently and clip away excess thread close to the fabric so the ends retract out of sight.

Some thick quilts, such as the Log Cabin, are difficult to quilt by hand or machine and must be **tied** (see Diagram 18). Using a length of quilting thread (or yarn if you wish), make a backstitch through all three layers of the quilt (a). Pull through so that the ends are even (b). Tie the ends into a knot (c), then make another knot over the first one (d). Pull tight and trim the ends close to the knot (e).

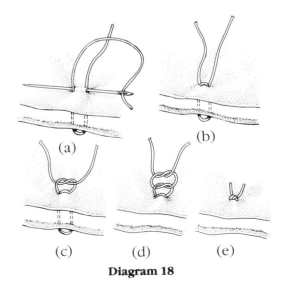

(a)

(b)

(c)   (d)   (e)

Diagram 18

Binding

The binding is the frame of your quilt, so choose the fabric carefully. Most of the quilts can be bound with fabric cut on the straight grain. However, the quilts with curved edges must be bound with bias binding. To make **bias binding**, cut a square of fabric on straight grain (the individual quilt instructions will tell you how big to cut the square – you may have to cut two squares, one the full width of the fabric plus a smaller one). Cut the square in half diagonally, then stitch the short straight edges together using a ¼ inch/6 mm seam (see Diagram 19). Press the seam allowance

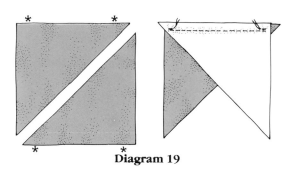

Diagram 19

open then, using a pencil and ruler, mark straight parallel lines 1½ inches/4 cm wide across the fabric (see Diagram 20). (**Note:** For Princess Feather on page 172, you will need to make a bias vine that is only 1 inch/2.54 cm wide.) With the right

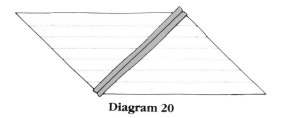

Diagram 20

sides facing, pin the diagonal edges of the fabric together, offsetting the edges so that the top of the fabric aligns with the first marked line (see

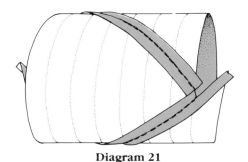

Diagram 21

Diagram 21). Stitch the diagonal edges together. Starting at the offset edge, cut through one thickness of the fabric along the marked lines to make one long continuous strip (see Diagram 22).

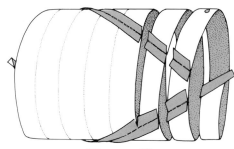

Diagram 22

To finish a quilt with a **separate binding**, press the binding strip in half with wrong sides facing and long raw edges even. Open up and press one raw edge ¼ inch/6 mm to the wrong side. Starting in the middle of one edge of the quilt, pin the end of the binding to the quilt edge with the right side of the binding facing the quilt top, and all raw edges even. Fold the end over as shown in Diagram 23. Stitch the binding to the

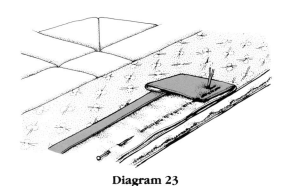

Diagram 23

quilt top using a ¼ inch/6 mm seam; as you reach the first corner, reduce the size of the stitches, stopping your stitching ¼ inch/6 mm from the corner. Lift the presser foot of your sewing machine and pivot the quilt to sew the next edge. Adjust the binding so the raw edge is even with the next edge of the quilt; do not catch the bit of extra fabric that forms in your stitching. Lower the presser foot and stitch for a short distance; adjust your stitch length and continue to the next corner (see Diagram 24). Continue stitching the binding to the quilt in this way. When you reach the beginning, allow the binding to overlap the

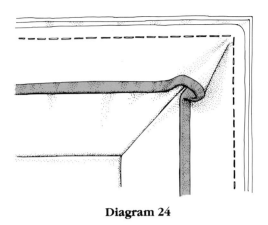

Diagram 24

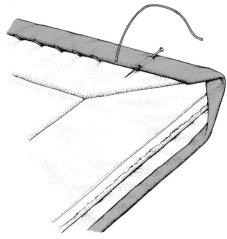

Diagram 25

folded edge by about ¼ inch/6 mm, then cut away any excess binding. Fold the binding over the raw edges of the quilt to the wrong side; slipstitch to the back of the quilt using matching thread. Miter the corners by carefully folding and stitching the excess fabric together at an angle on both the front and back of the quilt.

Some of the quilts have a **self binding**. Trim the quilt top and the batting/wadding so their edges are even. Finger-press the edges of the back ¼ inch/6 mm to the wrong side to make a folded edge. Then wrap the back over the raw edges of the top, pinning the folded edges in place (see Diagram 25). Using matching thread, slipstitch the folded edges of the back to the quilt top, mitering the corners.

Signing the Quilt

We would know a lot more about the quilts in this book if all the quiltmakers had signed their work. Be sure to sign your finished masterpiece either by embroidering your name and the date on the quilt, or by writing this information on the back with indelible ink.

CROWN OF THORNS

*The Crown of Thorns is one of the many pattern names which take
their inspiration from the Bible. This Amish quilt, beautifully stitched
entirely with black thread, was made in Ohio c.1940. The plain
black outer border is set off by elaborate rope quilting. The quilting
on the black blocks in the central portion of the quilt boasts a
beautiful curvilinear harp pattern.*

Skill Level: Easy

Size

Block is 10 inches/25.4 cm square
16 patchwork blocks and 9 quilted blocks are
needed for finished quilt
Finished quilt is 73 × 73 inches/185.4 × 185.4 cm

Materials

● 2 yards/meters bright fabric for borders,
patchwork blocks and binding
● 3¾ yards/meters dark fabric for borders,
patchwork blocks, quilted blocks, side triangles and
corner triangles
● 4 yards/meters coordinating fabric for back of
quilt

● 73½ × 73½ inch/186.7 × 186.7 cm piece of batting/wadding

● Make template (see page 108) for the following piece (measurements include a ¼ inch/6 mm seam allowance):
C: 10½ × 10½ inch/26.7 × 26.7 cm square

Cutting (per quilt)

Note: All measurements include a ¼ inch/6 mm seam allowance.

BACK OF QUILT

Cut two pieces coordinating fabric, each 37 × 73½ inches/94 × 186.7 cm

BORDERS

Two **F** strips 2 × 56½ inches/5 × 143.5 cm, bright fabric
Two **G** strips 2 × 59½ inches/5 × 151 cm, bright fabric
Two **H** strips 7½ × 59½ inches/19 × 151 cm, dark fabric
Two **J** strips 7½ × 73½ inches/19 × 186.7 cm, dark fabric

SIDE D TRIANGLES

From dark fabric, cut three 15¼ inch/38.7 cm squares; cut each square diagonally into four quarters to make twelve side triangles

CORNER E TRIANGLES

From dark fabric, cut two 7⅞ inch/20 cm squares; cut in half diagonally to make four corner triangles

BINDING

Cut bright fabric into seven 1½ inch/4 cm wide strips across the full width of the fabric and sew together to measure 8 yards/meters long

PATTERN PIECE	NUMBER OF PIECES

Note: Number of pieces for a single block is shown in parentheses.

A	(16) 256 bright
	(16) 256 dark
B	(4) 64 bright
	(5) 80 dark
C	9 dark
D	12 dark
E	4 dark

Piecing

CROWN OF THORNS BLOCKS

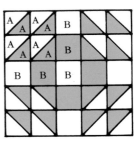

Block Assembly Diagram

1. Sew each bright A to a dark A along the diagonal edge to form a square as shown in Diagram 1.

Diagram 1

2. For the first row of the block, sew two pairs of A squares together, then sew to opposite sides of a dark B as shown in Diagram 2. Construct another row in the same manner for the fifth row.

Diagram 2

3. For the second row of the block, sew two pairs of A squares together, then sew to opposite sides of a bright B as shown in Diagram 3. Construct another row in the same manner for the fourth row of the block.

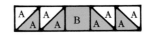

Diagram 3

4. For the third row, sew five Bs together, alternating dark and bright as shown in Diagram 4.

Diagram 4

5. Following Diagram 5, sew the first and second rows of the block together, matching seams carefully, then sew the third row to the second row. Sew the fourth and fifth rows together, again matching seams carefully, then sew to the other side of the third row to complete the block as shown in the Block Assembly Diagram.

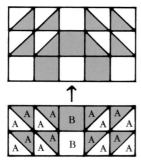

Diagram 5

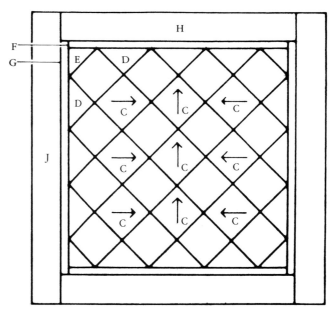

Diagram 6

6. Construct 15 more Crown of Thorns blocks in the same manner.

7. Complete the half-pattern for the harp quilting design. Following the instructions given on pages 108–9, enlarge the harp, flower and twisted rope quilting designs. Use each of the enlarged patterns to make a quilting template as directed on page 108. Make a quilting template from the lozenge quilting design (shown actual size).

8. Following the instructions on page 113, mark the harp design in the middle of each of the C squares. Mark the flower quilting design on each of the D side triangles and E corner triangles.

9. Mark the lozenge quilting design on the F and G pieces.

10. Mark the twisted rope quilting design on the H and J pieces.

Assembly

11. Following Diagram 6 and working on a large flat surface, arrange the patchwork blocks with the C blocks to form a checkerboard pattern. To copy the quilt in the color photograph exactly, turn the harps on the C blocks in the directions shown by the arrows on Diagram 6. (Or you can position them straight up if you wish.) Fill in the sides and corners of the quilt with the D and E triangles.

12. Note that the quilt is constructed in diagonal rows. Stitch the blocks together in rows starting in the middle and working outward. Be sure to sew a D or an E triangle to each end of each row.

13. Stitch the rows together, matching seams carefully at the intersections.

14. Sew the F borders to the top and bottom of the patchwork.

15. Sew the G borders to each side of the patchwork.

16. Sew the H borders to the F borders.

17. Sew the J borders to the G borders to complete the quilt top.

18. To make the quilt back, sew the two fabric pieces together along the long edges; press the seam allowance to one side.

19. Assemble the quilt top, batting/wadding and back as directed on page 113.

Finishing

20. Quilt the patchwork blocks with straight diagonal lines, spaced 1 inch/2.54 cm apart. Work a second set of diagonal lines in the opposite direction so that the quilting lines intersect.

21. Quilt each of the C blocks along the marked harp design.

22. Quilt each of the side and corner triangles along the marked flower design.

23. Quilt the lozenge design along the F and G borders, using a dark thread if you wish.

24. Quilt the twisted rope design on the H and J pieces.

25. Bind the quilt with a separate binding as directed on page 115.

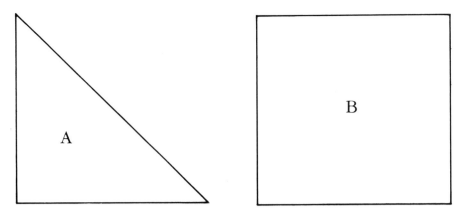

Note: These pattern pieces **do not** include seam allowance.

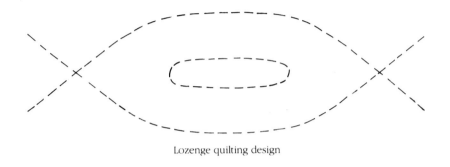

Lozenge quilting design

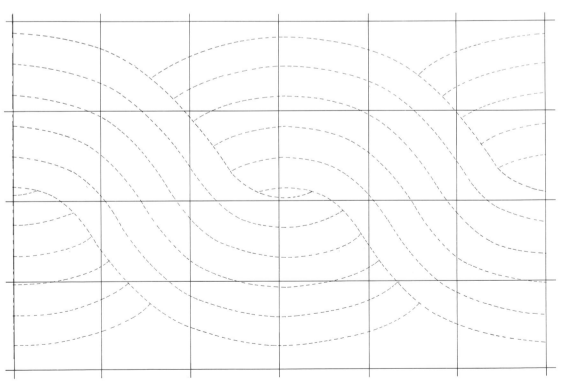

Twisted rope quilting design

each square = 2"/5 cm

half-pattern

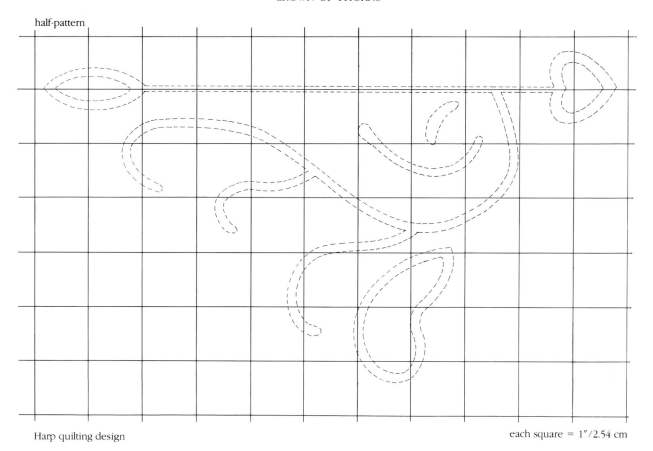

Harp quilting design

each square = 1″/2.54 cm

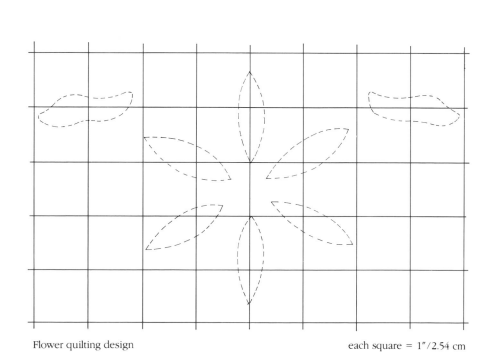

Flower quilting design

each square = 1″/2.54 cm

STRING OF FLAGS

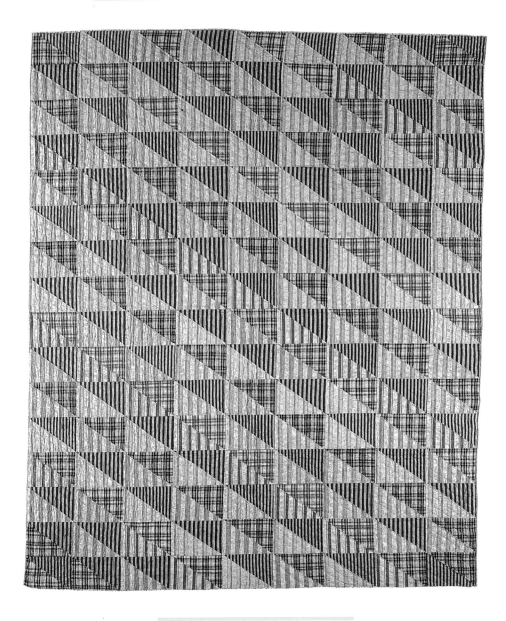

Made entirely of what appears to be patterned shirting material, this deceptively simple quilt is a variation on the ever-present triangle and is both 'homey' and sophisticated. The piecework was done by machine.

Skill Level: Easy

Size

Rectangle is 5½ × 8 inches/14 × 20.3 cm
144 rectangles are needed for finished quilt
Finished quilt is 72 × 88 inches/183 × 223.5 cm

Materials

Note: The quilt shown in the photograph above is actually a scrap quilt – different fabrics were used to construct each patchwork rectangle. The crisp image of flags snapping in the wind is achieved through the use of a variety of fabrics in contrasting shades; no solid fabrics were used to make this quilt – only stripes or plaids, which is why there is such a sense of movement. To make your fabric selection easier, you can use the same fabric for the light pieces throughout the quilt, which means you can concentrate on finding just the right plaids and stripes for the 'flags'.

● Total of 5 yards/meters light fabric (can be assorted scraps – see Note above)
● 2⅞ yards/meters dark fabric for flags (A on Diagram 3)
● 1¼ yards/meters medium-dark fabric for flags (B on Diagram 3)
● ¾ yard/meter medium fabric for flags (C on Diagram 3)
● ¾ yard/meter bright fabric for flags (D on Diagram 3)
● 5 yards/meters coordinating fabric for back of quilt and self-binding
● 72½ × 88½ inch/184 × 225 cm piece of batting/wadding

Cutting (per quilt)

Note: All measurements include a ¼ inch/6 mm seam allowance.

BACK OF QUILT AND SELF BINDING

Cut two pieces coordinating fabric, each 37 × 89½ inches/94 × 227.3 cm

PATTERN PIECE	NUMBER OF PIECES

Note: Number of pieces for a single rectangle is shown in parentheses. Use template A to mark the required number of pieces on the wrong side of the dark, medium and bright fabrics. Then completely reverse template A so that the left edge of the template is on the right and the top edge is at the bottom. Use this reversed pattern to mark the A pieces on the wrong side of the light fabric.

A	(1)	76 dark
	(1)	34 medium-dark
	(1)	18 medium
	(1)	16 bright
A reversed	(1)	144 light

Piecing

STRING OF FLAGS

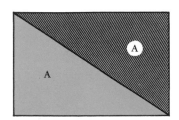

Block Assembly Diagram

1. Match a dark A to a reversed light A as shown in Diagram 1.

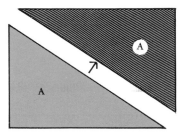

Diagram 1

2. With the long diagonal edges even, sew the two A pieces together, offsetting the corners by ¼ inch/6 mm as shown in Diagram 2.

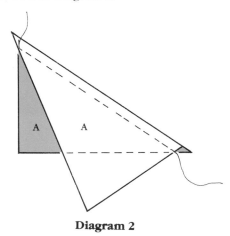

Diagram 2

3. Open up the fabrics to reveal a rectangle as shown in the Block Assembly Diagram. Press the seam allowance toward the dark fabric.
4. Construct 75 more dark (A) rectangles, 34 medium-dark (B) rectangles, 18 medium (C) rectangles and 16 bright (D) rectangles in the same manner as shown in Diagram 3.

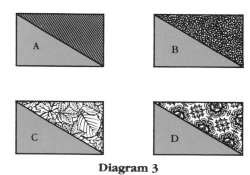

Diagram 3

Assembly

5. Following Diagram 4 and working on a large flat surface, arrange the rectangles in sixteen horizontal rows with nine rectangles in each row. You can

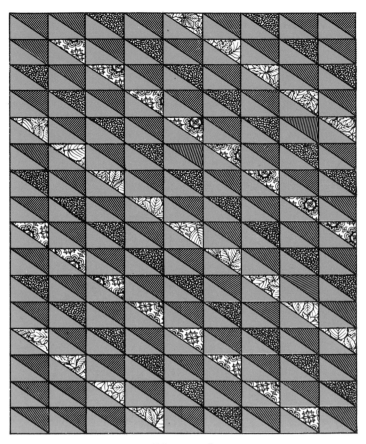

Diagram 4

follow Diagram 4 carefully to reconstruct the quilt exactly as it is in the photograph, or make up your own arrangement. Note that the top left rectangle does not follow the rest of the quilt. You can correct this or leave the deliberate 'mistake' the way the maker of this quilt did.

6. Stitch the rectangles together in horizontal rows.

7. Stitch the rows together, matching seams carefully at the intersections, to complete the quilt top.

8. To make the quilt back, sew the fabric pieces together along the long edges; press the seam allowances to one side.

9. Assemble the quilt top, batting/wadding and back as directed on page 113, centering the top and batting/wadding on the back which will be larger.

Finishing

10. Quilt diagonal lines across the quilt, following the diagonals created by the patchwork pieces and spacing the lines about 1 inch/2.54 cm apart across the quilt.

11. Following the directions on page 116 for a self binding, wrap the fabric from the back over onto the top of the quilt and bind off neatly.

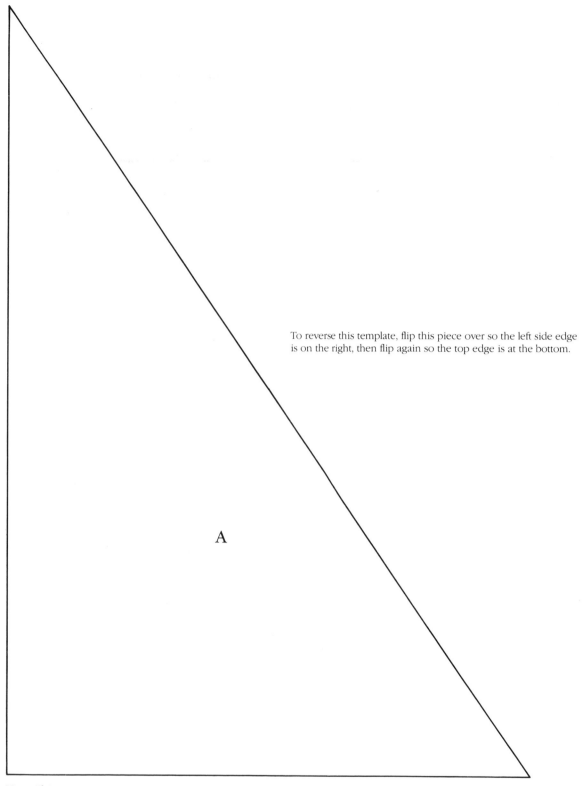

To reverse this template, flip this piece over so the left side edge
is on the right, then flip again so the top edge is at the bottom.

A

Note: This pattern
piece **does not** include
seam allowance.

ZIGZAG BRICKS

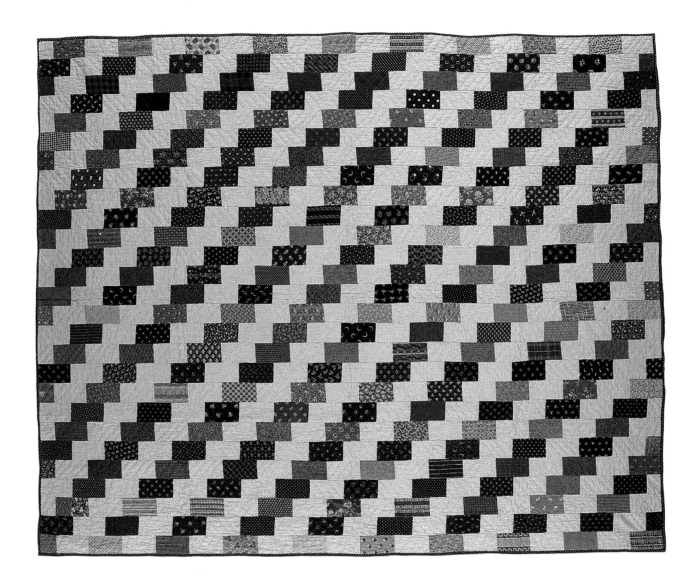

*Made in Missouri around 1880, this simple yet striking quilt displays
a fascinating array of textiles with the small-scale, rather sober prints
which were fashionable during the period. The quilt is constructed
in rows and is the easiest quilt in the book to make.*

Skill Level: Easy

Size

Finished quilt is 67½ × 83¼ inches/171.4 × 211.4 cm

Materials

● 2 yards/meters light fabric for bricks (use same fabric throughout)

● 2 yards/meters dark fabric for bricks (use assorted dark scraps)

● 4¾ yards/meters coordinating fabric for back of quilt

● ⅜ yard/meter coordinating dark fabric for binding

● 68 × 83¾ inch/172.7 × 212.7 cm piece of batting/wadding

126

Cutting (per quilt)

Note: All measurements include a ¼ inch/6 mm seam allowance.

BACK OF QUILT

Cut two pieces coordinating fabric, each 34½ × 83¾ inches/87.6 × 212.7 cm

BINDING

Cut coordinating dark fabric into seven 1½ inch/4 cm wide strips across the full width of the fabric and sew together to measure 8½ yards/meters long

PATTERN PIECE	NUMBER OF PIECES
A	243 light
	243 dark
B	13 light
	14 dark

Piecing

1. This very simple quilt is composed of twenty-seven rows of rectangles, with eighteen A rectangles and one B rectangle in each row. To achieve the design shown in the color photograph, you'll need to stitch the dark and light rectangles together in a pattern which repeats itself every four rows.

2. Begin Row 1 by sewing a dark B to a light A as shown in Diagram 1. Then, continue sewing dark and light As together in an alternating pattern until you have joined a total of eighteen As; end with a dark A. Make six more rows in the same way for a total of seven rows.

Diagram 1

3. Begin Row 2 by sewing a dark A to a light A. Continue sewing a total of eighteen As together in an alternating pattern as shown in Diagram 2; end with a dark B. Make six more rows in the same way for a total of seven rows.

Diagram 2

4. Begin Row 3 by sewing a light B to a dark A as shown in Diagram 3. Then continue sewing light and dark As together in an alternating pattern until you have joined a total of eighteen As; end with a light A. Make six more rows in the same way for a total of seven rows.

Diagram 3

5. Begin Row 4 by sewing a light A to a dark A. Continue sewing a total of eighteen As together in an alternating pattern as shown in Diagram 4; end with a light B. Make five more rows in the same way for a total of six rows.

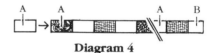

Diagram 4

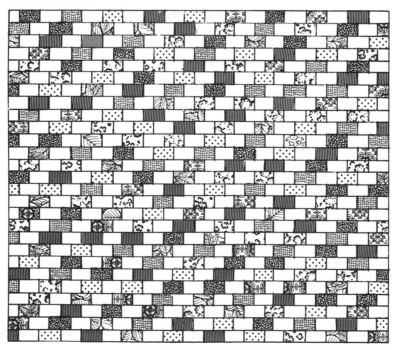

Diagram 5

Assembly

6. Following Diagram 5 on page 127 and working on a large flat surface, place Rows 1 through 4 next to one another vertically, starting at the left with Row 1, and working toward the right with Rows 2, 3 and 4. Sew the rows together, matching the edges of the strips at the beginning and the end of each row. While you do not need to match seams, try to position the seams in the middle of each A rectangle.

7. Following the directions in step 6, sew five more groups of Rows 1 through 4 together. For the seventh group, sew the remaining Rows 1 through 3 together.

8. Join the groups of rows together by sewing Row 4 of the first group to Row 1 of the next group. Continue until all the rows are joined.

9. To make the quilt back, sew the two fabric pieces together along the long edges; press the seam allowance to one side.

10. Assemble the quilt top, batting/wadding and back as directed on page 113.

Finishing

11. Following Diagram 6, quilt a chevron design on the quilt, with the diagonal lines going from upper left to lower right on Rows 1 and 3. On Rows 2 and 4, work the diagonal lines from lower left to upper right.

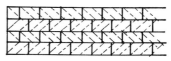

Diagram 6

12. Bind the quilt with a separate binding as directed on page 115.

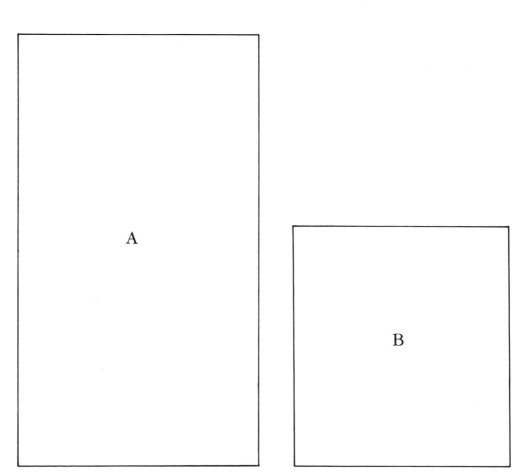

Note: These pattern pieces **do not** include seam allowance.

SCHOOLHOUSES

The schoolhouse has long been associated with frontier settlement and it represented, after the Church, the establishment of a stable community. The quilt pattern, based on the schoolhouse, was developed during the last years of the nineteenth century. This lively example was made c.1940 in Oklahoma and is composed of a number of period prints, including several patriotic designs. The bright blue sashing sports a lovely curved quilting design.

Skill Level: Easy

Size

Block is 12½ × 13¾ inches/31.7 × 35 cm
25 blocks are needed for finished quilt
Finished quilt is 74½ × 80¾ inches/189 × 205 cm

Materials

Note: The quilt shown in the photograph is actually a scrap quilt – different fabrics were used to construct each patchwork block. If you wish, you can follow the yardage given here and make every block exactly the same, or you can use up your scraps of fabric to make each block different. You'll need slightly less than ¼ yard/meter per house.

- 7 yards/meters light fabric for background of patchwork blocks and back of quilt
- 3½ yards/meters bright fabric for schoolhouses
- 2⅜ yards/meters medium fabric for sashing and binding
- 75 × 81¼ inch/190.5 × 206.3 cm piece of batting/wadding

Cutting (per quilt)

Note: All measurements include a ¼ inch/6 mm seam allowance.

BACK OF QUILT

Cut two pieces light fabric, each 37¾ × 81¼ inches/ 96 × 206.3 cm

SASHING

Twenty **P** sashing strips 3½ × 13 inches/9 × 33 cm, medium fabric

Four **Q** sashing strips 3½ × 81¼ inches/9 × 206.3 cm, medium fabric

BINDING

From medium fabric, cut seven 1½ inch/4 cm wide strips across the full width of the fabric and sew together to measure 8¾ yards/meters long

PATTERN PIECE	NUMBER OF PIECES

Note: Number of pieces for a single block is shown in parentheses.

A	(1) 25 light
B	(2) 50 bright
C	(2) 50 light
D	(1) 25 bright
E	(1) 25 light
F	(1) 25 light
F reversed	(1) 25 light
G	(1) 25 bright
H	(1) 25 light
	(2) 50 bright
J	(1) 25 bright
K	(1) 25 bright
L	(2) 50 light
	(3) 75 bright
M	(2) 50 bright
N	(1) 25 light
O	(1) 25 light

Piecing

SCHOOLHOUSE BLOCKS

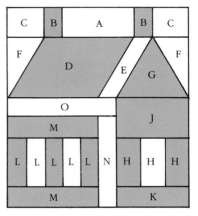

Block Assembly Diagram

1. For the chimney strip, sew a B to each side of A, then sew a C to each B as shown in Diagram 1.

Diagram 1

2. For the roof strip, following Diagram 2, sew an E to the right edge of D and an F to the left edge. Sew the reversed F to a G, then sew G–F to E.

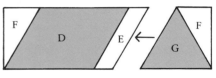

Diagram 2

3. Sew the roof strip to the chimney strip, matching seams carefully as shown in Diagram 3.

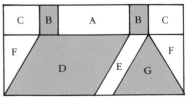

Diagram 3

4. For the front of the house, sew a bright H to each side of the light H. Sew a J to the top of the patchwork and a K to the bottom edge as shown in Diagram 4.

130

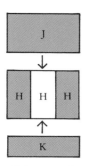

Diagram 4

5. For the side of the house, sew the L pieces together, alternating bright and light as shown in Diagram 5. Sew an M to the top and to the bottom of the patchwork.

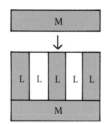

Diagram 5

6. Following Diagram 6, sew an N to the right edge of M–L–M. Then sew an O to the top edge.

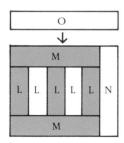

Diagram 6

7. Following Diagram 7, sew the side to the front to complete the bottom of the house.

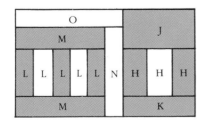

Diagram 7

8. Sew the bottom of the house to the roof strip to complete the patchwork block as shown in the Block Assembly Diagram.

9. Construct 24 more Schoolhouse blocks in the same manner.

Assembly

10. Following Diagram 8 and working on a large flat surface, arrange the patchwork blocks with the P and Q sashing strips in five rows with five blocks in each row. If you have used a variety of scraps for the patchwork, arrange the blocks to create a pleasing color scheme.

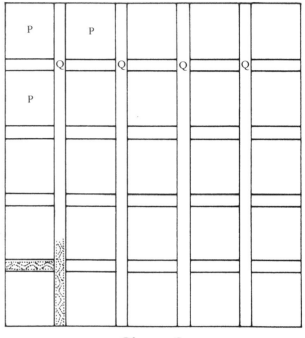

Diagram 8

11. When you are satisfied with your arrangement, join the blocks in vertical rows by sewing the blocks to the P sashing strips.

12. Next, complete the quilt top by sewing the vertical rows of blocks to each side of each Q sashing strip.

13. To make the quilt back, sew the two fabric pieces together along the long edges; press the seam allowance to one side.

14. Assemble the quilt top, batting/wadding and back as directed on page 113.

Finishing

15. Quilt ¼ inch/6 mm away from each seam on the patchwork blocks. Following Diagram 8, quilt a straight line along each side of the sashing strips, and a zigzag border design down the center of each strip.

16. Bind the quilt with a separate binding as directed on page 115.

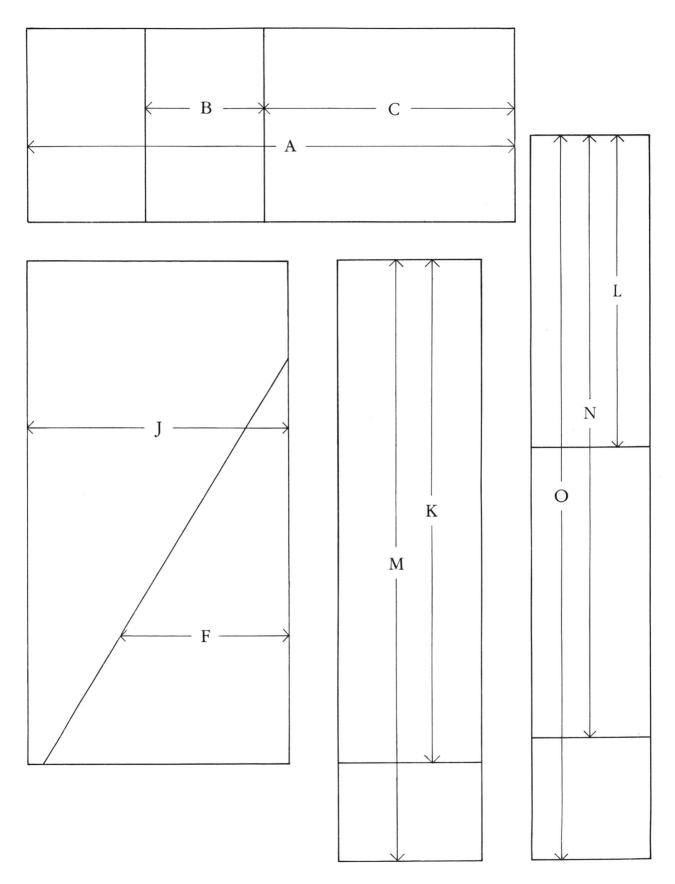

Note: These pattern pieces **do not** include seam allowance.

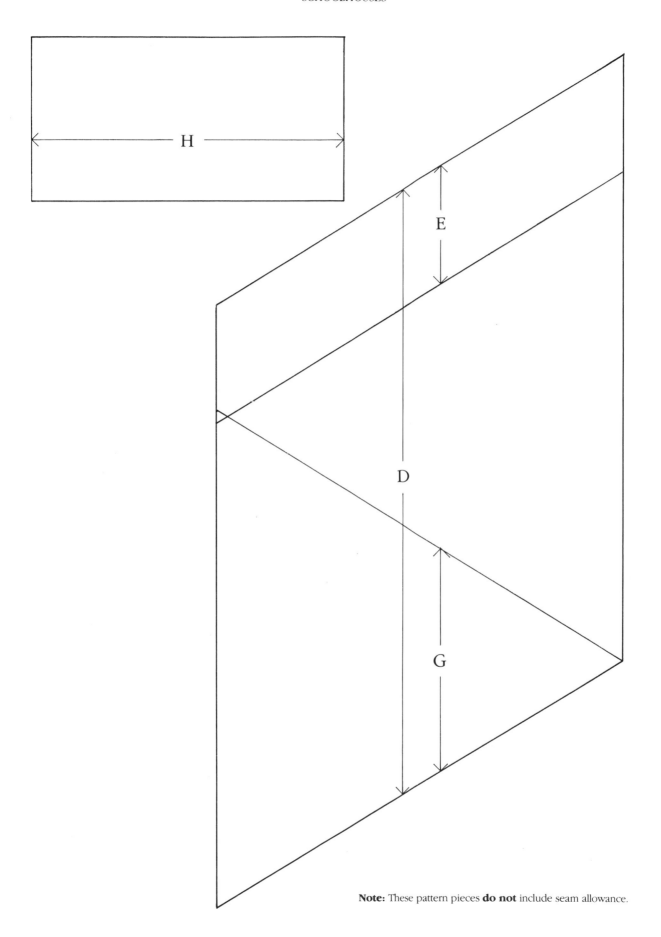

Note: These pattern pieces **do not** include seam allowance.

BLUEBIRD APPLIQUÉ

*Made in rural Tennessee in 1952, this charming quilt is timeless in
its general folk character and has a quality which appears
simultaneously modern and nostalgic. The large pieces and smooth
curves make this design relatively easy to appliqué.*

Skill Level: Intermediate

Size

Block is 13 inches/33 cm square
25 blocks are needed for finished quilt
Finished quilt is 83 × 83 inches/211 × 211 cm
square

Materials

Note: For clarity, the actual colors used in the quilt in the photograph have been listed below. Feel free to make color substitutions should you wish to do so.

● 8⅛ yards/meters white fabric for background of blocks and back of quilt
● 2¾ yards/meters red fabric for appliqué, sashing and binding
● 1⅜ yards/meters green fabric for appliqué
● ¾ yard/meter blue fabric for appliqué
● ½ yard/meter brown fabric for appliqué
● 1 spool No. 5 Pearl Cotton thread, gold
● 83½ × 83½ inch/212 × 212 cm piece of batting/wadding

● Make template (see page 108) for the following piece (measurements include a ¼ inch/6 mm seam allowance):
Background: 13½ × 13½ inches/34.3 × 34.3 cm square

Cutting (per quilt)

Note: All measurements include a ¼ inch/6 mm seam allowance.

BACK OF QUILT

Cut two pieces white fabric, each 42 × 83½ inches/106.7 × 212 cm

BINDING

Cut red fabric into eight 1½ inch/4 cm wide strips across the full width of the fabric and sew together to measure 9⅜ yards/meters long

SASHING

Thirty **F** strips 3½ × 13½ inches/9 × 34.3 cm, red fabric
Six **G** strips 3½ × 83½ inches/9 × 212 cm, red fabric

PATTERN PIECE	NUMBER OF PIECES

Note: Number of pieces for a single block is shown in parentheses.

A	(1) 25 brown
B	(3) 75 green
C	(2) 50 green
D	(1) 25 blue
E	(1) 25 red
Background	(1) 25 white

Piecing

BLUEBIRD APPLIQUÉ BLOCKS

Block Assembly Diagram

1. Prepare pieces A, B, C, D and E for appliqué as directed on page 112. You do not have to turn the bottom edges of the leaves or the left edge of the red breast under, as they will be tucked beneath other pieces.
2. Following Diagram 1, position the brown A branch on the background block; baste in position onto the background with a line of stitches down the middle of the branch as shown.

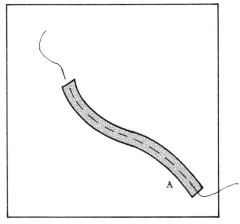

Diagram 1

3. Following Diagram 2 (next page), position the B and C leaves on each side of and at the tip of the branch, tucking the bottom edges of each leaf under the branch as shown by the dash lines on the diagram. Slipstitch the leaves and branch to the background with matching thread, making very small stitches.

135

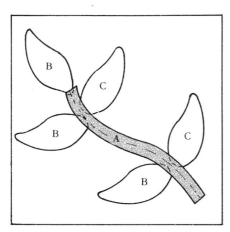

Diagram 2

4. Following Diagram 3, position the bluebird's body (D) across the branch at an angle; pin-baste in place. Then position the red breast (E) next to the body, tucking the edges of the breast beneath the body as shown by the dash lines on the diagram. Slipstitch the body and breast to the background with matching thread, making very small stitches.

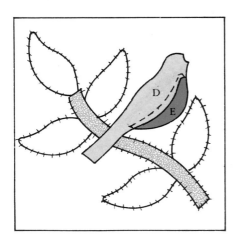

Diagram 3

5. Using one strand of the gold pearl cotton thread in an embroidery needle, work the bird's beak and eye in satin stitch as shown in Diagram 4.

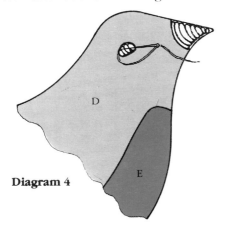

Diagram 4

6. Using one strand of gold pearl cotton thread in the embroidery needle, work the bird's legs in satin stitch as shown in Diagram 5.

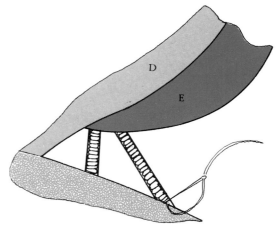

Diagram 5

7. Use the full-size quilting designs and make a template of each following the directions on page 108. Use the templates to mark four hearts and one star on the background of the block as shown in the Block Assembly Diagram.

8. Construct 24 more Bluebird Appliqué blocks in the same manner.

Assembly

9. Following Diagram 6 and working on a large flat surface, arrange the appliqué blocks in five rows with five blocks in each row; separate the blocks with the F and G sashing strips.

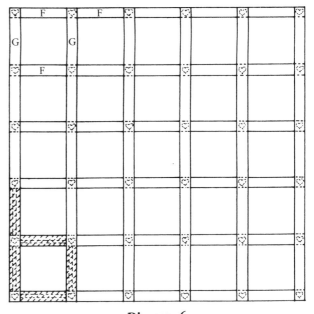

Diagram 6

10. Join the blocks in vertical rows by sewing an F sashing strip in between each one. Also sew an F strip to the top and bottom edges of each vertical row.

11. Join the vertical rows by sewing a G sashing strip to each side of each vertical row to complete the quilt top.

12. To make the quilt back, sew the two fabric pieces together along the long edges; press the seam allowance to one side.

13. Assemble the quilt top, batting/wadding and back as directed on page 113.

Finishing

14. Outline-quilt the bird, leaves and branches. Then, quilt the hearts and the star along the marked outlines.

15. Quilt a heart at each sashing intersection as shown in Diagram 6. Then quilt each sashing strip with two rows of lengthwise stitches and rows of diagonal stitches, spaced 1 inch/2.54 cm apart as shown in the lower left corner of Diagram 6.

16. Bind the quilt with a separate binding as directed on page 115.

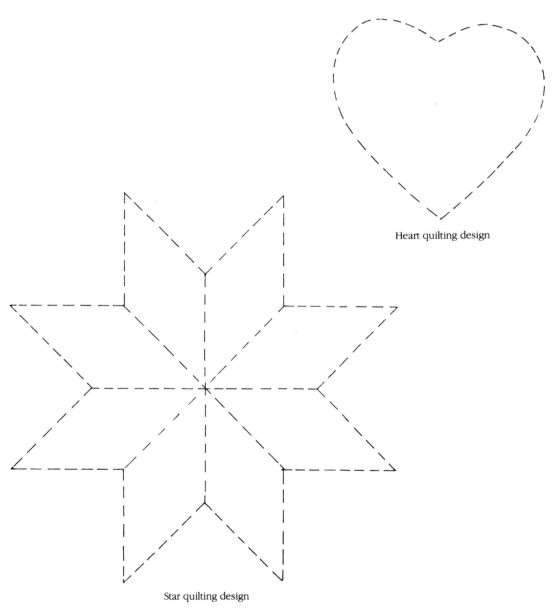

Heart quilting design

Star quilting design

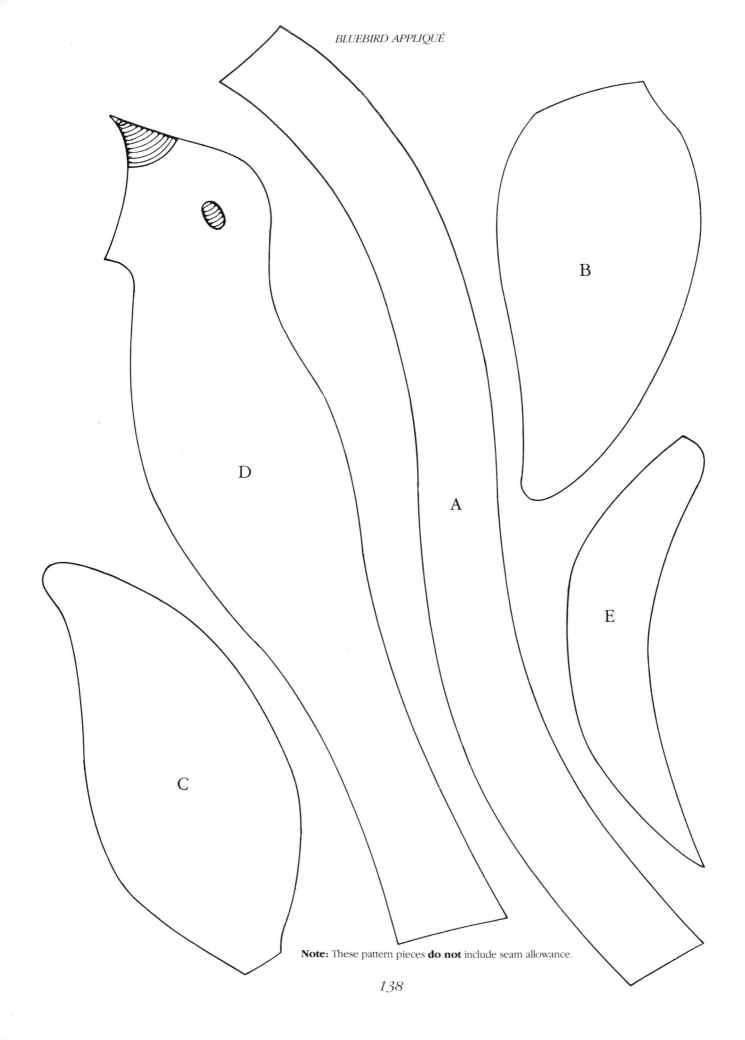

Note: These pattern pieces **do not** include seam allowance.

SNOW CRYSTALS

Pattern names are often idiosyncratic and this one is perhaps no
exception. This lovely quilt, made in Oklahoma during the 1920s, is
a variation of the star design. The pattern was probably originally
Arabic, and then spread to Europe with adaptations to Western
culture. Blue and white have been the most popular quilt colors
throughout the past century; this piece is particularly pleasing in that
it subtly exploits two contrasting shades of blue. The twenty blocks
are each given distinction by the darker blue sashing
with center white posts.
Courtesy: Tory Weil.

Skill Level: Advanced

Size

Block is 16 inches/40.6 cm square
20 blocks are needed for finished quilt
Finished quilt is 71½ × 90 inches/181.6 × 228.6 cm

Materials

● 9 yards/meters dark fabric for patchwork blocks,
sashing, back of quilt and self binding
● 3¼ yards/meters light fabric for patchwork blocks
and sashing
● 72 × 90½ inch/183 × 230 cm piece of batting/
wadding

Cutting (per quilt)

Note: Pattern piece B is used in two parts of the quilt – the sashing and the patchwork blocks. All measurements include a ¼ inch/6 mm seam allowance.

BACK OF QUILT AND SELF BINDING

Cut two pieces dark fabric, each 36¾ × 91½ inches/ 93.3 × 232.4 cm

SASHING

Twelve **B** squares (using template), light fabric
Thirty-one **F** strips 3 × 16½ inches/7.6 × 42 cm, dark fabric

PATTERN PIECE	NUMBER OF PIECES

Note: Number of pieces for a single block is shown in parentheses.

A	(16) 320 dark
A reversed	(16) 320 dark
B	(8) 160 light
C	(4) 80 light
D	(8) 160 light
E	(4) 80 light

Piecing

SNOW CRYSTALS BLOCKS

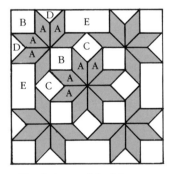

Block Assembly Diagram

1. Sew each A to a reversed A along the edges marked with an X to form a pair of petals as shown in Diagram 1.

Diagram 1

2. To form the central snow crystal, sew four pairs of petals together along the edges marked with dots, matching seams carefully in the middle as shown in Diagram 2.

Diagram 2

3. Inset a B into each corner of the central snow crystal as shown in Diagram 3. (See page 111 for instructions on insetting.)

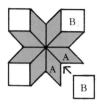

Diagram 3

4. Inset a C into the remaining angled edges of the central snow crystal as shown in Diagram 4.

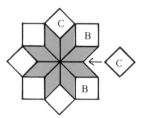

Diagram 4

5. To form a corner snow crystal, sew three pairs of petals together along the edges marked with dots, matching seams carefully in the middle as shown in Diagram 5.

Diagram 5

6. Following Diagram 6, inset a B into the corner of the snow crystal. Then inset a D into each of the two angles adjacent to B. Construct three more corner crystals in the same manner.

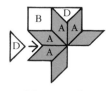

Diagram 6

7. Following Diagram 7, join the corner crystals to the central snow crystal by insetting the Bs from the central crystal into the angled A edges of the corner crystals. Then sew C from the central crystals to the A edges of the corner crystals.

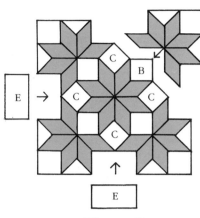

Diagram 7

8. To complete the block, inset an E into each of the four remaining open areas of the snow crystals as shown in Diagram 7 and the Block Assembly Diagram.

9. Construct 19 more Snow Crystals blocks in the same manner.

Assembly

10. Following Diagram 8 and working on a large flat surface, arrange the patchwork blocks in five horizontal rows with four blocks in each row. Place the F and B sashing pieces between the blocks as shown.

11. Stitch the blocks to the vertical F sashing strips to create five horizontal rows.

12. Stitch the horizontal F sashing strips to the B squares, creating four horizontal sashing rows.

13. Stitch the rows of blocks to the sashing rows, matching seams carefully, to complete the quilt top.

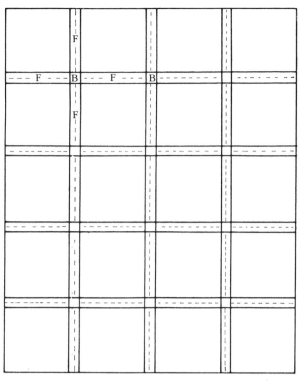

Diagram 8

14. To make the quilt back, sew the two fabric pieces together along the long edges; press the seam allowance to one side.

15. Assemble the quilt top, batting/wadding and back as directed on page 113.

Finishing

16. Outline-quilt each of the A pieces.

17. Outline-quilt the F and B sashing pieces, then quilt a straight line centered along the length of each F piece, as shown in Diagram 8.

18. Following the directions on page 116 for a self binding, wrap the fabric from the back over onto the top of the quilt and bind off neatly.

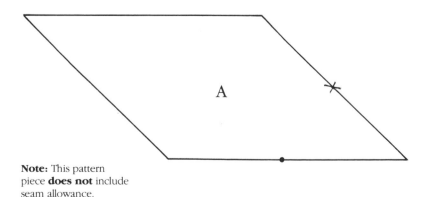

Note: This pattern piece **does not** include seam allowance.

141

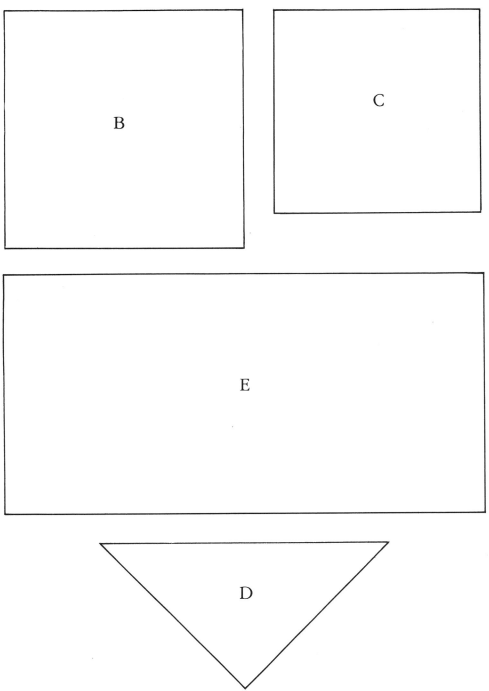

Note: These pattern pieces **do not** include seam allowance.

HEARTS AND GIZZARDS

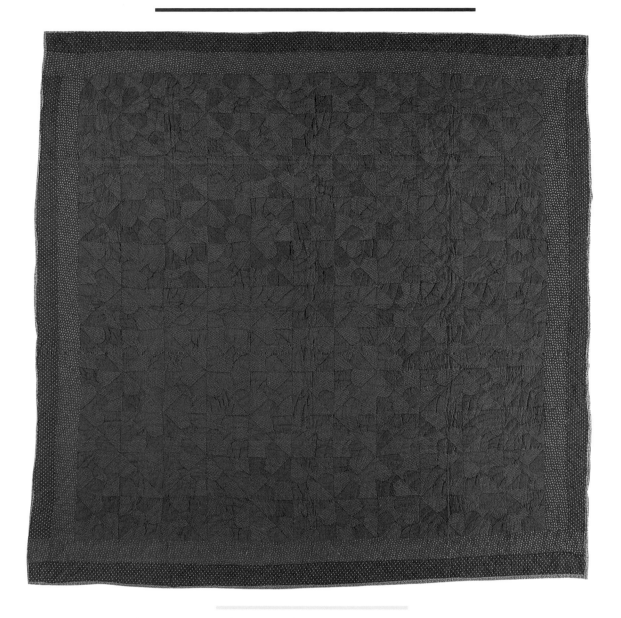

*This rare pattern, bearing such a curious name, is one of the most
visually pleasing. It has its roots in the Amish 'Puzzle' pattern. The
blocks themselves are composed of template designs in two boldly
contrasting colors which when alternated create an almost
kaleidoscopic effect. This marvelous example was skillfully stitched
around the turn of the century by Mrs Kunze from Illinois.*

Skill Level: Intermediate

Size

Block is 6 inches/15 cm square
121 blocks are needed for finished quilt
Finished quilt is 79 × 79 inches/200.6 × 200.6 cm

Materials

● 4¾ yards/meters medium fabric for patchwork
blocks and borders
● 4¾ yards/meters dark fabric for patchwork blocks
and borders

● 4½ yards/meters coordinating fabric for back of quilt
● ⅜ yard/meter coordinating fabric for binding
● 79½ × 79½ inch/202 × 202 cm piece of batting/ wadding

Cutting (per quilt)

Note: All measurements include a ¼ inch/6 mm seam allowance.

BACK OF QUILT

Cut two pieces coordinating fabric, each 40 × 79½ inches/101.6 × 202 cm

BORDERS

Two **C** strips 3¾ × 66½ inches/9.5 × 169 cm, medium fabric
Two **C** strips 3¾ × 66½ inches/9.5 × 169 cm, dark fabric
Two **D** strips 3¾ × 79½ inches/9.5 × 202 cm, medium fabric
Two **D** strips 3¾ × 79½ inches/9.5 × 202 cm, dark fabric

BINDING

Cut coordinating fabric into eight 1½ inch/4 cm wide strips across the full width of the fabric and sew together to measure 9 yards/meters long

PATTERN PIECE	NUMBER OF PIECES

Note: Number of pieces for a single block is shown in parentheses. It is essential that you place the templates with the arrows on the straight grain of fabric when marking and cutting out the patchwork pieces.

PATTERN PIECE	NUMBER OF PIECES
A	(1) 121 medium
	(1) 121 dark
A reversed	(1) 121 medium
	(1) 121 dark
B	(1) 121 medium
	(1) 121 dark

Piecing

HEARTS AND GIZZARDS BLOCKS

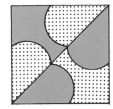

Block Assembly Diagram

1. Following Diagram 1, sew a medium A to each side of a dark B, matching the notches, to form a

triangle. (See page 111 for instructions on sewing curves.)

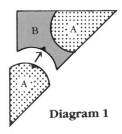

Diagram 1

2. Following Diagram 2, sew a dark A to each side of a medium B to form a triangle.

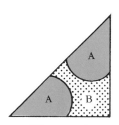

Diagram 2

3. Sew the two triangles together along the long edges, matching seams carefully, to complete the block as shown in the Block Assembly Diagram.
4. Construct 120 more Hearts and Gizzards blocks in the same manner.

Assembly

5. Following Diagrams 3 and 4, arrange the patchwork blocks on a large flat surface in eleven rows with eleven blocks in each row. Turn adjacent blocks in opposite directions as shown in Diagram 3.

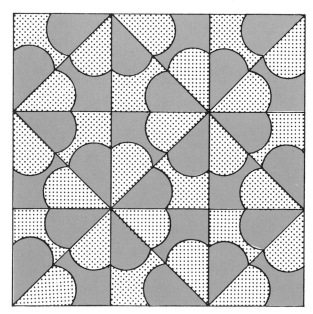

Diagram 3

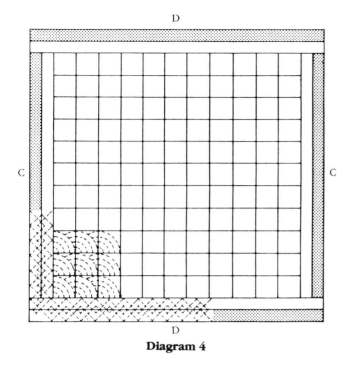

Diagram 4

6. Sew the blocks together in rows, matching seams carefully.

7. Sew the rows together, matching seams carefully.

8. Sew a dark C border to each side of the patchwork as shown in Diagram 4.

9. Sew a medium C border to each dark C border.

10. Sew a dark D border to the top and bottom of the patchwork as shown in Diagram 4.

11. Sew a medium D border to each dark D border to complete the quilt top.

12. To make the quilt back, sew the two fabric pieces together along the long edges; press the seam allowance to one side.

13. Assemble the quilt top, batting/wadding and back as directed on page 113.

Finishing

14. Following Diagram 4, quilt four curved lines across each block, creating a clamshell pattern. Continue the curved lines on adjacent blocks as shown in the diagram.

15. Quilt linked squares or some other border design along the C and D pieces as shown in Diagram 4.

16. Bind the quilt with a separate binding as directed on page 115.

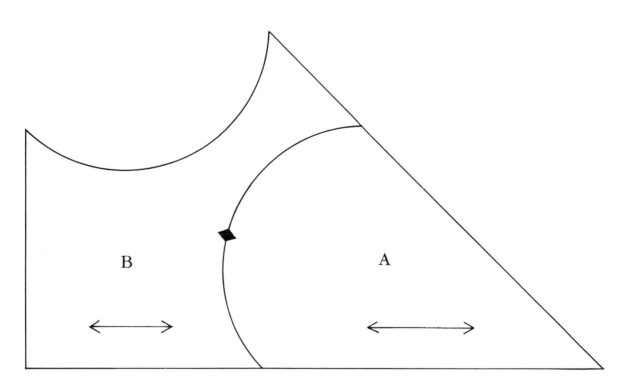

Note: These pattern pieces **do not** include seam allowance.

145

CHERRY BASKET

This colorful 1930s quilt is an exuberant example of a well-loved pattern. The slightly tipsy baskets have been pieced and then appliquéd onto a whole piece of fabric, creating a sense of warmth and spontaneity. The bright calico prints are typical of those which were printed during this period. The project has been made easier by translating the entire quilt into patchwork, with appliqué work only on the handles.

Skill Level: Easy

Size

Block is 15 × 14 inches/38 × 35.5 cm
24 blocks are needed for finished quilt
Finished quilt is 70 × 84 inches/178 × 213.4 cm

Materials

- 9½ yards/meters light fabric for patchwork blocks and back of quilt
- 2 yards/meters bright fabric for patchwork blocks
- 2 yards/meters dark fabric for patchwork blocks
- ⅜ yard/meter coordinating fabric for binding

● 70½ × 84½ inch/179 × 214.6 cm piece of batting/wadding

● Make templates (see page 108) for the following pieces (measurements include a ¼ inch/6 mm seam allowance):
C: 1¾ × 15½ inch/4.4 × 39.4 cm rectangle
D: 5¾ × 15½ inch/14.4 × 39.4 cm rectangle

Cutting (per quilt)

Note: All measurements include a ¼ inch/6 mm seam allowance.

BACK OF QUILT

Cut two pieces light fabric, each 42¾ × 70½ inches/108.6 × 179 cm

BORDERS

Two **G** strips 5½ × 84½ inches/14 × 214.6 cm, light fabric

BINDING

Cut coordinating fabric into seven 1½ inch/4 cm wide strips across the full width of the fabric and sew together to measure 8½ yards/meters long

PATTERN PIECE	NUMBER OF PIECES	
Note: Number of pieces for a single block is shown in parentheses.		
A	(15)	360 bright
	(12)	288 dark
B	(1)	24 light
B reversed	(1)	24 light
C	(1)	24 light
D	(1)	24 light
E	(1)	24 bright
F	(2)	48 dark

Piecing

CHERRY BASKET BLOCKS

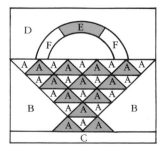

Block Assembly Diagram

1. Sew a bright A to a dark A along the diagonal edge to form a square as shown in Diagram 1.

Construct 9 more A–A squares in the same manner.

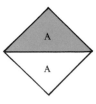

Diagram 1

2. Arrange the squares as shown in Diagram 2 and stitch together in four rows. Then, stitch a bright A triangle to the end of each row as shown; stitch the remaining bright A triangle to the right-hand corner of the single square.

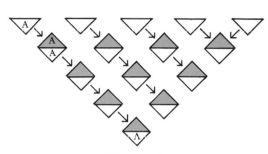

Diagram 2

3. Stitch the pieced rows together, matching seams carefully, to form the pieced basket.
4. Sew a dark A triangle to the diagonal edge of each B piece as shown in Diagram 3. Stitch A–B to each side of the basket.

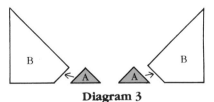

Diagram 3

5. Sew C to the bottom edge of the patchwork, as shown in the Block Assembly Diagram.
6. Sew an F to each end of E, matching the straight edges. Fold the raw edges ¼ inch/6 mm to the wrong side and press. Place the handle on the D piece, centered carefully between the side edges and with the raw edges even as shown in Diagram 4. Appliqué the handle to D following the directions on page 112.

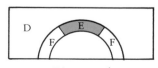

Diagram 4

7. Following the Block Assembly Diagram, sew D to the top edge of the basket, enclosing the raw edges of the handle in the seam, to complete the patchwork.

8. Construct 23 more Cherry Basket blocks in the same manner.

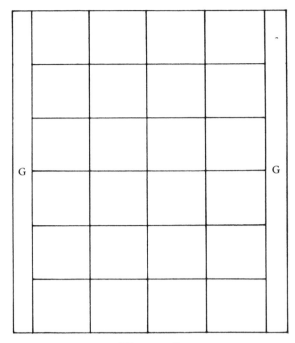

Diagram 5

Assembly

9. Following Diagram 5 and working on a large flat surface, arrange the blocks in six horizontal rows, with four blocks in each row. Stitch the blocks together in horizontal rows, carefully matching the seams of the baskets.

10. Stitch the rows together, matching seams carefully at the intersections.

11. Sew the G side borders to the right and left edges of the quilt top. There are no top and bottom borders.

12. To make the quilt back, sew the two fabric pieces together along the long edges; press the seam allowance to one side.

13. Assemble the quilt top, batting/wadding and back as directed on page 113.

Finishing

14. Outline-quilt the outer edges of the baskets and the handles. If you wish to quilt the background as shown in the photograph, quilt evenly spaced horizontal lines across the quilt; do not stitch on top of the patchwork. Then, work evenly spaced vertical or diagonal lines across the quilt. Alternatively, quilt a simple cherry motif in the open spaces between the baskets.

15. Bind the quilt with a separate binding as directed on page 115.

Note: These pattern pieces **do not** include seam allowance.

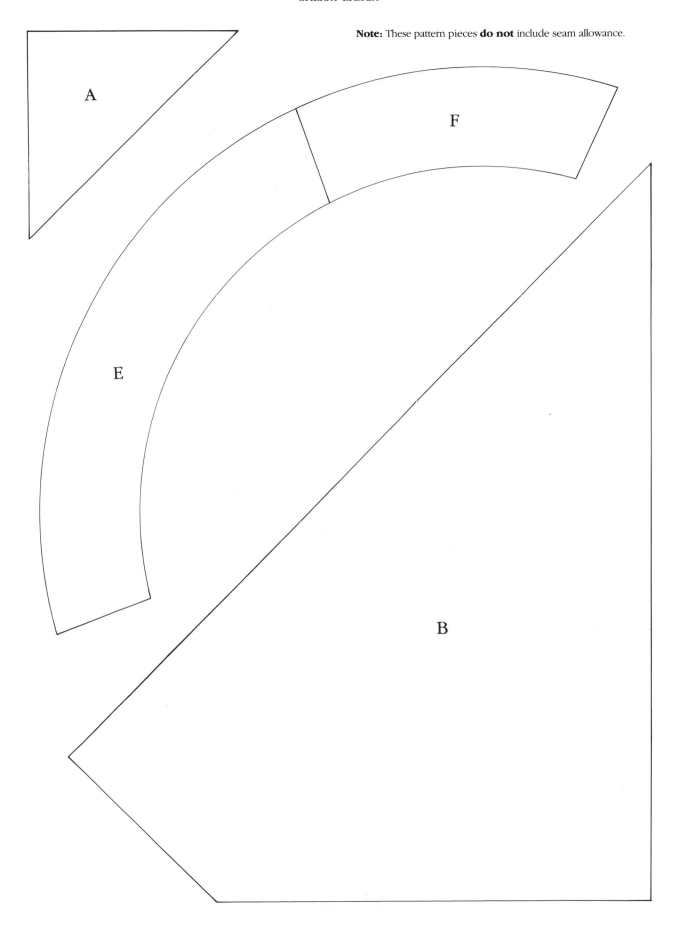

CAKE STAND

*This striking 1890s quilt has a real patchwork feel, while the design
is inspired by an important domestic accessory. The intricate
piecework and the attention paid to scale, direction and proportion
are effectively presented through a highly contrasting color scheme.*

Skill Level: Intermediate

Size

Block is 4½ inches/11.4 cm square
90 patchwork blocks and 72 plain blocks are needed
for finished quilt
Finished quilt is 68¼ × 74½ inches/173.4 × 189 cm

Materials

● 5⅝ yards/meters white fabric for patchwork
blocks, plain blocks, plain borders, back of quilt and
self binding
● 2½ yards/meters light fabric for patchwork blocks
and sawtooth border
● 4½ yards/meters dark fabric for patchwork blocks,
sawtooth border and plain border

● 68¾ × 75 inch/174.6 × 190.5 cm piece of batting/wadding

● Make template (see page 108) for the following piece (measurements include a ¼ inch/6 mm seam allowance):
F: 5 × 5 inches/12.7 × 12.7 cm square

Cutting (per quilt)

Note: All measurements include a ¼ inch/6 mm seam allowance.

BACK OF QUILT AND SELF BINDING

Cut two pieces white fabric, each 69¾ × 38¼ inches/177 × 97 cm

BORDERS

For sawtooth border: cut 270 light **B** triangles and 270 dark **B** triangles

Two **J** strips 2¼ × 59¾ inches/5.7 × 151.7 cm, white fabric

Two **K** strips 2¼ × 69½ inches/5.7 × 176.5 cm, white fabric

Two **L** strips 3¼ × 63¼ inches/8 × 160.7 cm, dark fabric

Two **M** strips 3¼ × 75 inches/8 × 190.5 cm, dark fabric

PATTERN PIECE	NUMBER OF PIECES

Note: Number of pieces for a single block is shown in parentheses.

A	(1)	90 light
	(1)	90 dark
B	(6)	540 light
	(8)	720 dark
C	(1)	90 light
D	(2)	180 light
E	(1)	90 light
F		72 white
G		34 white
H		4 white

Piecing

CAKE STAND BLOCKS

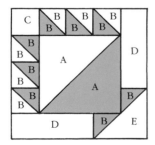

Block Assembly Diagram

1. Sew a light and dark A together along the diagonal edge to form a square as shown in Diagram 1.

2. Following Diagram 2, sew six light Bs to six dark Bs along the diagonal edges, forming six squares.

Diagram 1   **Diagram 2**

3. Following Diagram 3, sew three B squares together, then sew to one edge of the light A triangle with the dark Bs touching the light A.

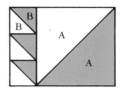

Diagram 3

4. Sew the remaining three B squares together, then sew a C to the dark B at one end as shown in Diagram 4. Sew this strip to the top edge of the patchwork, matching the seams at the corner carefully, to form the 'cake'.

Diagram 4

5. Sew a dark B to one end of each of two D rectangles as shown in Diagram 5.

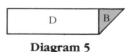

Diagram 5

6. Following Diagram 6, sew a D–B unit to the side and bottom edges of the cake. Then sew E to the straight edge formed by the two B triangles to complete the square.

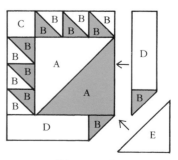

Diagram 6

151

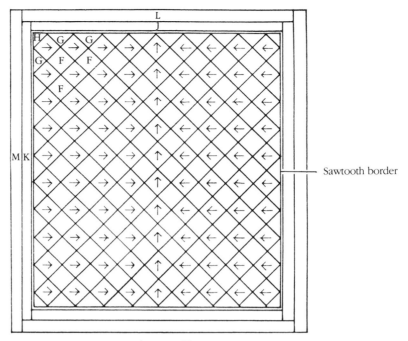

Diagram 7

7. Construct 89 more Cake Stand blocks in the same manner.

Assembly

8. Following Diagram 7 and working on a large flat surface, arrange the patchwork blocks with the plain F blocks to form a checkerboard pattern. The arrows on the diagram indicate the direction of the top of each patchwork block. Note that the blocks are straight up-and-down in the middle of the quilt; the remainder are positioned sideways. Fill in the side edges with the G triangles. Fill in the corners with the H triangles.

9. Note that the quilt is constructed in diagonal rows. Stitch the blocks together in rows, starting in the middle and working outward. Be sure to sew a G or an H triangle to each end of each row, as shown in Diagram 7.

10. Stitch the rows together, matching seams carefully at the intersections.

11. To construct the sawtooth border as shown in the color photograph on page 150, sew each remaining light B to a dark B along the diagonal edge, creating 270 squares. Sew the squares together to form two strips, each 63 squares long for the top and bottom edges of the quilt. For the side edges, construct two strips, each 72 squares long.

12. Following Diagram 8 (which shows a corner of the quilt), sew the short sawtooth borders to the top and bottom edges of the quilt top with the dark triangles against the quilt edge.

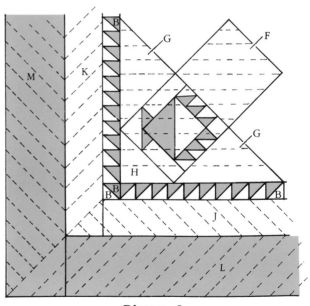

Diagram 8

13. Sew the long sawtooth borders to the side edges of the quilt top, again with the dark triangles against the quilt edge.

14. Using Diagrams 7 and 8 for reference, sew the white J strips to the top and bottom edges of the patchwork.

15. Sew the white K strips to the side edges of the patchwork.

16. Sew the dark L strips to the J strips.

17. Sew the dark M strips to the K strips to complete the quilt top.

18. To make the quilt back, sew the two fabric pieces together along the long edges; press the seam allowance to one side.

19. Assemble the quilt top, batting/wadding and back as directed on page 113, centering the quilt top and batting/wadding on the back, which will be larger.

Finishing

20. Following Diagram 8, quilt straight parallel lines across the quilt top up to but not including the sawtooth border; space the lines about ¾ inch/2 cm apart. Quilt the lines in a horizontal direction except for the central Cake Stand blocks which are positioned straight up and down. Quilt those blocks with straight parallel vertical lines.

21. Outline-quilt each of the triangles of the sawtooth border.

22. Quilt diagonal lines across the white and dark borders following Diagram 8, making each line about ¾ inch/2 cm apart.

23. Following the directions on page 116 for a self binding, wrap the fabric from the back over onto the top of the quilt and bind off neatly.

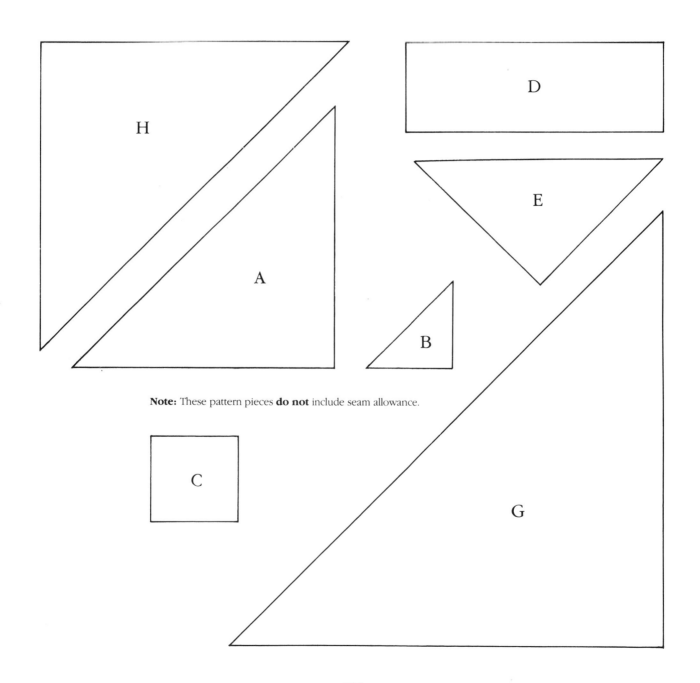

Note: These pattern pieces **do not** include seam allowance.

LOG CABIN

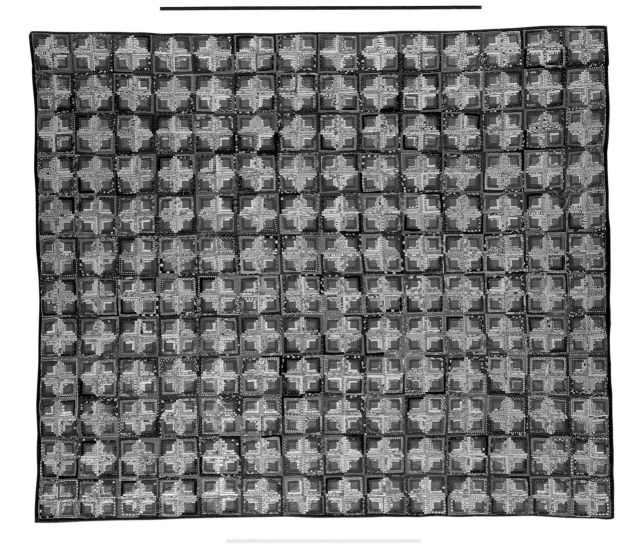

The dominant blue central block in this delightful turn-of-the-century Log Cabin quilt immediately sets this piece apart from most 'log cabins'. The careful placement of a bright red strip next to the middle square creates a sense of visual warmth and solidity in contrast to the hundreds of small-scale late-nineteenth- and early-twentieth-century printed cottons which make up the 766 individual blocks. That makes 9,192 strips!

Skill Level: Easy

Size

Block is 2½ inches/6.3 cm square
672 blocks are needed for finished quilt
Finished quilt is 60 × 70 inches/152.4 × 178 cm

Materials

Note: The quilt shown in the photograph above is unusual in that the center square of each block is blue, bordered on two sides by red strips. This creates a visually striking effect when the quilt is viewed as a whole. In order to duplicate this effect, you must use the same fabric for the blue and red throughout (although you do not necessarily have to use blue and red). The remainder of the block is divided as most Log Cabin blocks are, with half the block composed of light fabrics and the other half of dark fabrics.

A wide variety of fabrics in contrasting shades of light and dark were used to construct the quilt in the photograph, although in most cases the same fabric was used for adjoining right-angle pieces (see the Block Assembly Diagram). If you want to achieve an antique-looking quilt, use up your scraps of fabric to make each block different. Or, you can use the same fabrics for the light and dark pieces throughout the quilt, which will result in a very graphic effect; the exact yardage you'll need is given below.

- 1 yard/meter blue fabric (or color of your choice) for patchwork blocks
- 1¼ yards/meters red fabric (or color of your choice) for patchwork blocks
- Total of 4¼ yards/meters light fabric (if you are using scraps); if you are buying fabric and wish to make the rows the same on each block, you'll need the following:

  Rows B and C – 1⅛ yards/meters
  Rows F and G – 1½ yards/meters
  Rows K and L – 1¾ yards/meters

- Total of 3½ yards/meters dark fabric (if you are using scraps); if you are buying fabric and wish to make the rows the same on each block, you'll need the following:

  Rows H and J   1⅝ yards/meters
  Rows M and N – 1⅞ yards/meters

- 3¾ yards/meters muslin/calico for backing of blocks
- 3⅜ yards/meters coordinating fabric for back of quilt
- ¼ yard/meter dark fabric for binding
- 60½ × 70½ inch/153.6 × 179 cm piece of batting/wadding (optional – batting/wadding was not used in the quilt in the photograph)

- Make templates (see page 108) for the following pieces (measurements include a ¼ inch/6 mm seam allowance):

Block backing square: 3 × 3 inches/7.6 × 7.6 cm
A: 1½ × 1½ inches/4 × 4 cm

Cutting (per quilt)

Note: All measurements include a ¼ inch/6 mm seam allowance.

BACK OF QUILT

Cut two pieces coordinating fabric, each 35½ × 60½ inches/90 × 153.6 cm

BINDING

Cut dark fabric into six 1½ inch/4 cm wide strips across the full width of the fabric and sew together to measure 7¼ yards/meters long

Note: Because of the number of blocks required to make this quilt, it would be very tedious and time-consuming to cut out every strip individually. The following chart directs you to cut a number of strips the full width of the fabric for pieces B through N; cut every strip ¾ inch/2 cm wide. The instructions that follow will then tell you how to use the strips. If you have one, use a rotary cutter and rotary ruler to cut the strips; see page 110 for instructions. If you do not have a rotary cutter, measure and mark the fabrics carefully with a ruler and pencil before cutting the strips with sharp scissors.

PATTERN PIECE	NUMBER OF PIECES
Block Backing	672 muslin/calico
A	672 blue
B	23 light strips
C	27 light strips
D	27 red strips
E	31 red strips
F	31 light strips
G	36 light strips
H	36 dark strips
J	40 dark strips
K	40 light strips
L	42 light strips
M	42 dark strips
N	48 dark strips

Piecing

LOG CABIN BLOCKS

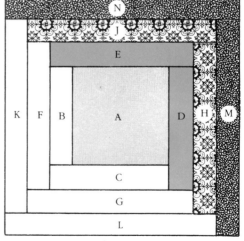

Block Assembly Diagram

1. Following Diagram 1 (next page) and using a pencil and ruler, draw diagonal lines across a block backing square. Center one A square, right side up, in the middle of the backing square; baste in place close to the raw edges. (It will not be necessary to remove these basting stitches later.) **Note:** The backing square will not be drawn in the remainder of the diagrams.

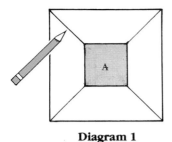

Diagram 1

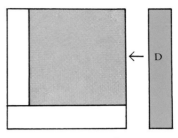

Diagram 4

2. Following Diagram 2, sew a light B to the left edge of A. First, place your B strip on top of A with right sides facing and the raw top and side edges even; stitch together, then turn B to the right side and press open onto the backing square. Trim off the excess B strip extending below your stitching, even with the bottom raw edge of A. Continue to use the remainder of this B strip with the other A squares until the strip is used up. Continue with the next strip in the same way. **Note:** Sew all the strips of the Log Cabin block in this manner, cutting away the excess fabric of each strip, even with the pieced center.

5. Following Diagram 5, sew a dark E to the top edge of the pieced center.

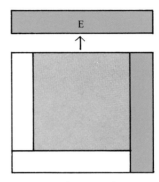

Diagram 5

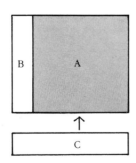

Diagram 2

3. Following Diagram 3, sew a light C to the bottom edge of the pieced center.

6. Following Diagram 6, sew a light F to the left edge of the pieced center.

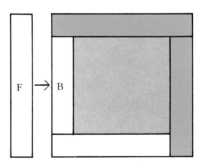

Diagram 6

7. Following Diagram 7, sew a light G to the bottom edge of the pieced center.

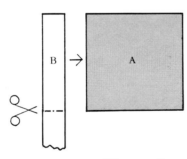

Diagram 3

4. Following Diagram 4, sew a dark D to the right edge of the pieced center.

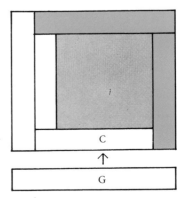

Diagram 7

8. Following Diagram 8, sew a dark H to the right edge of the pieced center.

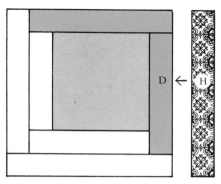

Diagram 8

9. Following Diagram 9, sew a dark J to the top edge of the pieced center.

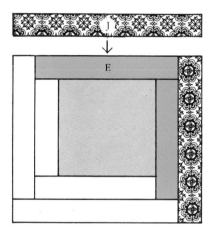

Diagram 9

10. Following Diagram 10, sew a light K to the left edge of the pieced center.

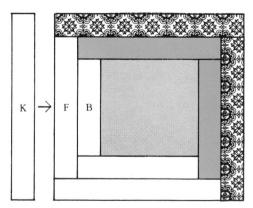

Diagram 10

11. Following Diagram 11, sew a light L to the bottom edge of the pieced center.

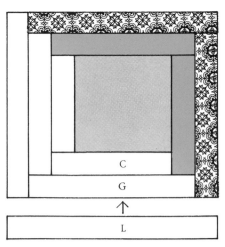

Diagram 11

12. Following Diagram 12, sew a dark M to the right edge of the pieced center.

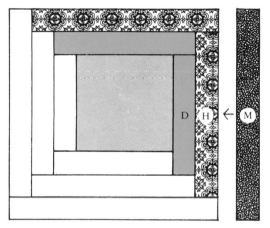

Diagram 12

13. Following Diagram 13, sew a dark N to the top edge of the pieced center.

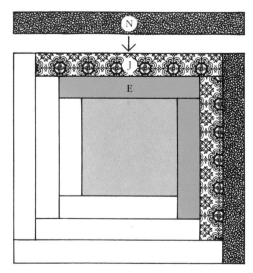

Diagram 13

14. Construct 671 more Log Cabin blocks in the same manner.

15. Following the Block Unit Assembly Diagram, sew the blocks together in groups of four, positioning the light pieces in the middle as shown. When finished, you will have a total of 168 block units.

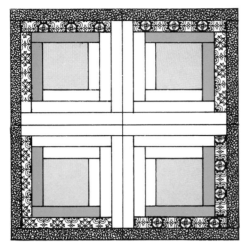

Block Unit Assembly Diagram

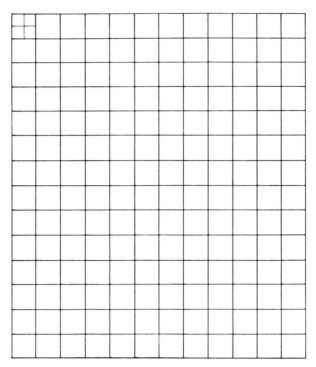

Diagram 15

Assembly

16. Following Diagram 14 and working on a large flat surface, arrange the patchwork block units from step 15 in fourteen rows with twelve block units in each row.

17. Stitch the block units together in rows.

18. Stitch the rows together, matching seams carefully at the intersections to complete the quilt top.

19. To make the quilt back, sew the two fabric pieces together along the long edges; press the seam allowance to one side.

20. Assemble the quilt top, batting/wadding (if using) and back as directed on page 113.

Finishing

21. Because of the thickness of the fabric, it would be very difficult to hand-quilt through all the layers of this quilt. So either machine-quilt around each block to secure the three layers together, or tie the quilt at each of the corners of each block. (See page 114 for instructions on machine-quilting and tying.)

22. Bind the quilt with a separate binding as directed on page 115.

BEAR'S PAW

The Bear's Paw is one of those well-loved patterns which both typified and celebrated the romance of rural life. This example, c.1880 from the Midwest, is well-balanced and harmonious in the overall scale of design and color combinations. There are quite a few pieces to assemble because of the small scale of the design; however, the sewing is straight and relatively simple.

Skill Level: Intermediate

Size

Block is 6 inches/15 cm square
54 patchwork and 54 plain blocks are needed for finished quilt
Finished quilt is 54 × 72 inches/137 × 183 cm

Materials

Note: The quilt shown in the color photograph is actually a scrap quilt – different fabrics were used to construct each patchwork block. For simplicity, the instructions divide the fabrics into bright (for the 'claws') and contrasting (for the main portion of the 'paws' and the central square of the block). If you wish, you can make every block exactly the same, or you can use up your scraps of fabric to make each block different.

- 1¾ yards/meters light fabric for background of patchwork blocks
- 4½ yards/meters medium fabric for plain blocks and back of quilt
- ¾ yard/meter bright fabric for patchwork blocks
- 1 yard/meter contrasting fabric for patchwork blocks and binding
- 54½ × 72½ inch/138.4 × 184 cm piece of batting/wadding
- Make template (see page 108) for the following piece (measurements include a ¼ inch/6 mm seam allowance):

E: 6½ × 6½ inch/16.5 × 16.5 cm square

Cutting (per quilt)

Note: All measurements include a ¼ inch/6 mm seam allowance.

BACK OF QUILT

Cut two pieces medium fabric, each 27½ × 72½ inches/70 × 184 cm

BINDING

Cut contrasting fabric into six 1½ inch/4 cm wide strips across the full width of the fabric and sew together to measure 7 yards/meters long

PATTERN PIECE	NUMBER OF PIECES

Note: Number of pieces for a single block is shown in parentheses.

A	(16) 864 light
	(16) 864 bright
B	(5) 270 contrasting
C	(4) 216 light
D	(4) 216 light
E	(1) 54 medium

Piecing

BEAR'S PAW BLOCKS

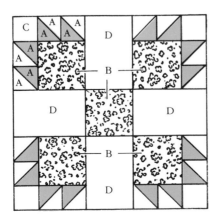

Block Assembly Diagram

1. Sew each light A to a bright A along the diagonal edge to form a square as shown in Diagram 1.

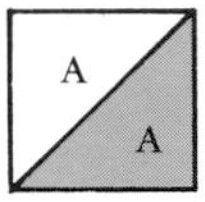

Diagram 1

2. Following Diagram 2, sew two A–A squares together, then sew to B with the bright As touching B.

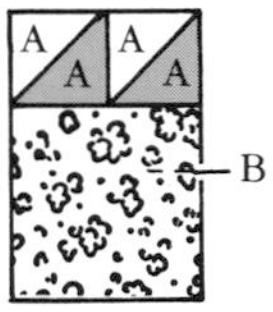

Diagram 2

3. Following Diagram 3, sew two A–A squares together, then sew a C to the bright end. Stitch to the side of A–B, matching the seam at the top corner. This will complete one 'paw'. Make a total of four paws in this manner.

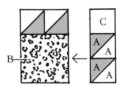

Diagram 3

4. Sew a paw to each side of D as shown in Diagram 4 for the upper row of the patchwork block. Repeat in same manner for the lower row.

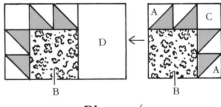

Diagram 4

5. For the middle row, sew a D to each side of the remaining B as shown in Diagram 5.

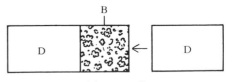

Diagram 5

6. Stitch the upper and lower rows to each side of the middle row as shown in the Block Assembly Diagram to complete the block.

7. Construct 53 more Bear's Paw blocks in the same manner.

8. Following Diagram 6 and using a compass, mark three curved quilting lines around each corner of each E block.

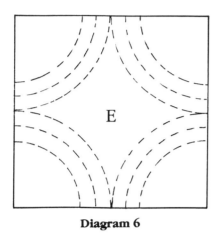

Diagram 6

Assembly

9. Following Diagram 7 and working on a large flat surface, arrange the blocks in twelve horizontal rows, with nine blocks in each row. Alternate the patchwork and plain blocks to create a checkerboard pattern as shown. Stitch the blocks together in horizontal rows.

	E		E		E		E	
E		E		E		E		E
	E		E		E		E	
E		E		E		E		E
	E		E		E		E	
E		E		E		E		E
	E		E		E		E	
E		E		E		E		E
	E		E		E		E	
E		E		E		E		E
	E		E		E		E	
E		E		E		E		E

Diagram 7

10. Stitch the rows together, matching seams carefully at the intersections.

11. To make the quilt back, sew the two fabric pieces together along the long edges; press the seam allowance to one side.

12. Assemble the quilt top, batting/wadding and back as directed on page 113.

Finishing

13. Outline-quilt the paws and the central B square on each patchwork block.

14. Quilt along the marked curved lines on each of the plain E blocks.

15. Bind the quilt with a separate binding as directed on page 115.

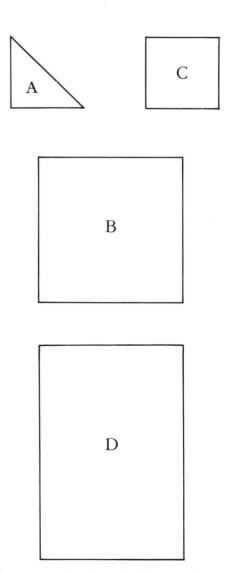

Note: These pattern pieces **do not** include seam allowance.

DRUNKARD'S PATH

*This fascinating quilt with alternating blocks of faded brown and
cherry red creates a sophisticated optical puzzle where focus is
constantly shifting. The entire design is well disciplined by the use of
an intricately pieced triangular border. It was made in Ohio
c.1880.*

Skill Level: Advanced

Size

Block is 10 inches/25.4 cm square
42 blocks are needed for finished quilt
Finished quilt is 65 × 75 inches/165 × 190.5 cm

Materials

● 3½ yards/meters light fabric for patchwork blocks
● 3¾ yards/meters dark fabric for patchwork blocks
and binding
● 4¼ yards/meters coordinating fabric for back of
quilt
● 65½ × 75½ inch/166 × 192 cm piece of batting/
wadding

Cutting (per quilt)

Note: All measurements include a ¼ inch/6 mm seam allowance.

BACK OF QUILT

Cut two pieces coordinating fabric, each 33 × 75½ inches/84 × 192 cm

BINDING

Cut dark fabric into seven 1½ inch/4 cm wide strips across the full width of the fabric and sew together to measure 8 yards/meters long

PATTERN PIECE	NUMBER OF PIECES

Note: Number of pieces for a single block is shown in parentheses. It is essential that you place the templates with the arrows on the straight grain of fabric when marking and cutting out the patchwork pieces.

A	(8) 336 light
	(8) 336 dark
B	(8) 336 light
	(8) 336 dark
C	108 light
	108 dark

Piecing

DRUNKARD'S PATH BLOCKS

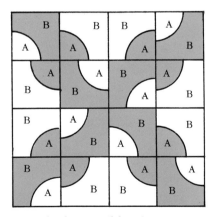

Block Assembly Diagram

1. Following Diagram 1, sew a light A to a dark B, matching the notches, to form a square. (See page 111 for instructions on sewing curves.) Construct 7 more A–B squares in the same manner.

Diagram 1

2. Following Diagram 2, sew a dark A to a light B to form a square. Construct 7 more A–B squares in the same manner.

Diagram 2

3. Sew four A–B squares together to make the first row of the block, following Diagram 3 carefully for the exact placement of the curved corners. Construct another row in the same manner for the fourth row.

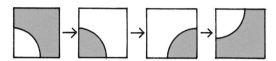

Diagram 3

4. Sew four A–B squares to make the second row of the block, following Diagram 4 carefully for the exact placement of the curved corners. Construct another row in the same manner for the third row.

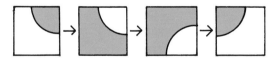

Diagram 4

5. Following the Block Assembly Diagram carefully, arrange the rows exactly as shown, turning the third and fourth rows upside-down. Then sew the rows together, matching seams carefully.

6. Construct 41 more Drunkard's Path blocks in the same manner.

Assembly

7. Following Diagram 5 (next page), arrange the patchwork blocks on a large flat surface in seven horizontal rows with six blocks in each row.

8. Sew the blocks together in rows, matching seams carefully.

9. Sew the rows together, matching seams carefully.

10. Sew each light C to a dark C triangle to form 108 squares. Sew the squares together to make two strips of 28 squares for the side borders and two strips of 26 squares for the top and bottom borders of the quilt.

11. With the dark triangles placed against the edge of the quilt, sew the side borders to the patchwork as shown in Diagram 5 (next page).

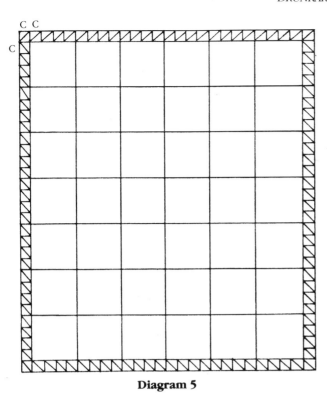

C C

C

Diagram 5

12. With the dark triangles placed against the edge of the quilt, sew the top and bottom borders to the patchwork to complete the quilt top as shown in Diagram 5.

13. To make the quilt back, sew the two fabric pieces together along the long edges; press the seam allowance to one side.

14. Assemble the quilt top, batting/wadding and back as directed on page 113.

Finishing

15. Quilt straight diagonal lines across the entire quilt, spacing the lines about 1 inch/2.54 cm apart.

16. Quilt a second set of straight diagonal lines across the quilt in the opposite direction to form a diamond pattern.

17. Bind the quilt with a separate binding as directed on page 115.

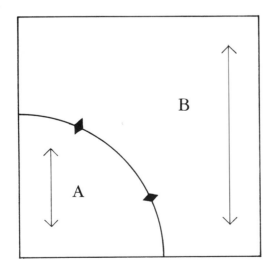

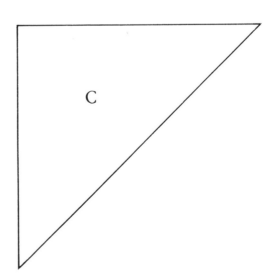

Note: These pattern pieces **do not** include seam allowance.

NEW YORK BEAUTY

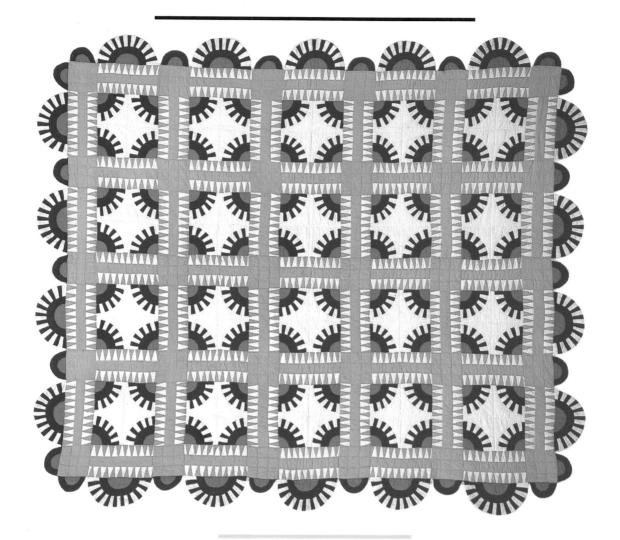

Made in Michigan, sometime in the 1920s or 1930s, this energetic masterpiece translates a nineteenth-century design into a very Art-Deco quilt. The generous scalloped border complements the internal curved seams which radiate out in bands of orange, red, and red and white stripes. One of the most interesting features of this quilt is the intricate green and white pieced border which comprises two of the three layers of the central sashing. The overall effect of the green/white and red/white stripes is reminiscent of a child's board game.

Skill Level: Advanced

Size

Block is 11 inches/28 cm square
20 blocks are needed for finished quilt
Finished quilt is about 80 × 96 inches/203 × 244 cm including curved edging; 69 × 85 inches/175 × 216 cm without edging

Materials

Note: For clarity, the actual colors used in the quilt in the photograph have been listed in parentheses below.

● 12¼ yards/meters light fabric (white) for patchwork blocks, sashing, optional edging, back of quilt and straight or bias binding
● 3¾ yards/meters medium fabric (green) for sashing

- ¾ yard/meter bright fabric (orange) for patchwork blocks and optional edging
- 2⅝ yards/meters dark fabric (red) for patchwork blocks and optional edging
- 80½ × 96½ inch/204.4 × 245 cm piece of batting/wadding

- Make template (see page 108) for the following piece (measurements include a ¼ inch/6 mm seam allowance):

G: 2¼ × 11½ inches/5.7 × 29 cm

Cutting (per quilt)

Note: All measurements include a ¼ inch/6 mm seam allowance.

BACK OF QUILT

Cut two pieces light fabric, each 40¾ × 96½ inches/103.5 × 245 cm

SASHING

Forty-nine **G** strips, medium fabric
Thirty **H** squares, medium fabric

BIAS BINDING

See page 115 for instructions on cutting bias binding. Cut one 44 inch/111.7 cm square and one 30 inch/76 cm square piece light fabric into 1½ inch/4 cm wide bias strips and sew together to measure 13¾ yards/meters long; see Note about binding the quilt in Step 12

STRAIGHT BINDING

Cut light fabric into seven 1½ inch/4 cm wide strips across the full width of the fabric and sew together to measure 8½ yards/meters long

PATTERN PIECE	NUMBER OF PIECES

Note: Number of pieces for a single block, strip or edging piece is shown in parentheses. It is essential that you place the templates with the arrows on the straight grain of fabric when marking and cutting out the patchwork pieces.

A	(20)	400 light
	(20)	400 dark
B	(4)	80 dark
C	(4)	80 bright
D	(4)	80 light

For Sashing

E	(9)	882 light
	(9)	882 medium
F	(1)	49 light
	(1)	49 medium
F reversed	(1)	49 light
	(1)	49 medium

For Edging (optional – see Step 12)

J	(10)	180 light
	(10)	180 dark
K	(1)	18 dark
L	(1)	18 bright
M	(1)	22 dark
N	(1)	22 bright

Piecing

NEW YORK BEAUTY BLOCKS

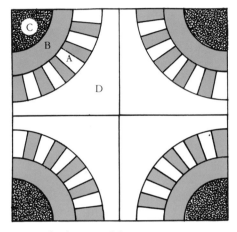

Block Assembly Diagram

1. Each New York Beauty block is composed of four pieced squares, sewn together with the light D pieces in the middle and the curved 'suns' in the corners. The following directions will first instruct you to make a single pieced square, then the entire block. (See page 111 for instructions on sewing curves.)

2. Following Diagram 1, sew five light and five dark As together, alternating light and dark as shown to form a curved strip.

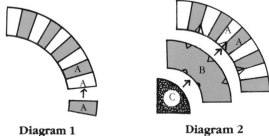

Diagram 1   **Diagram 2**

3. Following Diagram 2, sew a B to the A strip, matching the notches on B to the second, fifth and eighth seams of the A strip. Then sew a C to the B-A unit, matching the open circles.

4. Sew a D to the A strip, matching the Xs on D to the second, fifth and eighth seams of A as shown in Diagram 3.

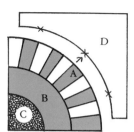

Diagram 3

5. Make three more pieced squares in the same manner. Following the Block Assembly Diagram, arrange the four squares on a flat surface with the light D pieces meeting in the middle. Stitch together in two rows, then stitch the rows together, matching seams carefully in the middle, to create one New York Beauty block.

6. Construct 19 more New York Beauty blocks in the same manner.

SASHING

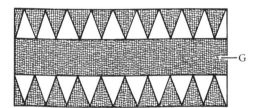

Sashing Assembly Diagram

7. The sashing strips are composed of a medium G strip sandwiched on each side by a pieced E–F strip; see the Sashing Assembly Diagram.

8. Each E–F strip is composed of nine light and nine medium Es. Sew the E pieces together, alternating light and medium, as shown in Diagram 4.

Diagram 4

9. Sew a light and medium F to opposite sides of the E strip as shown in Diagram 5.

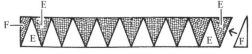

Diagram 5

10. With the light E pieces touching G, sew an E strip to each long edge of G as shown in the Sashing Assembly Diagram.

11. Construct 48 more sashing strips in the same manner.

Edging (optional)

12. Much of the charm of this quilt derives from the unusual curved edging. However, if you do not wish to add an edging, go on to step 18.

13. If you wish to add the edging, first make the large pieced 'suns' as follows. Sew ten light and ten dark J pieces together, alternating light and dark to form a curved strip as shown in Diagram 6.

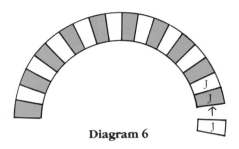

Diagram 6

14. Following Diagram 7, sew K to the J strip, matching the notches on K to the fifth, tenth and fifteenth seams of the J strip. Then sew L to K matching the dots.

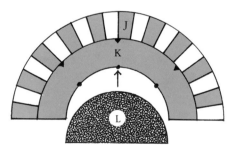

Diagram 7

15. Construct 17 more large suns in the same manner.

16. Follow Diagram 8 to make the small 'suns'. Sew M to N matching the ovals.

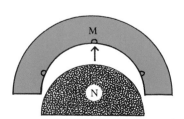

Diagram 8

17. Construct 21 more small suns in the same manner.

Assembly

18. Following Diagram 9 and working on a large flat surface, arrange the patchwork blocks with the pieced sashing, H squares and edging (if using).

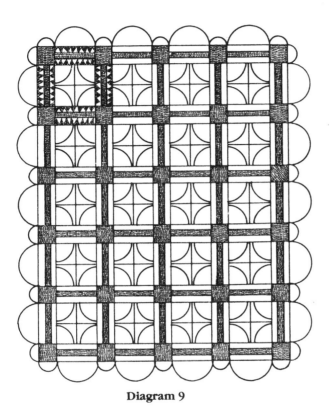

Diagram 9

19. Assemble the quilt in horizontal rows, ignoring the top and bottom edging suns for the moment. Following Diagram 10, sew five H and four pieced sashing strips together, alternating the pieces as shown. If you are using the curved edging, sew a

small edging sun to the H at each end of the row. Construct 5 more rows of sashing in the same manner.

20. Following Diagram 11, sew five pieced sashing strips and four New York Beauty blocks together, alternating the pieces as shown. If using the edging, sew a large edging sun to the sashing strips at each end of the row. Construct 4 more rows of blocks in the same manner.

21. Following Diagram 9, sew the rows of sashing and blocks together, matching seams carefully.

22. To complete the quilt top if you are using the edging, sew the small and large edging suns to the top and bottom edges as shown in Diagrams 9 and 12. (H is shown in white on Diagram 12 for clarity.)

23. To make the quilt back, sew the two fabric pieces together along the long edges; press the seam allowance to one side.

24. Assemble the quilt top, batting/wadding and back as directed on page 113. Trim the edges of the back to follow the curved lines of the edging.

Finishing

25. Outline-quilt all the curved seams of the patchwork, including the sashing strips. (It is not necessary to outline-quilt the A, E, F or J pieces.) Quilt each H square as shown on the template and Diagram 12.

26. If you are not using the curved edging, you will need a straight binding, cut from the light fabric. Bind the quilt with a separate binding as directed on page 115.

27. If you have added the curved edging, bind the quilt with a separate bias binding as directed on page 115, easing the binding around the curves and making a small pleat in each 'valley' between the curves.

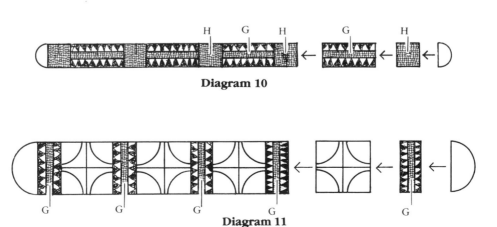

Diagram 10

Diagram 11

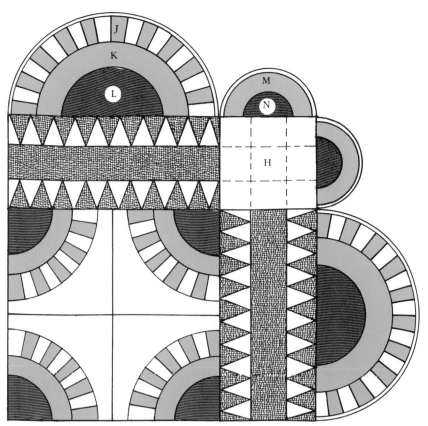

Diagram 12

Note: This pattern piece **does not** include seam allowance.

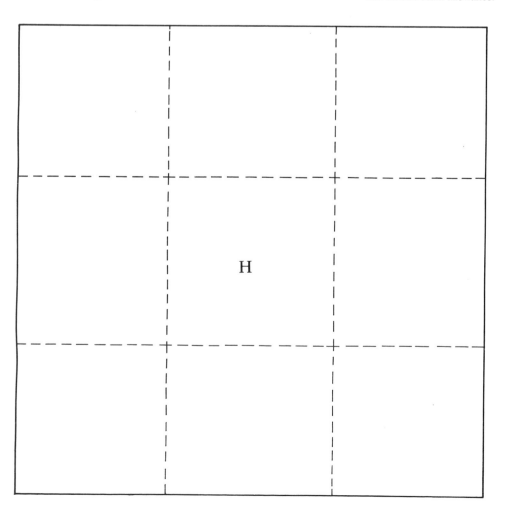

H

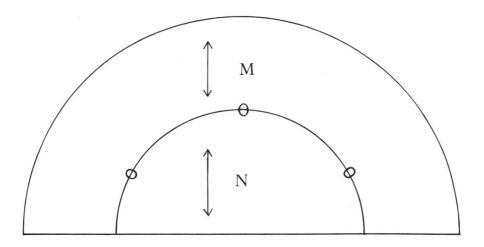

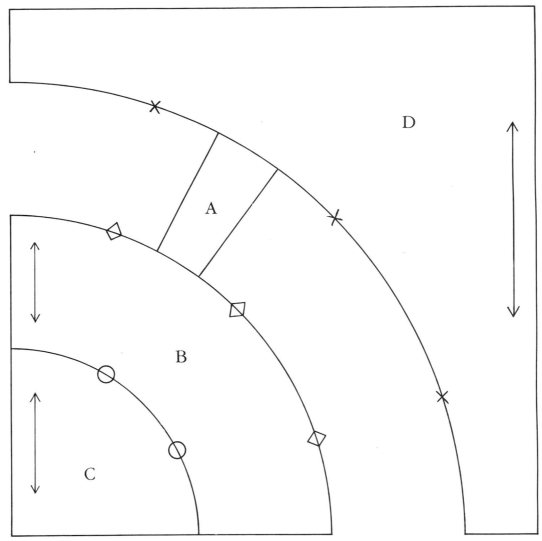

Note: These pattern pieces **do not** include seam allowance.

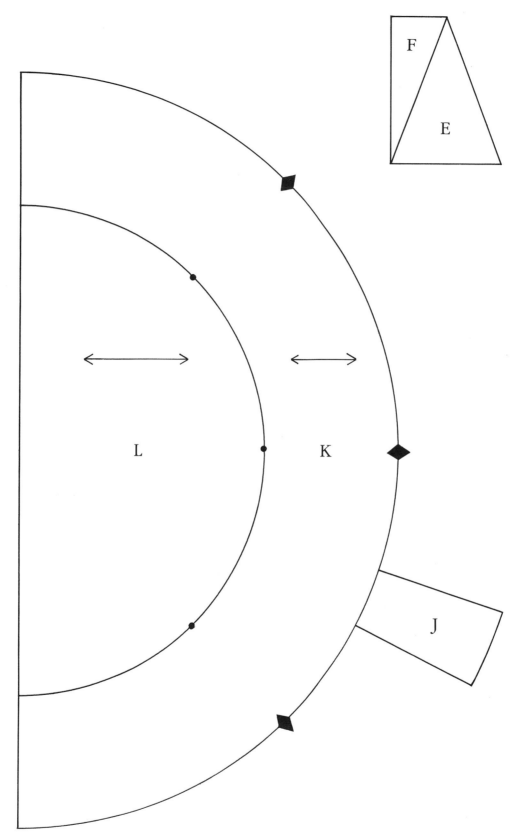

Note: These pattern pieces **do not** include seam allowance.

PRINCESS FEATHER

This delightful mid-nineteenth-century quilt exudes a sense of harmony and excitement. The nine circles of plumes are each punctuated by a central eight-pointed star, and are visually connected by the chrome orange trapunto circles on the end of each plume. The trapunto work is cleverly echoed by the stuffed berries on the winding vine border. The stems are embroidered with home-dyed pink wool.

Skill Level: Advanced

Size

Block is 21 inches/53.3 cm square
9 blocks are needed for finished quilt
Finished quilt is 73 × 73 inches/185.4 × 185.4 cm

Materials

Note: For clarity, the actual colors used in the quilt in the photograph have been listed below; feel free to make color substitutions should you wish to do so.

● 8 yards/meters white fabric for patchwork blocks, border, back of quilt and binding

- 2⅜ yards/meters pink (or red) fabric for patchwork blocks and border
- 2½ yards/meters green fabric for patchwork blocks and border
- ¼ yard/meter gold fabric for patchwork blocks
- 73½ × 73½ inch/186.7 × 186.7 cm piece of batting/wadding
- cotton or polyester fiberfill and small crochet hook for stuffing D circles and H berries
- green or pink crewel embroidery wool for embroidering stems on border pieces
- embroidery needle

- Make templates (see page 108) for the following pieces:

Background: 21½ × 21½ inches/54.6 × 54.6 cm square (measurements include a ¼ inch/6 mm seam allowance)

D: 1⅛ inch/2.8 cm diameter circle (does not include seam allowance; make template without a seam allowance)

H: 1 inch/2.54 cm diameter circle (does not include seam allowance; make template without a seam allowance)

Cutting (per quilt)

Note: All measurements include a ¼ inch/6 mm seam allowance.

BACK OF QUILT

Cut two pieces white fabric, each 37 × 73½ inches/94 × 186.7 cm

BORDERS

Two **E** strips 5½ × 63½ inches/14 × 161.3 cm, white fabric

Two **F** strips 5½ × 73½ inches/14 × 186.7 cm, white fabric

BIAS-STRIP VINE FOR BORDERS

From green fabric, cut one 30 inch/76 cm square piece of fabric into 1 inch/2.54 cm wide bias strips; sew the strips together to measure 8¾ yards/meters long (see page 115 for instructions on cutting bias binding)

BINDING

Cut white fabric into seven 1½ inch/4 cm wide strips across the full width of the fabric and sew together to measure 8 yards/meters long

PATTERN PIECE	NUMBER OF PIECES

Note: Number of pieces for a single block is shown in parentheses. It is essential that you place the templates with the arrows on the straight grain of fabric when marking and cutting out the appliqué feather pieces.

For Blocks:

Background	(1)	9 white
A	(1)	9 pink
B	(8)	72 green
C	(8)	72 pink
D	(9)	81 gold (add seam allowance)

For Borders:

| **G** | | 96 green |
| **H** | | 270 pink (add seam allowance) |

Piecing

PRINCESS FEATHER BLOCKS

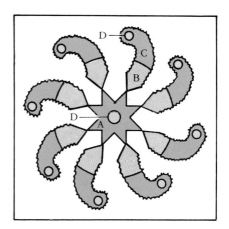

Block Assembly Diagram

1. Following Diagram 1, sew each B to a C along the straight edges to make eight feathers.

Diagram 1

2. Prepare one A star and the feathers for appliqué as directed on page 112.

3. Following Diagram 2, fold the background fabric in half diagonally in both directions and press so that you can position the pieces accurately. Position one A star in the exact center of the background block. Appliqué the star to the background block (see page 112 for instructions on how to appliqué).

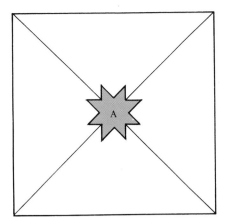

Diagram 2

4. Following Diagram 3, position the pieced feathers on the background, matching the pointed end of B to each tip of the A star. Pin the feathers to the background so that you can adjust them perfectly once all eight are in place. When you are satisfied with their position, appliqué the feathers to the background block.

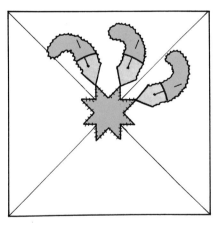

Diagram 3

5. To make the D circles, first work a round of basting stitches close to the raw edges of one D circle as shown in Diagram 4.

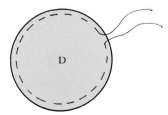

Diagram 4

6. Center template D on the wrong side of the fabric circle and pull the basting stitches to gather the

edges of the fabric tightly around the template as shown in Diagram 5.

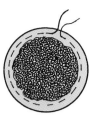

Diagram 5

7. Press the fabric circle gently, then pop out the cardboard template without disturbing the pressed shape of the appliqué.

8. Appliqué D in the middle of the A star, leaving an opening along the edge as shown in Diagram 6. Then, using the blunt end of a crochet hook, or the eraser end of a pencil, stuff the appliqué firmly and evenly with some cotton or polyester fiberfill. After stuffing, slipstitch the remaining edge of the appliqué to the star, securing the stuffing inside.

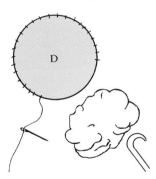

Diagram 6

9. Repeat step 8 to sew and stuff a D circle on the tip of each C feather in the position shown on the actual-size template and the Block Assembly Diagram.

10. Construct 8 more Princess Feather blocks in the same manner.

Appliquéd Borders

11. It is easier to appliqué the borders before sewing them to the quilt top; just take care not to fray the edges of the border fabrics. You may wish to zigzag-stitch the edges to keep them from fraying while you work.

12. First study Diagram 7 to see how the border design works. On the E pieces, the vine has ten curves; on the F pieces, the vine has thirteen curves. Press or lightly mark your E borders so that they are divided evenly into five sections. Do the same with the F pieces, adding two extra markings 5¼ inches/ 13.3 cm from each end.

Diagram 7

13. Cut your bias strip vine into two 72 inch/183 cm pieces for the E borders, and two 84 inch/213.4 cm pieces for the F borders. Press both long edges of each vine ¼ inch/6 mm to the wrong side, being careful not to stretch the strips out of shape as you press. The finished width of the vine will be ½ inch/ 13 mm.

14. Then, following Diagram 7, pin one vine to the E border, making ten curves as shown. This might take some time, but be patient and it will work. When you start, align the raw edge of the bias strip with the raw edge of the border. You may have a bit of extra fabric once you get to the end; simply cut this off, even with the raw edge of the border. When you are satisfied with the curves, baste the vine to the border, then press very carefully so that the curves are smooth with no puckers. Appliqué the vine to the border. Repeat for the other E border.

15. For the F border, pin the vine to F making

thirteen curves as shown in Diagram 7. Again, you may have a bit of extra fabric left over; simply trim it away. Baste, press and appliqué the vine to F as you did for E. Repeat for the other F border.

16. Prepare all the G leaves for appliqué as directed on page 112, turning all edges under because the leaves will not be placed beneath the vines but will just touch them.

17. Following steps 5, 6 and 7, prepare all the H berries for appliqué.

18. Following Diagram 7, position the leaves and the berries on the E and F borders, pinning them in place as shown. You will need 22 leaves and 60 berries for each E border, and 26 leaves and 75 berries for each F border. Once you are satisfied with their position, appliqué the leaves and berries to the borders. Stuff each of the berries before sewing closed as described in step 8.

19. Once all the pieces are sewn in place,

embroider a chain-stitch stem from the vine to the central berry in the cluster as shown in Diagram 7. Use one strand of crewel wool in the needle as shown in Diagram 8.

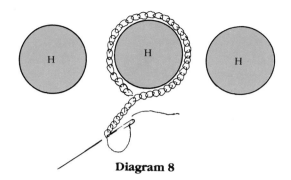

Diagram 8

Assembly

20. Following Diagram 7 and working on a large flat surface, arrange the appliquéd blocks in three rows with three blocks in each row.

21. Sew the blocks together in rows, then sew the rows together, matching seams carefully at the intersections.

22. Sew an E border to each side of the appliquéd center.

23. Sew an F border to the top and bottom edges to complete the quilt top.

24. To make the quilt back, sew the two fabric pieces together along the long edges; press the seam allowance to one side.

25. Assemble the quilt top, batting/wadding and back as directed on page 113.

Finishing

26. Quilt the A star and B–C feather pieces as shown on the actual-size templates. Outline-quilt each D circle.

27. Quilt the background blocks with intersecting diagonal lines, spaced about ¾ inch/2 cm apart; do not quilt on top of the appliqués or into the borders.

28. Quilt each G leaf as shown on the actual-size template; then outline-quilt each leaf.

29. Outline-quilt each H berry, then work a second line ¼ inch/6 mm away from each berry; where the quilting lines will intersect with an adjacent berry, simply stop the quilting to form a cloud effect around the berries.

30. Outline-quilt the vines.

31. Bind the quilt with a separate binding as directed on page 115.

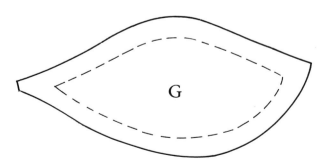

Note: The dotted line shown on pattern piece G indicates the quilting (see step 28). It is **not** the seam allowance.

Note: This pattern piece **does not** include seam allowance.

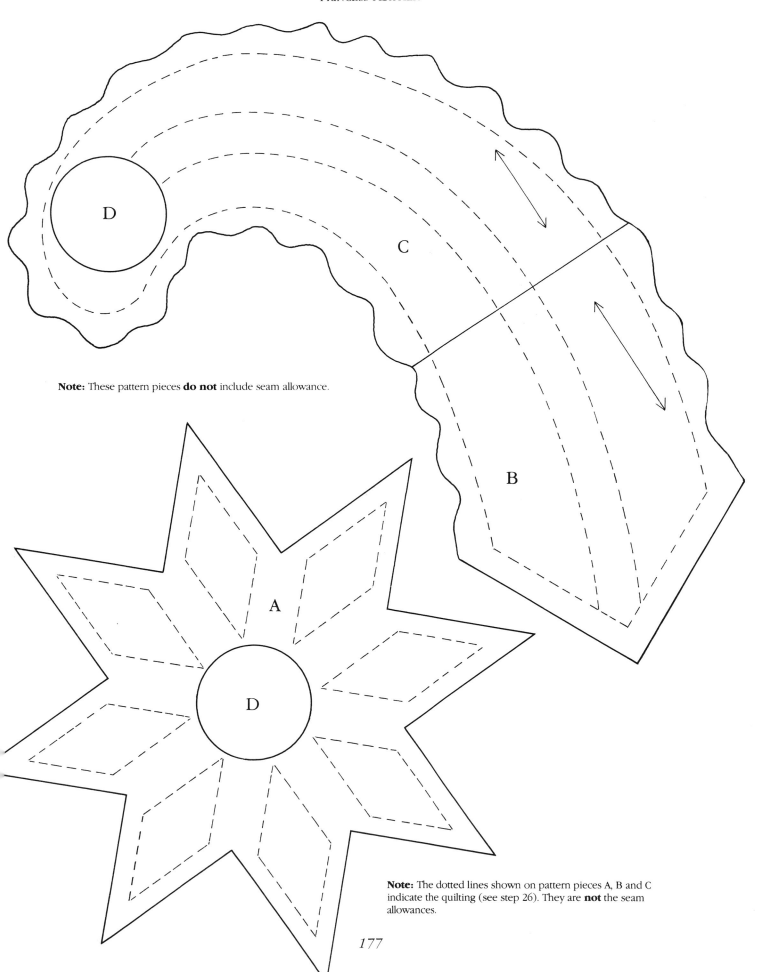

Note: These pattern pieces **do not** include seam allowance.

Note: The dotted lines shown on pattern pieces A, B and C indicate the quilting (see step 26). They are **not** the seam allowances.

RAYED STAR

This 1900s, well-ordered Mennonite quilt boasts elaborate feather quilting around a pieced design of deceptively simple triangles. The strong sense of symmetry is charmingly offset by a wide scalloped border.

Skill Level: Intermediate

Size

Block is an equilateral triangle, about 6¾ inches/17 cm per side
209 triangles and 22 half-triangles are needed for finished quilt
Finished quilt is 82 × 83½ inches/208.3 × 212 cm

Materials

● 10½ yards/meters light fabric for patchwork blocks, borders and back of quilt
● 2¾ yards/meters bright fabric for patchwork blocks
● 3 yards/meters dark fabric for patchwork blocks and bias binding
● 82½ × 84 inch/209.5 × 213.4 cm piece of batting/wadding

Cutting (per quilt)

Note: All measurements include a ¼ inch/6 mm seam allowance.

BACK OF QUILT

Cut two pieces light fabric, each 41½ × 84 inches/ 105.4 × 213.4 cm

BORDERS

Two **G** strips 8½ × 68 inches/21.6 × 172.7 cm, light fabric

Two **H** strips 8½ × 82½ inches/21.6 × 209.5 cm, light fabric

BIAS BINDING

See page 115 for instructions on cutting bias binding. Cut one 44 inch/111.7 cm square and one 13 inch/33 cm square piece of dark fabric into 1½ inch/4 cm wide bias strips and sew together to measure 10⅜ yards/meters long

PATTERN PIECE	NUMBER OF PIECES

Note: Number of pieces for a single block is shown in parentheses.

Complete Triangle

A	(1)	209 bright
B	(3)	627 light
C	(3)	627 dark

Half-Triangle

B	(1)	22 light
C	(1)	22 dark
D	(1)	11 bright
D reversed	(1)	11 bright
E	(1)	11 light
E reversed	(1)	11 light
F	(1)	22 dark

Piecing

RAYED STAR TRIANGLES

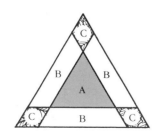

Triangle Assembly Diagram

1. Sew a B to one edge of A as shown in Diagram 1.

2. Sew a C to one end of a B as shown in Diagram 2.

Diagram 1   **Diagram 2**

3. Sew B–C to A–B as shown in Diagram 3.

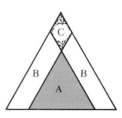

Diagram 3

4. Sew a C to each end of a B as shown in Diagram 4.

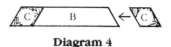

Diagram 4

5. Sew C–B–C to the bottom edge of the B–A–B to complete the triangle as shown in the Triangle Assembly Diagram.

6. Construct 208 more Rayed Star triangles in the same manner.

RAYED STAR HALF-TRIANGLES

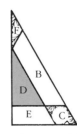

Half-triangle Assembly Diagram

7. Sew E to D as shown in Diagram 5.

8. Sew F to the left end of B, and C to the right end of B as shown in Diagram 6.

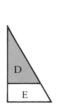

Diagram 5   **Diagram 6**

9. Sew F–B–C to the right edge of D–E to form a half-triangle as shown in the Half-Triangle Assembly Diagram.

10. Construct 10 more half-triangles in the same manner. Then construct 11 mirror-image triangles using the reversed D and E pieces.

Assembly

11. Following Diagrams 7 and 8 and working on a large flat surface, arrange the patchwork triangles and half-triangles in eleven horizontal rows with nineteen complete triangles in each row. Place a half-triangle at each end of each row as shown.

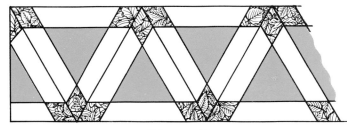

Diagram 7

12. Stitch the triangles together in rows, matching seams carefully as shown in Diagram 7.

13. Stitch the rows together, matching seams carefully.

14. Following Diagram 8, stitch a G border strip to the top and bottom edges of the patchwork.

15. Stitch an H border strip to each side of the patchwork to complete the quilt top.

16. Following the directions on pages 108–9, enlarge the feather quilting design and use the enlarged pattern to make a quilting template. Following the directions on page 113, mark the feather design on the G and H pieces. First mark the feather design in each of the four corners, then connect the corners by repeating the quilting design across the borders to form a continuous curve.

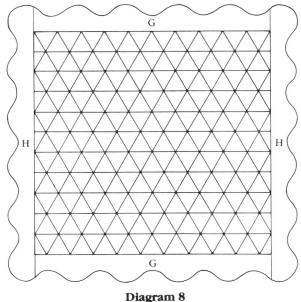

Diagram 8

17. To make the quilt back, sew the two fabric pieces together along the long edges; press the seam allowance to one side.

18. Assemble the quilt top, batting/wadding and back as directed on page 113.

Finishing

19. Outline-quilt each of the A, C, D and F pieces.

20. Quilt the feather border on the G and H pieces. Then, quilt straight diagonal lines from the inner edge of the feather border to the edge of the patchwork; space the lines about ¾ inch/2 cm apart.

21. After all the quilting is done, trim the edge of the quilt 1¼ inches/3 cm away from the outer stitching lines of the quilting on the G and H pieces.

22. Bind the quilt with a separate bias binding as directed on page 115, easing the binding carefully around the corners and the curved edges.

Feather quilting design

each square = 2″/5 cm

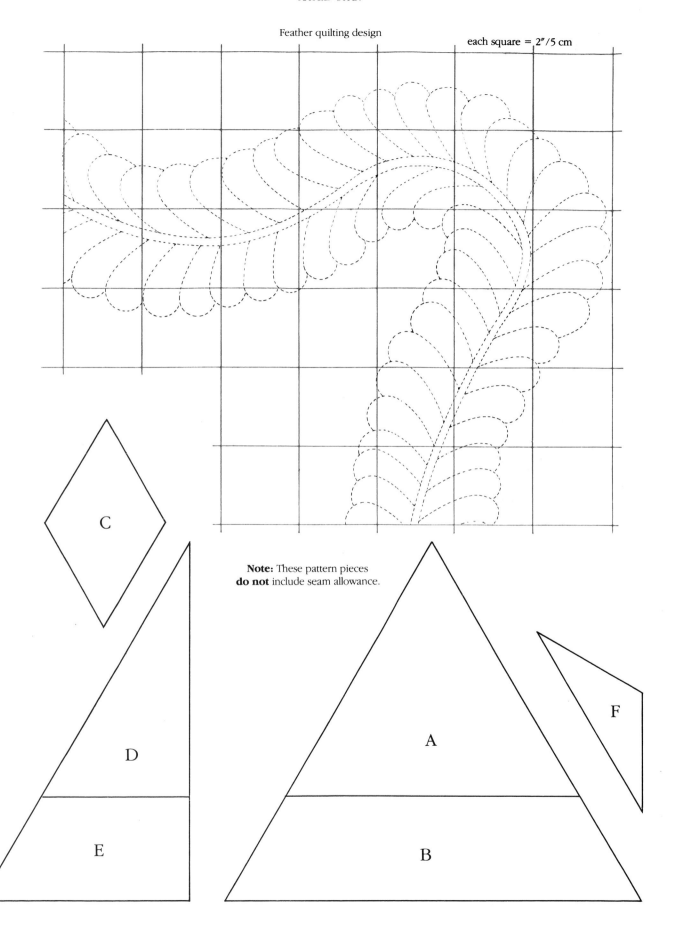

C

D

E

Note: These pattern pieces **do not** include seam allowance.

A

B

F

AMISH UNKNOWN

The remarkable muted colors of the soft wools used in this quilt, from forest green to blue, burgundy, mauve, brown, grey and butternut, create a rich, almost earthy feeling. The irregular placement of mauve, grey and blue in the internal blocks presents a spontaneous yet beautifully disciplined quality. This quilt boasts five separate quilting patterns, all stitched with great regularity and skill.

Skill Level: Easy

Size

Block is 12 inches/30.5 cm square
12 blocks are needed for finished quilt
Finished quilt is 68 × 85 inches/172.7 × 216 cm

Materials

Note: For clarity, the actual colors used to make the quilt pictured in the photograph above have been listed in parentheses below.

● 2 yards/meters light (mauve) fabric for patchwork blocks and sashing

● 1½ yards/meters bright (purple) fabric for patchwork blocks

● 1¼ yards/meters dark (gold-brown) fabric for patchwork blocks and sashing

● 1½ yards/meters medium (maroon) fabric for sashing and border OR ¾ yard/meter if you don't mind having a pieced border (see Borders: G)

● 5 yards/meters coordinating (blue) fabric for border, back of quilt and binding

● 2 yards/meters coordinating (dark green) fabric for border

● 68½ × 85½ inch/174 × 217 cm piece of batting/wadding

● Make templates (see page 108) for the following pieces (measurements include a ¼ inch/6 mm seam allowance):

D: 5½ × 12½ inches/14 × 31.7 cm
E: 5½ × 5½ inches/14 × 14 cm

Cutting (per quilt)

Note: All measurements include a ¼ inch/6 mm seam allowance.

BACK OF QUILT

Cut two pieces coordinating fabric, each 34½ × 85½ inches/87.6 × 217 cm (blue in photograph)

BORDERS

Two **F** strips 3½ × 63½ inches/9 × 161.3 cm, coordinating fabric (blue in photograph)

Two **G** strips 3½ × 52½ inches/9 × 133.4 cm, medium fabric (maroon in photograph), OR for a pieced border (to save fabric): four strips 3½ × 26½ inches/9 × 67.3 cm; stitch two pairs of strips together at the short ends to make two strips, each 52½ inches/133.4 cm long

Two **H** strips 8½ × 69½ inches/21.6 × 176.5 cm, coordinating fabric (dark green in photograph)

Two **J** strips 8½ × 68½ inches/21.6 × 174 cm, coordinating fabric (dark green in photograph)

SASHING

D: Eleven light, six medium, using template
E: Six dark, using template

BINDING

Cut coordinating fabric into seven 1½ inch/4 cm wide strips across the full width of the fabric and sew together to measure 8½ yards/meters long (blue in photograph)

PATTERN PIECE	NUMBER OF PIECES	
Note: Number of pieces for a single block is shown in parentheses. See special instructions for cutting the A pieces (steps 1 through 3 below).		
A	(10)	120 light
	(10)	120 bright
B	(4)	48 dark
C	(6)	72 light
	(6)	72 bright
	(8)	96 dark

Piecing

PATCHWORK BLOCKS

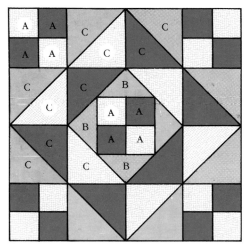

Block Assembly Diagram

1. No pattern piece is needed for the A pieces. Instead you will be constructing the A checkerboard units by cutting and sewing strips together as directed in steps 1 through 4. Measure and cut ten strips, each 3½ inches/9 cm wide, across the full width from each of your light and bright fabrics.

2. Following Diagram 1, sew each light strip to a bright one; press the seam allowances toward the bright fabric.

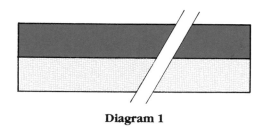

Diagram 1

3. Following Diagram 2, measure and cut twelve strips, each 3½ inches/9 cm wide, from each pieced strip made in step 2, until you have a total of 120 light/bright strips.

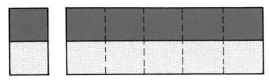

Diagram 2

4. Following Diagram 3, sew a pair of strips together, turning one of the strips so that the light and bright pieces are opposite one another. You will end up with a 3½ inch/9 cm square. Construct 59 more checkerboard squares in the same manner. You will need 5 checkerboard squares for the first block; set aside the other 55 squares.

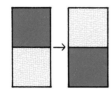

Diagram 3

5. Following Diagram 4, sew a dark B to each edge of one checkerboard square to form the central square.

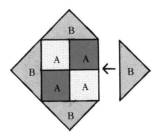

Diagram 4

6. Following Diagram 5, sew two light Cs and two bright Cs to opposite edges of the central square as shown.

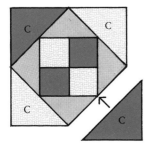

Diagram 5

7. Sew four light Cs to four dark Cs along the diagonal edge to form four squares as shown in Diagram 6. Then sew four bright Cs to four dark Cs in the same manner.

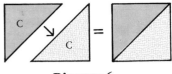

Diagram 6

8. Sew a light and bright C square together to form a rectangle as shown in Diagram 7. Repeat three more times for a total of four rectangles.

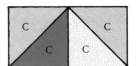

Diagram 7

9. Following Diagram 8, sew a C rectangle to each side of the central square, making sure that the light and bright pieces do not touch one another.

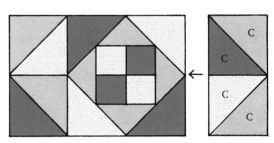

Diagram 8

10. Following Diagram 9, sew a checkerboard square to each side of the two remaining C rectangles, positioning the squares so that the light pieces are at the outer corners.

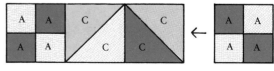

Diagram 9

11. Sew the strips just made to the top and bottom of the central square, matching seams carefully to complete the block as shown in the Block Assembly Diagram.

12. Construct 11 more patchwork blocks in the same manner.

13. Following the directions on pages 108–9, enlarge the feather quilting design and use the enlarged design to make a quilting template. Following the directions on page 113, use the template to mark the feather quilting design on each of the D sashing strips.

14. Enlarge the star quilting design and mark in the middle of each of the E squares in the same way.

15. Enlarge the lozenge quilting design on page 217 and mark along each of the F and G strips as shown in Diagram 10 in the same way.

16. Note: Because the leaf quilting design begins in a corner, mark the design on the H and J pieces *after* the quilt top has been completed. See Step 23.

Assembly

17. Following Diagram 10 and working on a large flat surface, arrange the patchwork blocks with the D and E sashing pieces. Sew the patchwork blocks to the D sashing pieces to form four horizontal rows with three blocks in each row. Sew the D and E sashing pieces together to form three horizontal sashing rows.

18. Sew the patchwork rows to the sashing rows, matching seams carefully at the intersections, to complete the central portion of the quilt top.

19. Sew an F strip to each side of the patchwork.

20. Sew a G strip to the top and bottom edges of the patchwork.

21. Sew an H strip to each side of the patchwork.

22. Sew a J strip to the top and bottom of the patchwork to complete the quilt top.

23. Following the directions on pages 108–9, enlarge the leaf quilting design and use the enlarged design to make a quilting template. Following the directions on page 113, use the template to mark the leaf quilting design on the H and J strips.

24. To make the quilt back, sew the two fabric pieces together along the long edges; press the seam allowance to one side.

25. Assemble the quilt top, batting/wadding and back as directed on page 113.

Finishing

26. Quilt the patchwork blocks with straight diagonal lines, as shown in the lower left corner of Diagram 10, using a dark quilting thread if you wish.

27. Quilt each of the D sashing strips along the marked feather design.

28. Quilt each E square with the marked star design.

29. Quilt the lozenge design along the F and G borders.

30. Quilt the curved leaf design along the H and J borders.

31. Bind the quilt with a separate binding as directed on page 115.

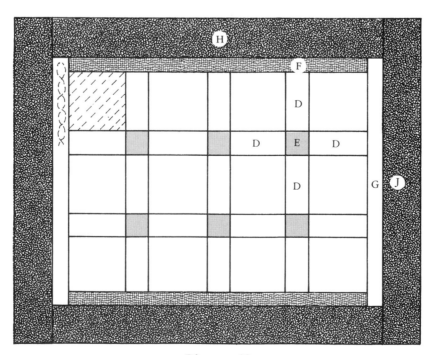

Diagram 10

185

Note: These pattern pieces **do not** include seam allowance.

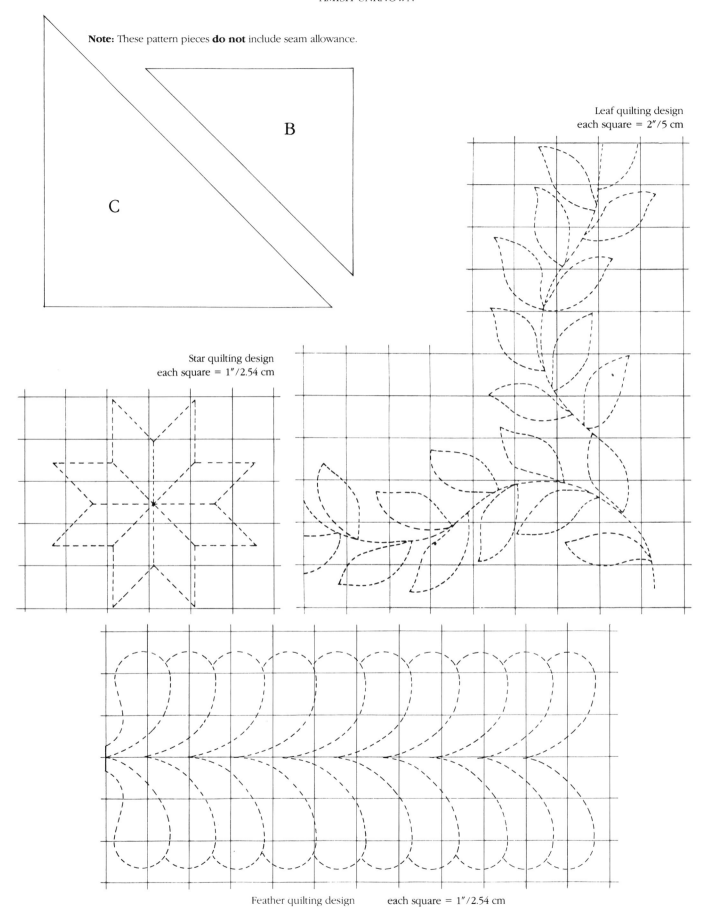

B

C

Leaf quilting design
each square = 2″/5 cm

Star quilting design
each square = 1″/2.54 cm

Feather quilting design   each square = 1″/2.54 cm

SPOOLS

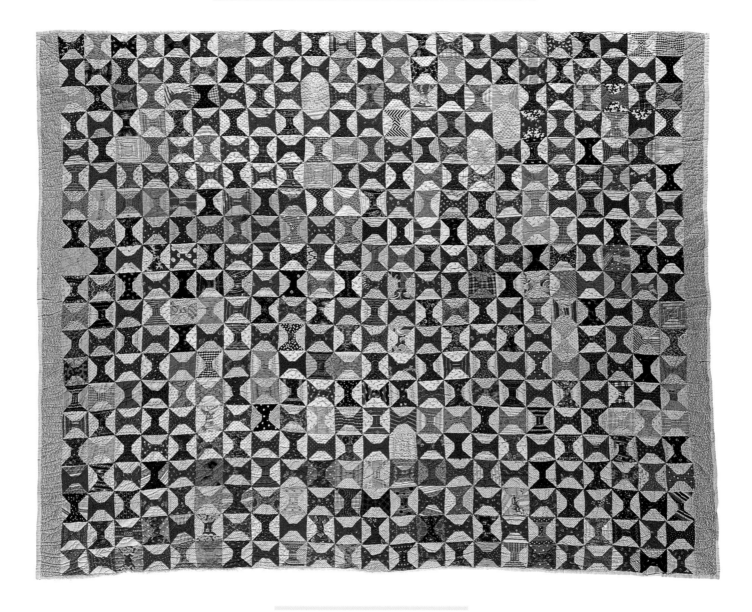

*This lovely quilt was made in Kansas in the last years of the
nineteenth century; it features a catalog of interesting fabrics and a
name which speaks of a woman's close relationship with
needlework. Spools was a popular frontier scrap pattern.*

Skill Level: Intermediate

Size

Block is 3 inches/7.6 cm square
460 blocks are needed for finished quilt
Finished quilt is 60 × 74 inches/152.4 × 188 cm

Materials

Note: The quilt shown in the photograph is actually a scrap quilt
– different fabrics were used to construct each patchwork block.
If you wish, you can follow the yardage given here and make
every block exactly the same, which will result in a very modern,
graphic effect; or you can use up your scraps of fabric to make
each block different. For simplicity, the instructions divide the
fabrics into light and dark.

- 3¾ yards/meters light fabric for patchwork blocks
- 4¼ yards/meters dark fabric for patchwork blocks
- 3⅜ yards/meters bright fabric for borders and back of quilt
- ¼ yard/meter coordinating fabric for binding
- 60½ × 74¼ inch/153.6 × 188.6 cm piece of batting/wadding

Cutting (per quilt)

Note: All measurements include a ¼ inch/6 mm seam allowance.

BACK OF QUILT

Cut two pieces bright fabric, each 37½ × 60½ inches/95 × 153.6 cm

BORDERS

Two **C** strips 3 × 60½ inches/7.6 × 153.6 cm, bright fabric

BINDING

Cut coordinating fabric into six 1½ inch/4 cm wide strips across the full width of the fabric and sew together to measure 7½ yards/meters long

PATTERN PIECE	NUMBER OF PIECES

Note: Number of pieces for a single block is shown in parentheses.

A	(1) 460 dark
B	(2) 920 dark
	(2) 920 dark

Piecing

SPOOLS BLOCKS

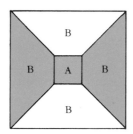

Block Assembly Diagram

1. Sew a dark B to each side of A as shown in Diagram 1.

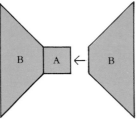

Diagram 1

2. Inset a light B into each side of B–A–B as shown in Diagram 2 to complete the block. (See page 111 for instructions on insetting.)

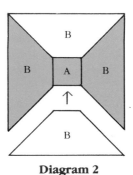

Diagram 2

3. Construct 459 more Spools blocks in the same manner.

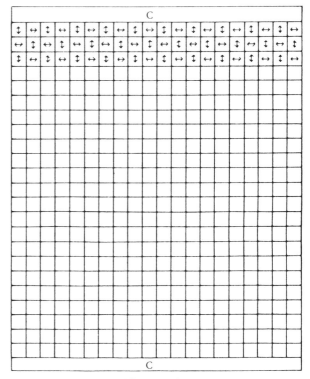

Diagram 3

Assembly

4. Following Diagram 3 and working on a large flat surface, arrange the patchwork blocks in twenty-three horizontal rows with twenty blocks in each row. Alternate the direction of the blocks as shown by the arrows on the diagram.

5. Stitch the blocks together in rows.

6. Stitch the rows together, matching seams carefully at the intersections.

7. Stitch a C border strip to the top and bottom edges of the patchwork to complete the quilt top.

8. Following the directions on pages 108–9, enlarge the wave quilting design and use the enlarged pattern to make a quilting template. Following the directions on page 113, use the template to mark the wave design across the entire quilt top, including the borders.

9. To make the quilt back, sew the two fabric pieces together along the long edges; press the seam allowance to one side.

10. Assemble the quilt top, batting/wadding and back as directed on page 113.

Finishing

11. Quilt the marked wave design.

12. Bind the quilt with a separate binding as directed on page 115.

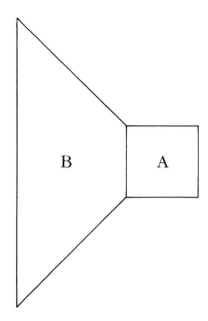

Note: These pattern pieces **do not** include seam allowance.

CARPENTER'S SQUARE

*Sources of inspiration for many quilts are either domestic objects like
cake stands and baskets or natural elements like flowers and birds. It is
unusual to find a quilt which is directly named after a household
tool. Another interesting feature of this late-nineteenth-century quilt
is the curved machine quilting, a point which testifies to the growing
pride which accompanied the ownership of a sewing machine.*

Skill Level: Advanced

Size

Block is 13¾ inches/35 cm square
12 blocks are needed for finished quilt
Finished quilt is 59¾ × 75¼ inches/152 × 191 cm

Materials

● 3¾ yards/meters light fabric for patchwork blocks,
sashing, borders and back of quilt
● 3 yards/meters dark fabric for patchwork blocks,
borders and binding
● 60¼ × 75¾ inch/153 × 192.4 cm piece of batting/
wadding

Cutting (per quilt)

Note: All measurements include a ¼ inch/6 mm seam allowance.

BACK OF QUILT

Cut two pieces light fabric, each 30⅜ × 75¾ inches/ 77 × 192.4 cm

BORDERS

Two **K** strips 1¾ × 44¼ inches/4.4 × 112.4 cm, light fabric

Two **L** strips 1¾ × 61¾ inches/4.4 × 157 cm, light fabric

Two **M** strips 1¾ × 46¾ inches/4.4 × 118.7 cm, dark fabric

Two **N** strips 1¾ × 64¼ inches/4.4 × 163 cm, dark fabric

Two **O** strips 1¾ × 49¼ inches/4.4 × 125 cm, light fabric

Two **P** strips 1¾ × 66¾ inches/4.4 × 169.5 cm, light fabric

Two **Q** strips 1¾ × 51¾ inches/4.4 × 131.4 cm, dark fabric

Two **R** strips 1¾ × 69¼ inches/4.4 × 176 cm, dark fabric

Two **S** strips 3½ × 54¼ inches/9 × 138 cm, light fabric

Two **T** strips 3½ × 75¼ inches/9 × 191 cm, light fabric

SASHING

Nine **H** strips (using template given), light fabric

Two **J** strips 1¾ × 45½ inches/4.4 × 115.6 cm, light fabric

BINDING

Cut dark fabric into seven 1½ inch/4 cm wide strips across the full width of the fabric and sew together to measure 7½ yards/meters long

PATTERN PIECE	NUMBER OF PIECES

Note: Number of pieces for a single block is shown in parentheses.

A	(5) 60 light
	(8) 96 dark
B	(3) 36 light
	(2) 24 dark
C	(3) 36 light
D	(2) 24 dark
E	(2) 24 dark
F	(1) 12 light
G	(1) 12 light
	(2) 24 dark
H	(2) 24 dark
	9 light (sashing)

Piecing

CARPENTER'S SQUARE BLOCKS

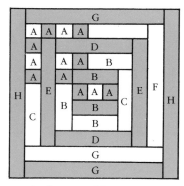

Block Assembly Diagram

1. Sew a dark A to each side of a light A as shown in Diagram 1.

 **Diagram 1**

2. Sew a dark B to the top and bottom of the pieced A strip as shown in Diagram 2.

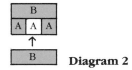 **Diagram 2**

3. Following Diagram 3, sew a light B to the bottom of the pieced center. Sew a dark A to one end of the light B. Sew to the left side edge of the pieced center as shown.

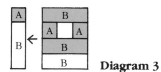 **Diagram 3**

4. Sew a C to the right side edge of the pieced center as shown in Diagram 4.

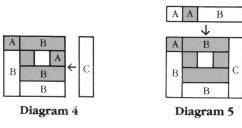

Diagram 4   **Diagram 5**

5. Following Diagram 5, sew a dark A between a light A and a light B, then sew to the top of the pieced center.

6. Sew a D to the top and bottom edges of the pieced center as shown in Diagram 6.

7. Sew an E to each side edge of the pieced center as shown in Diagram 7.

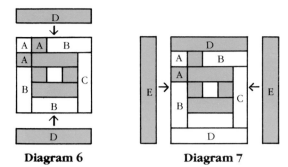

Diagram 6   **Diagram 7**

8. Following Diagram 8, sew a light A between two dark As, then stitch to the end of a C strip. Sew to the top edge of the pieced center.

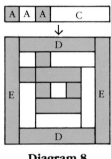

Diagram 8

9. Following Diagram 9, sew four As together, alternating light and dark, then sew the dark end of the pieced A strip to one end of a C strip. Sew to the left side edge of the pieced center. Then, sew an F to the right side edge.

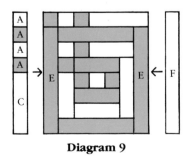

Diagram 9

10. Following Diagram 10, sew a dark G to the top edge of the pieced center. Sew a light and dark G together as shown, then sew the light G to the bottom edge of the pieced center.

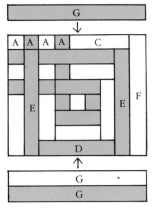

Diagram 10

11. Sew a dark H to each side edge of the pieced center as shown in Diagram 11 to complete the patchwork block.

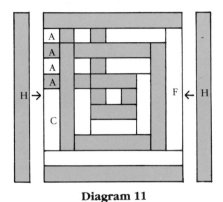

Diagram 11

12. Construct 11 more Carpenter's Square blocks in the same manner.

Assembly

13. Following Diagram 12 and the color photograph and working on a large flat surface, arrange the blocks in three vertical rows, with four blocks in each row. Make sure the blocks are in exactly the same position on each row. Place a light H sashing strip between each of the blocks making up the vertical rows, then stitch the blocks to the sashing strips.

14. Place a J sashing strip between the vertical rows as shown in Diagram 12. Stitch the rows to each side of the sashing strip to complete the central portion of the quilt top.

15. Next, add the border strips, following Diagram 12 for placement. Sew a K strip to the top and bottom edges of the quilt top; sew an L strip to each side edge.

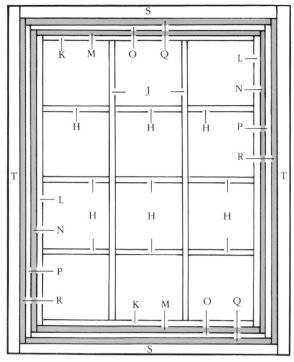

Diagram 12

Diagram 13

16. Sew an M strip to each K strip; sew an N strip to each L strip.

17. Sew an O strip to each M strip; sew a P strip to each N strip.

18. Sew a Q strip to each O strip; sew an R strip to each P strip.

19. Sew an S strip to each Q strip; sew a T strip to each R strip to complete the quilt top.

20. To make the quilt back, sew the two fabric pieces together along the long edges; press the seam allowance to one side.

21. Assemble the quilt top, batting/wadding and back as directed on page 113.

Finishing

22. If you wish to exactly copy the quilt shown in the color photograph on page 190, machine-quilt the central portion of the patchwork with wavy vertical lines.

23. Machine-quilt freestyle small, three-petaled 'flowers' around the outer border following the simple design shown in Diagram 13, and making your stitching continuous around the whole border.

24. Alternatively, you can outline-quilt the dark pieces by hand or machine to emphasize the geometric quality of the design.

25. Bind the quilt with a separate binding as directed on page 115.

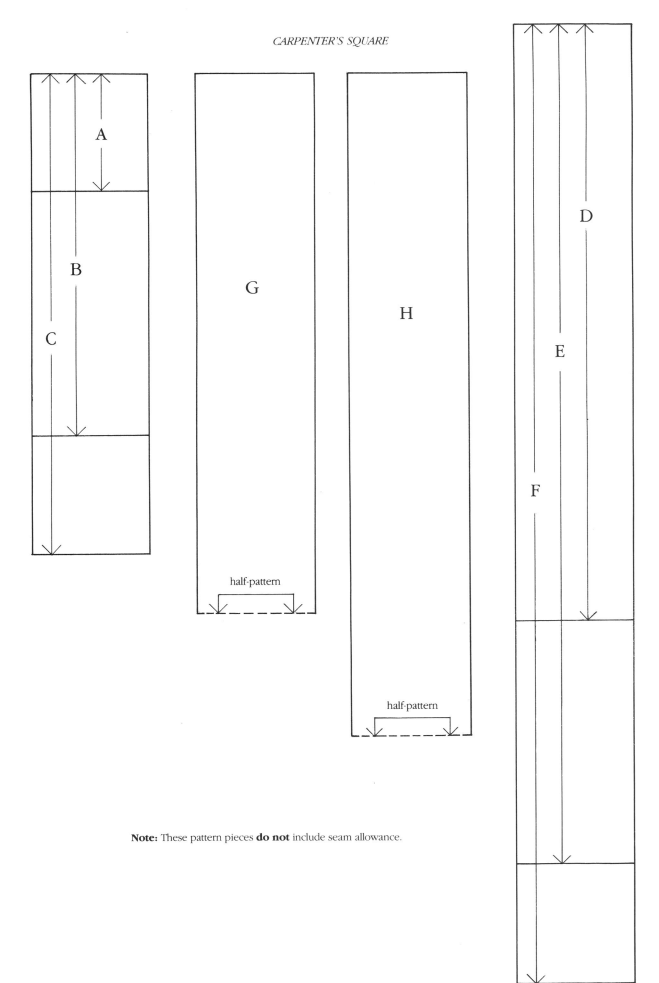

A

B

C

G

H

D

E

F

half-pattern

half-pattern

Note: These pattern pieces **do not** include seam allowance.

MARINER'S COMPASS

This quilt was made in New York State around the 1860s. It is considered to be quite a difficult pattern to construct because the design depends on the narrowness and sharpness of the points. The use of contrasting colors, the dark tones for the main compass points and the lighter shades for the secondary points, creates a three-dimensional effect.

Skill Level: Advanced

Size

Block is 21 inches/53.3 cm square
9 blocks are needed for finished quilt
Finished quilt is 81 inches/205.7 cm square

Materials

● 5¾ yards/meters pale fabric for patchwork blocks, sashing, back of quilt and self binding
● 4 yards/meters white fabric for patchwork blocks and sashing squares
● 1⅛ yards/meters light fabric for patchwork blocks

- 1 yard/meter medium fabric for patchwork blocks
- ⅝ yard/meter bright fabric for patchwork blocks
- ⅝ yard/meter dark fabric for patchwork blocks
- 81½ × 81½ inch/207 × 207 cm piece of batting/wadding

- Make templates (see page 108) for the following pieces (measurements include a ¼ inch/6 mm seam allowance):

G: 5¼ inch/13.3 cm diameter circle

H: 21½ × 21½ inch/54.6 × 54.6 cm square with a 19¼ inch/49 cm diameter circle drawn in the middle of it; divide the square into four equal quarters, then cut out along the curved line (see Diagram 8) for template H

K: 5 × 5 inches/12.7 × 12.7 cm

Cutting (per quilt)

Note: All measurements include a ¼ inch/6 mm seam allowance.

BACK OF QUILT AND SELF BINDING

Cut two pieces pale fabric, each 41½ × 82½ inches/105.4 × 209.5 cm

SASHING

Twenty-four **J** strips 5 × 21½ inches/12.7 × 54.6 cm, pale fabric

Sixteen **K** squares, using template, white fabric (cut these from the discarded central circle of the H pieces)

PATTERN PIECE	NUMBER OF PIECES

Note: Number of pieces for a single block is shown in parentheses.

A	(16) 144 light
B	(16) 144 white
B reversed	(16) 144 white
C	(8) 72 medium
D	(4) 36 bright
E	(4) 36 dark
F	(6) 54 pale
G	(1) 9 white
H	(4) 36 white

Piecing

MARINER'S COMPASS BLOCKS

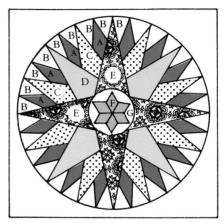

Block Assembly Diagram

1. Following Diagram 1, sew a B and a reversed B to adjacent sides of A, matching the notches. Construct 15 more A–B units in the same manner.

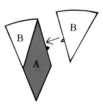

Diagram 1

2. Following Diagram 2, sew an A–B unit to each side of eight Cs, matching the seam of A–B to the marked dot on C.

Diagram 2

3. Following Diagram 3, sew an A–B–C unit to each side of four Ds, matching the seams of A–B and A–C with the marked open diamonds on D.

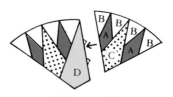

Diagram 3

4. Following Diagram 4, sew an E to each side of two A–B–C–D units, matching the seams to the marked circles on E.

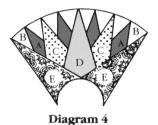

Diagram 4

5. Following Diagram 5, sew an A–B–C–D unit to each side of one of the units shown in Diagram 4, creating an almost complete circle. Then sew the remaining E unit into the opening, to complete the circle.

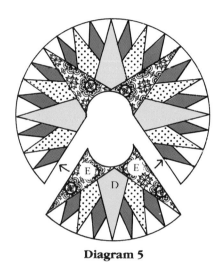

Diagram 5

6. Following Diagram 6, sew three F pieces together, matching the marked Xs. Repeat to make two sets of three F pieces.

Diagram 6   **Diagram 7**

7. Sew the two sets of F pieces together, matching the seams carefully in the middle as shown in Diagram 7. Fold the raw outer edges of the F star ¼ inch/6 mm to the wrong side and press carefully. Center the F star on a G circle and appliqué in place following the directions on page 112.

8. Fold and press the raw edges of the G circle ¼ inch/6 mm to the wrong side. Press carefully to eliminate any irregular points that may form. Pin G over the raw edges in the middle of the patchwork unit completed in step 5. Carefully slipstitch G to the patchwork using matching thread and making very small stitches.

9. Following Diagram 8, sew four H pieces together along the short straight edges to form the frame of the patchwork block. Fold and press the raw edges of the inner circle ¼ inch/6 mm to the wrong side, again pressing carefully to eliminate any irregular points.

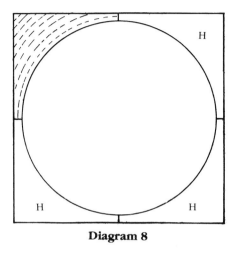

Diagram 8

10. Place the fabric frame on top of the patchwork, matching the seams on the frame to the points of each E piece as shown in the Block Assembly Diagram. Pin together, then carefully slipstitch H to the patchwork using matching thread and making very small stitches.

11. Construct 8 more Mariner's Compass blocks in the same manner.

Assembly

12. Following Diagram 9 and working on a large flat surface, arrange the patchwork blocks in three rows with three squares in each row. Then place the J strips and K squares around the blocks as shown.

13. First join the blocks to the J pieces in horizontal rows, sewing a J to each side of each patchwork block. Then join the pieces of the sashing rows, by sewing a K between each J.

14. Sew the rows of patchwork and sashing together, matching the seams carefully at the intersections.

15. To make the quilt back, sew the two fabric pieces together along the long edges; press the seam allowance to one side.

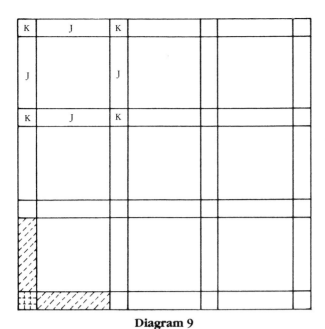

Diagram 9

16. Assemble the quilt top, batting/wadding and back as directed on page 113, centering the top and batting/wadding on the back which will be larger.

Finishing

17. Outline-quilt the F star in the middle of each patchwork block.

18. Quilt evenly spaced straight lines down the center of each A, B, C, D and E spike radiating outward from the central G circle to the edges of the patchwork; do not quilt within the G circle or into the H frame.

19. Following Diagram 8, quilt curved lines on each H piece.

20. Following Diagram 9, quilt diagonal lines on the J pieces and criss-cross lines on each K piece.

21. Following the directions on page 116 for a self binding, wrap the fabric from the back over onto the top of the quilt and bind off neatly.

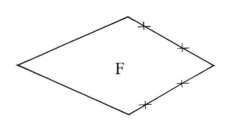

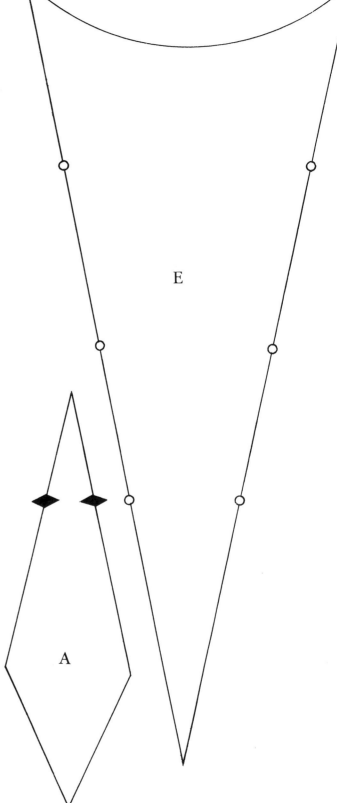

Note: These pattern pieces **do not** include seam allowance.

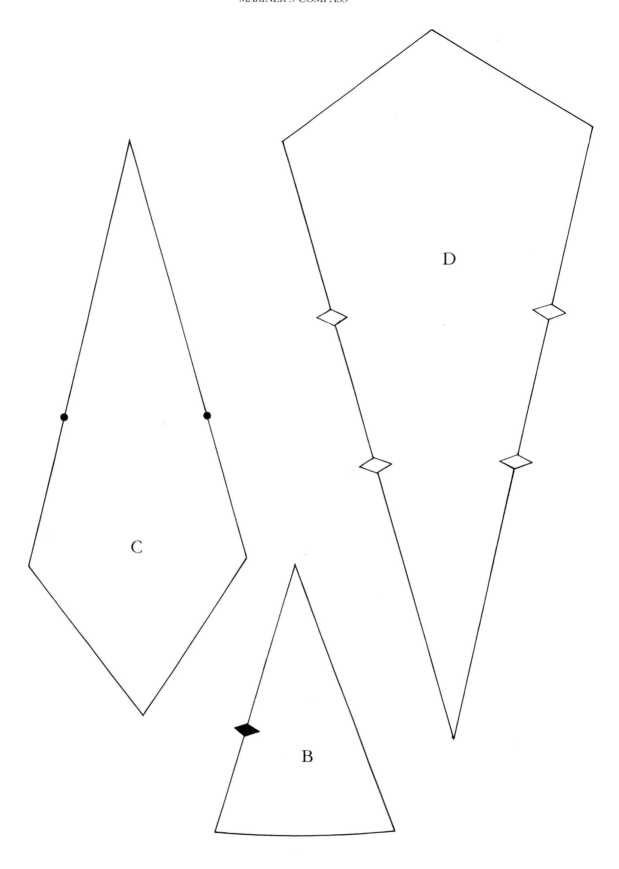

Note: These pattern pieces **do not** include seam allowance.

OCEAN WAVES

The Ocean Waves pattern is one of the more complicated pieced patterns which were developed during the final years of the nineteenth century. It is visually interesting, not only because it translates a natural scene into an abstraction, but because it reflects a strong concern for overall graphic effect. The piecework on this quilt was, like many of the period, done by machine.

Skill Level: Easy

Size

Block is 20 inches/50.8 cm square
12 blocks and 12 side units are needed for finished quilt
Finished quilt is about 89½ inches/227.3 cm square

Materials

Note: The quilt shown in the color photograph is actually a scrap quilt – different fabrics were used to construct each patchwork block, and the wonderful, sparkling ocean waves effect is achieved through the use of a wide variety of fabrics in highly contrasting shades of light and dark. If you wish, you can use the same fabric for the light and dark pieces throughout the quilt, which will result in a very graphic, modern-looking effect; the exact yardage you'll need is given below. Or, if you want to achieve an antique-looking quilt, use up your scraps of fabric to make each block different. However, you must use the same *bright* fabric throughout.

● 7½ yards/meters pale fabric for patchwork blocks, side units, border and back of quilt
● 2¾ yards/meters light fabric for patchwork blocks and side units
● ⅜ yard/meter bright fabric for patchwork blocks and side units
● 2¾ yards/meters dark fabric for patchwork blocks and side units
● ⅜ yard/meter coordinating fabric for binding
● 90 × 90 inch/228.6 × 228.6 cm piece of batting/wadding

● Make template (see page 108) for the following piece (measurements include a ¼ inch/6 mm seam allowance):
B: 8½ × 8½ inches/21.6 × 21.6 cm square

Cutting (per quilt)

Note: All measurements include a ¼ inch/6 mm seam allowance.

BACK OF QUILT

Cut three pieces pale fabric, each 30½ × 90 inches/77.4 × 228.6 cm

BORDERS

Four **D** strips 3½ × 90½ inches/9 × 230 cm, pale fabric

BINDING

Cut coordinating fabric into eight 1½ inch/4 cm wide strips across the full width of the fabric and sew together to measure 10 yards/meters long

PATTERN PIECE	NUMBER OF PIECES

Note: Number of pieces for a single block or unit is shown in parentheses.

Blocks	
A	(40) 480 light
	(4) 48 bright
	(40) 480 dark
B	(1) 12 pale
Side Units	
A	(20) 240 light
	(2) 24 bright
	(20) 240 dark
C	(1) 12 pale

Piecing

OCEAN WAVES BLOCKS

Note: All the small triangles in the step-by-step diagrams are A pieces; we have left the labels off for clarity.

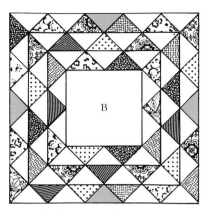

Block Assembly Diagram

1. Following Diagram 1, sew three A triangles (two dark and one light) together in a row, alternating light and dark as shown. Sew a dark A to the top to create a larger triangle. Make one more triangle in the same way.
2. Construct two more triangles, but this time use three light A triangles and one dark A so the finished triangle resembles Diagram 2.

Diagram 1   **Diagram 2**

3. Sew the four pieced triangles to opposite sides of a B square as shown in Diagram 3.
4. Construct two corner units by sewing three rows of As together, alternating the position of the triangles and the light and dark pieces as shown in Diagram 4. Sew the rows together, matching seams carefully.

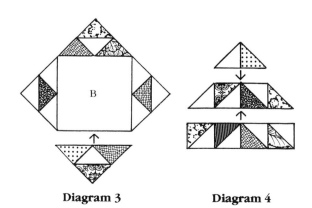

Diagram 3   **Diagram 4**

5. Sew the corner units to opposite sides of the A–B square as shown in Diagram 5, making sure that the pieces alternate light and dark.

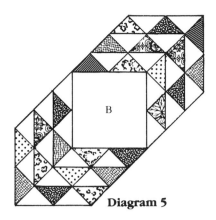

Diagram 5

6. Following Diagram 4, construct two more corner triangles as directed in step 4, but with the light and dark triangles in the opposite positions as shown in Diagram 6. Then add a bright A triangle to each end as shown in Diagram 6.

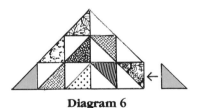

Diagram 6

7. Sew the corner triangles just made to the remaining sides of the A–B square as shown in the Block Assembly Diagram, again making sure that the pieces alternate light and dark.
8. Construct 11 more Ocean Waves blocks in the same manner.

OCEAN WAVES SIDE UNITS

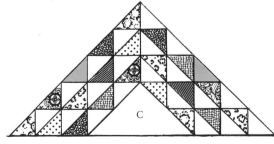

Side Assembly Diagram

9. Following Diagram 7, sew two rows of six A triangles together, alternating light and dark. Sew the rows together, matching seams carefully. Construct

another parallelogram in the same manner, but with the light and dark triangles in the opposite positions as shown on the left in Diagram 8.

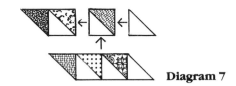

Diagram 7

10. Following Diagram 8, sew the parallelograms just made to each short side edge of a C triangle.

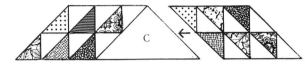

Diagram 8

11. Following step 6 and Diagram 6, construct a corner triangle, making sure to position a bright A triangle at each corner as shown.
12. Stitch the corner triangle to the top of A–C, completing a side unit as shown in the Side Assembly Diagram.
13. Construct 11 more Ocean Waves side units in the same manner.

Assembly

14. Following Diagram 9 and working on a large flat surface, arrange the patchwork blocks and the side units to form the quilt top, making sure that the light and dark triangles alternate.

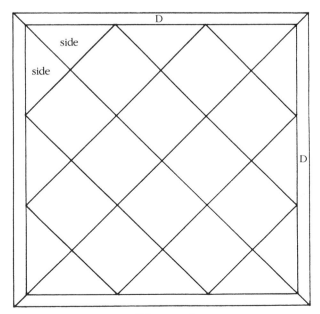

Diagram 9

15. Note that the quilt is constructed in diagonal rows. Stitch the blocks together in rows starting with the middle ones and working outward. Be sure to sew a side unit to each end of each row. Sew two side units together to create the corners.

16. Stitch the rows together, matching seams carefully at the intersections.

17. Stitch a border strip to each side of the quilt top, allowing the ends of the borders to extend beyond the top for mitering.

18. Miter the corners of the border, following the directions on page 112.

19. To make the quilt back, sew the three fabric pieces together along the long edges; press the seam allowances to one side.

20. Assemble the quilt top, batting/wadding and back as directed on page 113.

Finishing

21. Outline-quilt each seam of the quilt top. Quilt a curving border design on each of the borders as shown in the color photograph on page 200, or using one of the many border quilting patterns given in this section of the book.

22. Bind the quilt with a separate binding as directed on page 115.

Note: These pattern pieces **do not** include seam allowance.

C

A

CHARLES LINDBERGH COMMEMORATIVE

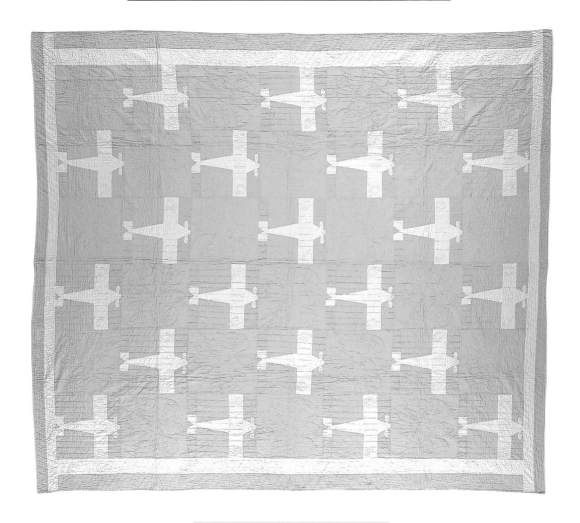

When Charles A. Lindbergh made his historic solo flight across the Atlantic in 1927, a quilt pattern followed suit which popularized the exploits of this modern-day folk hero. This quilt is dated 1930. The blocks between the white airplane patches are quilted in a subtle eagle pattern which testifies to Lindbergh's national identity as 'The Lone Eagle'. The patchwork pieces are easily assembled, but the small appliquéd propeller will require care.

Skill Level: Intermediate

Size

Block is 11 inches/28 cm square
21 patchwork blocks and 21 eagle-quilted blocks are needed for finished quilt
Finished quilt is 76 × 83 inches/193 × 211 cm

Materials

● 2¼ yards/meters light fabric for airplane blocks and borders
● 9¼ yards/meters bright fabric for airplane blocks, plain blocks, border, back of quilt and self binding
● 76½ × 83½ inch/194.3 × 212 cm piece of batting/wadding

● Make template (see page 108) for the following piece (measurements include a ¼ inch/6 mm seam allowance):

L: 11½ × 11½ inch/29 × 29 cm square

Cutting (per quilt)

Note: All measurements include a ¼ inch/6 mm seam allowance.

BACK OF QUILT AND SELF BINDING

Cut two pieces bright fabric, each 39 × 84½ inches/ 99 × 214.6 cm

BORDERS

Two **M** strips 3 × 77½ inches/7.6 × 197 cm, light fabric

Two **M** strips 3 × 77½ inches/7.6 × 197 cm, bright fabric

Two **N** strips 2 × 76½ inches/5 × 194.3 cm, light fabric

Two **N** strips 2 × 76½ inches/5 × 194.3 cm, bright fabric

PATTERN PIECE	NUMBER OF PIECES

Note: Number of pieces for a single block is shown in parentheses.

A	(1) 21 light
B	(1) 21 bright
B reversed	(1) 21 bright
C	(1) 21 light
D	(1) 21 light
E	(1) 21 bright
E reversed	(1) 21 bright
F	(1) 21 bright
G	(1) 21 light
H	(1) 21 light
J	(2) 42 bright
K	(1) 21 light
L	21 bright

Piecing

AIRPLANE BLOCKS

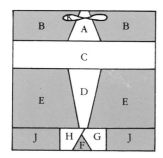

Block Assembly Diagram

1. For the nose of the airplane, sew a B and a reversed B to each side of A as shown in Diagram 1.

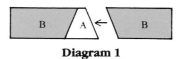

Diagram 1

2. Sew the nose strip to the wing (C) as shown in Diagram 2.

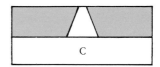

Diagram 2

3. Sew an E and a reversed E to each side of D to form the airplane's body as shown in Diagram 3.

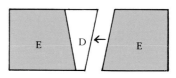

Diagram 3

4. To construct the airplane's tail, sew F to G as shown in Diagram 4.

5. Sew H to F–G as shown in Diagram 5.

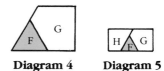

Diagram 4   **Diagram 5**

6. Sew a J to each side of H–F–G to complete the tail strip as shown in Diagram 6.

Diagram 6

7. Sew the body section to the tail strip as shown in Diagram 7.

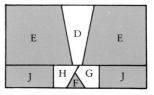

Diagram 7

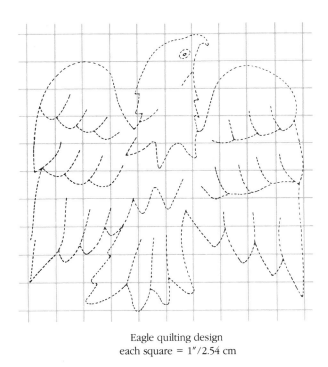

Eagle quilting design
each square = 1″/2.54 cm

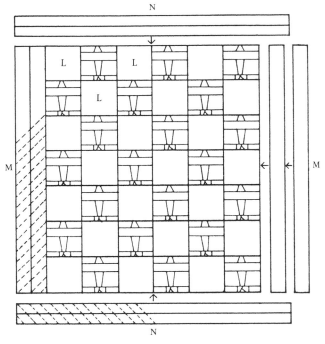

Diagram 8

8. Sew the body section to the wing as shown in the Block Assembly Diagram.

9. Appliqué the propeller (K) to the nose of the airplane, following the directions on page 112, to complete the patchwork block.

10. Construct 20 more Airplane Blocks in the same manner.

11. Following the directions on pages 108–9, enlarge the eagle quilting design, and use the enlarged pattern to make a quilting template. Make a quilting template for the double circle quilting design given on piece C. Following the directions on page 113, transfer the eagle design to the middle of each L block, and the circle design to each side of each C piece.

Assembly

12. Following Diagram 8 and working on a large flat surface, arrange the patchwork and eagle blocks in seven horizontal rows with six blocks in each row, forming a checkerboard pattern.

13. Stitch the blocks together in rows.

14. Stitch the rows together, matching seams carefully at the intersections.

15. Sew the light M strips to each side edge of the patchwork.

16. Sew the bright M strips to each of the light M strips.

17. Sew the light N strips to the top and bottom edges of the patchwork.

18. Sew the bright N strips to each of the light N strips to complete the quilt top.

19. To make the quilt back, sew the two bright fabric pieces together along the long edges; press the seam allowance to one side.

20. Assemble the quilt top, batting/wadding and back as directed on page 113, centering the top and batting/wadding on the back which will be larger.

Finishing

21. Using a contrasting thread (such as red) quilt the double circle design on each side of each airplane wing.

22. Quilt each airplane block with straight vertical lines, spaced 1 inch/2.54 cm apart; do not quilt on top of the circle designs.

23. Quilt the eagle design on each of the plain blocks.

24. Quilt diagonal lines, spaced 1 inch/2.54 cm apart along the borders as shown in Diagram 8.

25. Following the directions on page 116 for a self binding, wrap the fabric from the back over onto the top of the quilt and bind off neatly.

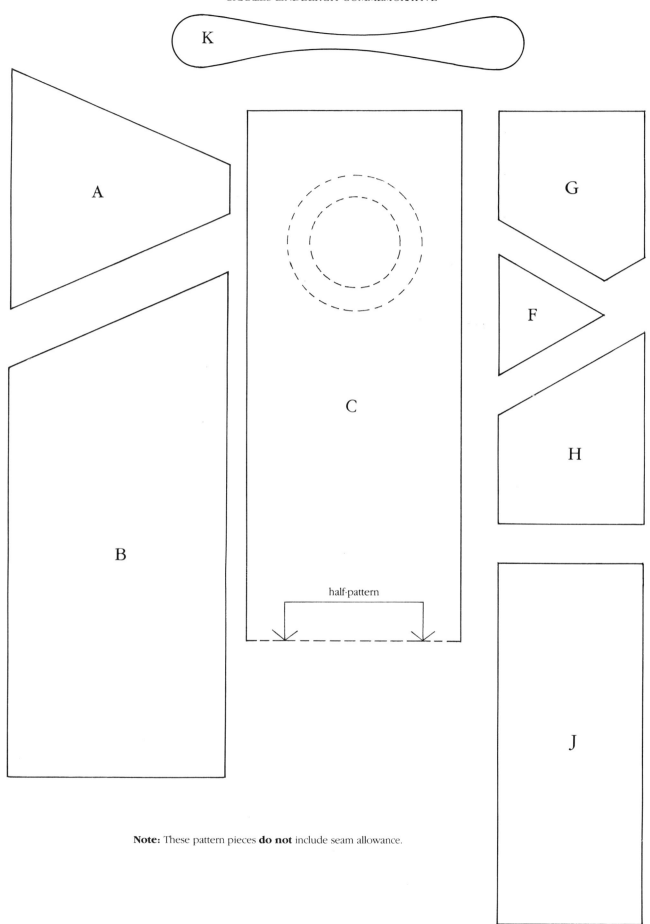

K

A

C

B

G

F

H

J

half-pattern

Note: These pattern pieces **do not** include seam allowance.

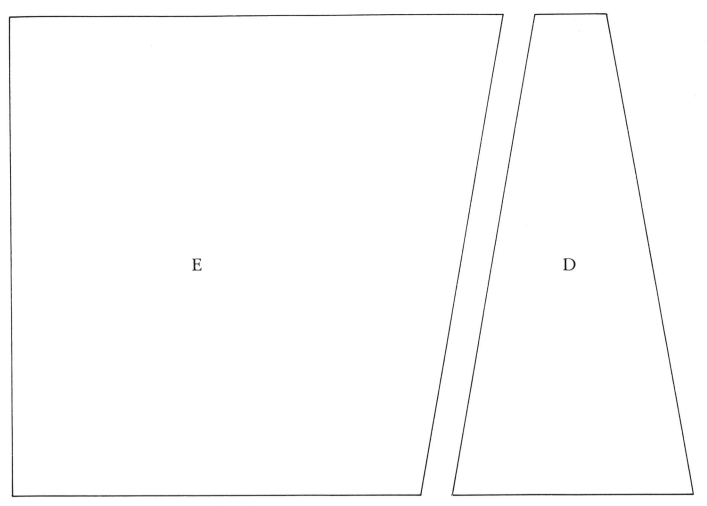

Note: These pattern pieces **do not** include seam allowance.

OHIO STAR

Stars were one of the earliest and most favored motifs used in American quilts. This Ohio Star quilt, c.1880, is from Vermont and features mattress ticking in an overall red, white and blue patriotic setting. Although the blocks are easy to piece, insetting is required along the border, which may present a challenge to some quilters!

Skill Level: Intermediate

Size

Block is 9½ inches/24 cm square
32 blocks, 14 side units and 4 corner units are needed for finished quilt
Finished quilt is 81½ × 100½ inches/207 × 255.3 cm

Materials

● 5½ yards/meters light fabric for patchwork and sashing (use a striped fabric to achieve the interwoven effect seen on the quilt in the color photograph)
● 4 yards/meters dark fabric for background of patchwork
● 5¾ yards/meters coordinating fabric for back of quilt

- ⅜ yard/meter coordinating fabric for binding
- 82 × 101 inch/208.3 × 256.5 cm piece of batting/wadding

Cutting (per quilt)

Note: All measurements include a ¼ inch/6 mm seam allowance.

BACK OF QUILT

Cut two pieces coordinating fabric, each 41½ × 101 inches/105.4 × 256.5 cm

SASHING

Note: If you are using a striped fabric, cut the sashing strips with the stripe running the *length* of the strip; yardage has been allowed for this.

Forty **L** strips 4½ × 10 inches/11.4 × 25.4 cm, light fabric

One **M** strip 4½ × 112½ inches/11.4 × 285.7 cm, light fabric

Two **N** strips 4½ × 99 inches/11.4 × 251.5 cm, light fabric

Two **O** strips 4½ × 72 inches/11.4 × 183 cm, light fabric

Two **P** strips 4½ × 45 inches/11.4 × 114.3 cm, light fabric

Two **Q** strips 4½ × 18 inches/11.4 × 45.7 cm, light fabric

BINDING

Cut coordinating fabric into nine 1½ inch/4 cm wide strips across the full width of the fabric and sew together to measure 10 yards/meters long

PATTERN PIECE	NUMBER OF PIECES	

Note: Number of pieces for a single block or unit is shown in parentheses.

Blocks

A	(8)	256 light
	(8)	256 dark
B	(1)	32 light
	(4)	128 dark

Side Units

C	(4)	56 light
	(4)	56 dark
D	(2)	28 light
	(2)	28 dark
E	(1)	14 dark
F	(1)	14 dark

Corner Units

G	(4)	16 light
	(4)	16 dark

H	(2)	8 light
	(2)	8 dark
J	(1)	4 dark
K	(1)	4 dark

Piecing

OHIO STAR BLOCKS

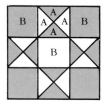

Block Assembly Diagram

1. Following Diagram 1, sew two light As and 2 dark As together along the straight edges to form two triangles. Sew the triangles together along the long diagonal edges, alternating the dark and light pieces, to form a square. Repeat three more times to make four A squares.

Diagram 1

2. To make the top and bottom rows of the block, sew a dark B to each side of one A square, sewing the Bs to the light A pieces as shown in Diagram 2.

Diagram 2

3. To make the middle row of the block, sew an A square to each side of one light B square, sewing the dark A pieces to B as shown in Diagram 3.

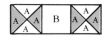

Diagram 3

4. Sew the top and bottom rows to the middle row to complete the block as shown in the Block Assembly Diagram; be sure to match the seams carefully as you sew.

5. Construct 31 more Ohio Star blocks in the same manner.

OHIO STAR SIDE UNITS

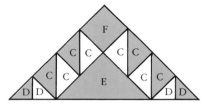

Side Assembly Diagram

6. Sew a light C to a dark C along the diagonal edge as shown in Diagram 4. Repeat three more times for a total of four C squares.

Diagram 4

7. Following Diagram 5, sew a dark and light pair of Ds together, forming a triangle. Repeat once more for a total of two triangles.

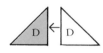

Diagram 5

8. Sew two pairs of C squares together; sew a D triangle to one end as shown in Diagram 6. For the other strip, construct a mirror image of Diagram 6.

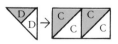

Diagram 6

9. Sew the mirror-image strip to the right side of the E triangle as shown in Diagram 7. Sew an F square to the remaining patchwork strip, then sew to the left side of E to complete the side unit.

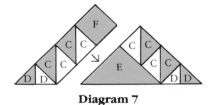

Diagram 7

10. Construct 13 more side units in the same manner.

OHIO STAR CORNER UNITS

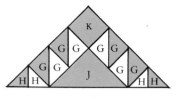

Corner Assembly Diagram

11. The corner units are constructed in exactly the same way as the side units using different-sized patchwork pieces. Refer to the Corner Unit Assembly Diagram for the letters of the patchwork pieces, then construct four corner units following Diagrams 4 through 7 and substituting G for C, H for D, J for E and K for F.

Assembly

12. Following Diagrams 8 and 9 (next page) and working on a large flat surface, arrange the patchwork blocks with the sashing strips.

13. Note that the quilt is constructed in diagonal rows. Stitch the L sashing strips to the patchwork blocks, then sew the blocks together in rows, starting with the middle rows and working outward to the corners.

Diagram 8

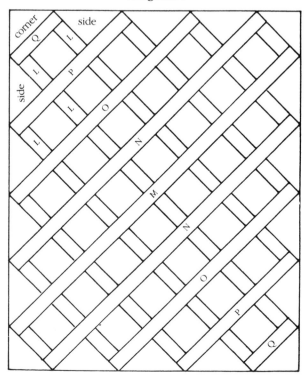

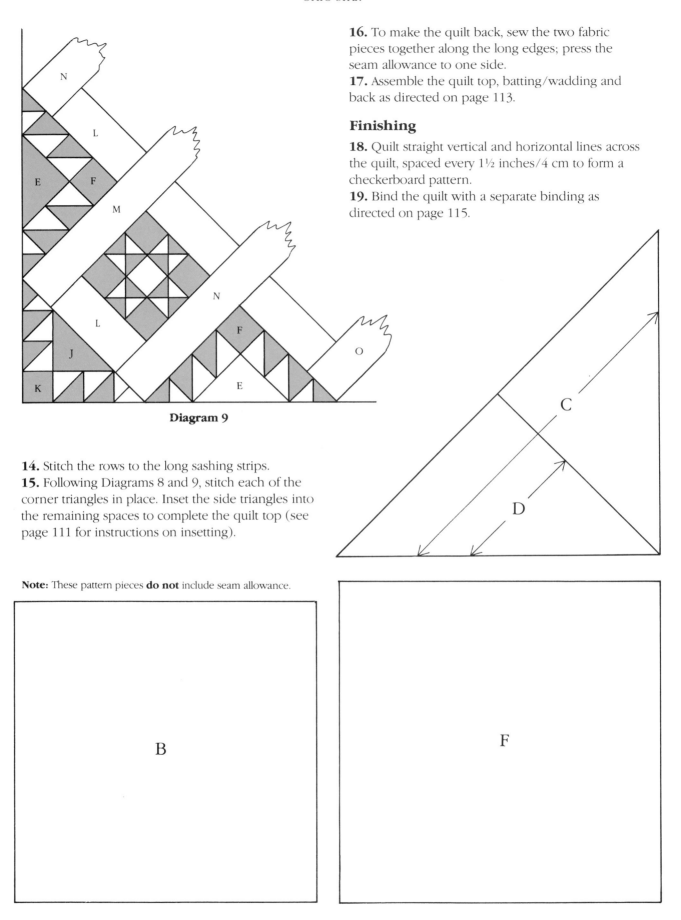

Diagram 9

16. To make the quilt back, sew the two fabric pieces together along the long edges; press the seam allowance to one side.

17. Assemble the quilt top, batting/wadding and back as directed on page 113.

Finishing

18. Quilt straight vertical and horizontal lines across the quilt, spaced every 1½ inches/4 cm to form a checkerboard pattern.

19. Bind the quilt with a separate binding as directed on page 115.

14. Stitch the rows to the long sashing strips.

15. Following Diagrams 8 and 9, stitch each of the corner triangles in place. Inset the side triangles into the remaining spaces to complete the quilt top (see page 111 for instructions on insetting).

Note: These pattern pieces **do not** include seam allowance.

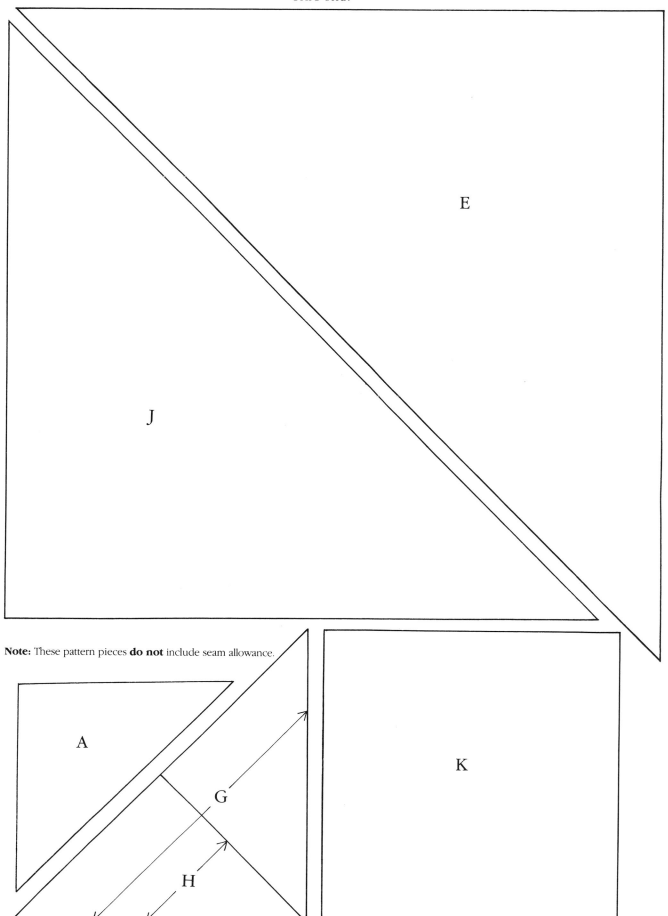

E

J

Note: These pattern pieces **do not** include seam allowance.

A

G

H

K

YOUNG MAN'S FANCY

This handsome quilt was made in the early part of the twentieth century in New England. Probably its most dominant feature is the vivid and clever use of a red, white and blue color scheme. A series of tiny blue and white blocks, composed in a traditional nine-patch arrangement, is strikingly placed within a frame of long, narrow, red and white bands set off by large triangles. The nine-patch theme is cunningly echoed in the posts within the sashing, while the scalloped edge provides a welcome relief from the sharp columns of the triple border.

Skill Level: Intermediate

Size

Block is 11¼ inches/28.6 cm square
12 blocks are needed for finished quilt
Finished quilt is 55¼ × 70¼ inches/140.3 × 178.4 cm

Materials

Note: For clarity, the actual colors used in the quilt in the photograph have been listed in parentheses below.

● 3 yards/meters dark fabric (red) for patchwork blocks, sashing, borders and binding
● 4⅝ yards/meters light fabric (white) for patchwork blocks, sashing, borders and back of quilt

- 2 yards/meters medium fabric (blue) for patchwork blocks, sashing and borders
- 55¾ × 70¾ inch/141.6 × 179.7 cm piece of batting/wadding

- Make templates (see page 108) for the following pieces (measurements include a ¼ inch/6 mm seam allowance):
E: 5¼ × 5¼ inches/13.3 × 13.3 cm square
F: 1¾ × 1¾ inches/4.4 × 4.4 cm square
G: 4¼ × 11¾ inches/11 × 30 cm rectangle

Cutting (per quilt)

Note: All measurements include a ¼ inch/6 mm seam allowance.

BACK OF QUILT

Cut two pieces white fabric, each 28 × 70¾ inches/ 71 × 179.7 cm

BORDERS

Two **H** strips 2½ × 61¼ inches/6.3 × 155.6 cm, red fabric
Two **J** strips 2½ × 46¼ inches/6.3 × 117.5 cm, red fabric
Two **K** strips 2½ × 65¼ inches/6.3 × 165.7 cm, white fabric
Two **L** strips 2½ × 50¼ inches/6.3 × 127.6 cm, white fabric
Two **M** strips 3½ × 71¼ inches/9 × 181 cm, blue fabric
Two **N** strips 3½ × 56¼ inches/9 × 143 cm, blue fabric

SASHING

Thirty **F** squares, white
Twenty-four **F** squares, red
Seventeen **G** rectangles, blue

BINDING

See page 115 for instructions on cutting bias binding. Cut one 44 × 44 inch/111.7 × 111.7 cm square of red fabric into 1½ inch/4 cm wide bias strips and sew together to measure 7½ yards/meters long

PATTERN PIECE	NUMBER OF PIECES	

Note: Number of pieces for a single block is shown in parentheses.

A	(8)	96 red
	(12)	144 white
	(4)	48 blue
B	(20)	240 white
	(16)	192 blue
C	(8)	96 red
	(4)	48 white
D	(4)	48 white
E	(1)	12 white

Piecing

YOUNG MAN'S FANCY BLOCKS

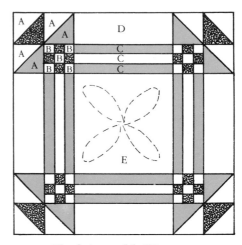

Block Assembly Diagram

1. Sew eight white As to eight red As, and four white As to four blue As along the diagonal edge to form twelve squares as shown in Diagram 1.

Diagram 1

2. Following Diagram 2, stitch the B squares together in rows of three as shown, then stitch the rows together, matching seams carefully, to form one checkerboard B square. Repeat three more times to make four checkerboard B squares.

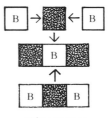

Diagram 2

3. Following Diagram 3, arrange two red and white A squares, one blue and white A square and one checkerboard B square as shown. Stitch the blue and red A squares together; stitch the remaining A square to the checkerboard. Then stitch the two

215

rows together, to make a corner unit. Repeat three more times to make a total of four corner units.

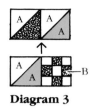

Diagram 3

4. Stitch a white C between two red Cs as shown in Diagram 4. Repeat three more times.

5. Stitch a D to each of the C–C–C pieces as shown in Diagram 5 to make four C–D units.

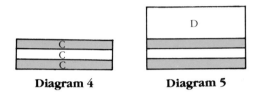

Diagram 4   **Diagram 5**

6. Following Diagram 6, arrange a corner unit on each side of one horizontal C–D unit. Stitch together matching seams carefully for the top row of the block. Repeat once more to construct the bottom row.

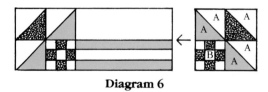

Diagram 6

7. To make the middle row, stitch a vertical C–D unit to each side of E as shown in Diagram 7.

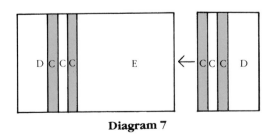

Diagram 7

8. Following the Block Assembly Diagram, stitch the top and bottom rows to the middle row to complete the patchwork block.

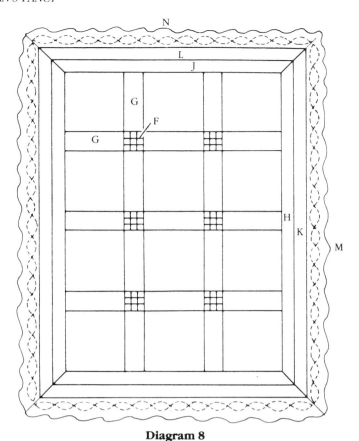

Diagram 8

9. Construct 11 more Young Man's Fancy blocks in the same manner.

Assembly

10. Following Diagram 8 and working on a large flat surface, arrange the blocks in four horizontal rows with three blocks in each row. Place a G sashing strip vertically between each of the blocks. Stitch the blocks to the sashing strips to complete each row.

11. To make the horizontal sashing strips, first stitch the F squares together in three rows with three squares in each row to make a checkerboard unit, alternating the red and white squares as shown. Then stitch three G strips together with the checkerboard units in between to make each horizontal sashing strip. Make two more horizontal sashing strips in the same manner.

12. Sew the patchwork rows to the sashing rows, matching seams carefully at the intersections.

13. Center a red H border strip along one side edge of the patchwork top so that the excess fabric on the H strip extends evenly beyond the top and bottom edges. Stitch in place. Repeat for the other side.

14. Center and sew the red J strips to the top and bottom edges of the quilt top in the same way.

15. Center and sew the white K strips to each H strip in the same way.

16. Center and sew the white L strips to each J strip in the same way.

17. Center and sew the blue M strips to each K strip in the same way.

18. Center and sew the blue N strips to each L strip in the same way.

19. To complete the quilt top, miter the border strips together at each of the corners, following the directions on page 112; match the seams carefully and use matching thread when sewing each of the different-color border strips together.

20. Following the directions on pages 108–9, enlarge the flower and lozenge designs and make a quilting template for each. Then, following the directions given on page 113, mark the quilting designs on the quilt top as follows: mark the flower design in the middle of each E piece. Mark the lozenge design along each of the three border strips using the full-size pattern and ending the design at each corner as shown in Diagram 8. (**Note:** The lozenge design is illustrated only on the outer border pieces in the diagram; these pieces are blue, which is not shown on the diagram.)

21. To make the quilt back, sew the two fabric pieces together along the long edges; press the seam allowance to one side.

22. Assemble the quilt top, batting/wadding and back as directed on page 113.

Finishing

23. Outline-quilt each of the red and blue pieces on each patchwork block.

24. Outline-quilt the outer edges of each patchwork block and the red F pieces on the sashing.

25. Quilt the marked flower design in the middle of each E piece.

26. Quilt the marked lozenge design on each of the borders.

27. After all the quilting is done, trim the edge of the quilt ½ inch/13 mm away from the outer stitching lines of the quilting on the M and N pieces, as shown on the lozenge quilting design.

28. Bind the quilt with a separate bias binding as directed on page 115, easing the binding carefully around the curved edges.

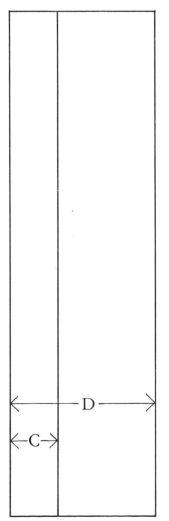

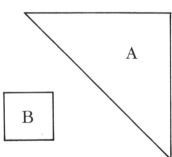

Note: These pattern pieces **do not** include seam allowance.

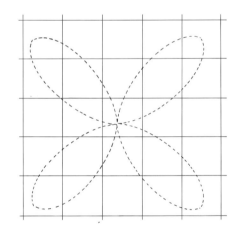

Flower quilting design   each square = 1"/2.54 cm

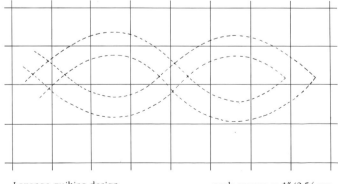

Lozenge quilting design   each square = 1"/2.54 cm

TREE OF LIFE

The Tree of Life motif was a popular Indo-European pattern which
translated into a Pine Tree design. The Pine Tree came to represent,
for many pioneers who settled in the stark Midwest, a remembrance
of life back home. This well-padded example, dated 1911, is from the
Blue Ridge Mountain area and is made out of a rough denim.

Skill Level: Intermediate

Size

Block is 8 inches/20.3 cm square
30 patchwork blocks and 20 plain blocks are needed
for finished quilt
Finished quilt is about 61¾ × 74½ inches/157 ×
189 cm

Materials

● 6 yards/meters light fabric for patchwork blocks
and back of quilt
● 1¼ yards/meters dark fabric for patchwork blocks
● 2¼ yards/meters medium fabric for plain blocks,
side triangles, corner triangles and border
● ⅜ yard/meter coordinating fabric for binding
● 62¼ × 75 inch/158 × 190.5 cm piece of batting/
wadding

● Make template (see page 108) for the following piece (measurements include a ¼ inch/6 mm seam allowance):

G: 8½ × 8½ inches/21.6 × 21.6 cm square

Cutting (per quilt)

Note: All measurements include a ¼ inch/6 mm seam allowance.

BACK OF QUILT

Cut two pieces light fabric, each 31⅜ × 75 inches/ 79.7 × 190.5 cm

BORDERS

Two **K** strips 2½ × 68⅛ inches/6.3 × 173 cm, medium fabric
Two **L** strips 3¼ × 61¾ inches/8 × 157 cm, medium fabric

SIDE H TRIANGLES

Cut four 12⅝ inch/32 cm squares from medium fabric; cut each square diagonally into four quarters to make sixteen triangles; use one triangle as a pattern to cut two additional triangles

CORNER J TRIANGLES

Cut two 6½ inch/16.5 cm squares from medium fabric; cut each square diagonally in half to make four corner triangles

BINDING

Cut coordinating fabric into seven 1½ inch/4 cm wide strips across the full width of the fabric and sew together to measure 7¾ yards/meters long

PATTERN PIECE	NUMBER OF PIECES	
Note: Number of pieces for a single block is shown in parentheses.		
A	(24)	720 light
	(30)	900 dark
B	(3)	90 light
C	(3)	90 light
	(1)	30 dark
D	(1)	30 light
D reversed	(1)	30 light
E	(2)	60 dark
F	(1)	30 dark
G		20 medium
H		18 medium
J		4 medium

Piecing

TREE OF LIFE BLOCKS

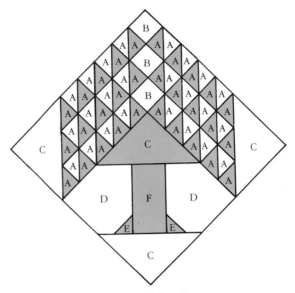

Block Assembly Diagram

1. Sew each light A to a dark A along the diagonal edge to form a square as shown in Diagram 1.

Diagram 1

2. Following Diagram 2, arrange nine A squares in three rows, with two squares in the top row, three in the middle and four at the bottom. Sew the squares together, then sew a dark A triangle to the left end of each row. Sew the rows together, matching seams carefully.

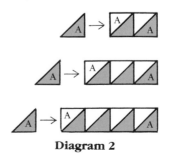

Diagram 2

219

3. Following Diagram 3, sew a light C to the diagonal edge of the patchwork. This is the left side of the tree top. Set aside.

Diagram 3

4. Sew four A squares together as shown in Diagram 4, then sew a B to the left end and a dark A triangle to the right end. This is the top strip. Repeat twice more for a total of three patchwork strips.

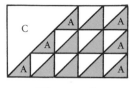

Diagram 4

5. Following Diagram 5, sew the dark edge of an A square to B for the middle strip.

Diagram 5

6. Following Diagram 6, sew two A squares together, then sew the dark edge of an A square to B for the bottom strip.

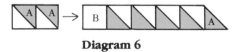

Diagram 6

7. Sew the top, middle and bottom strips together, matching seams carefully as shown in Diagram 7. Then sew a light C to the diagonal edge of the patchwork. This is the right side of the tree top. Set aside.

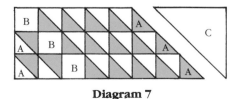

Diagram 7

8. Sew an E to the lower diagonal edge of each D as shown in Diagram 8.

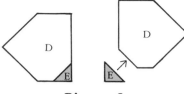

Diagram 8

9. Sew D–E to each side of F as shown in Diagram 9.

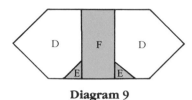

Diagram 9

10. Following Diagram 10, sew a dark C to the top of D-F-D, and a light C to the bottom edge.

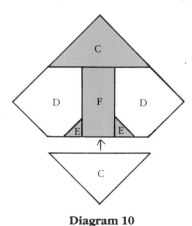

Diagram 10

11. Sew the left side of the tree top to C–D–F as shown in Diagram 11.

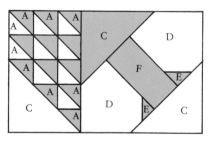

Diagram 11

12. Sew the right side of the tree top to the patchwork, matching seams carefully, to complete the block as shown in the Block Assembly Diagram.
13. Construct 29 more Tree of Life blocks in the same manner.

Assembly

14. Following Diagram 12 and working on a large flat surface, arrange the patchwork blocks with the

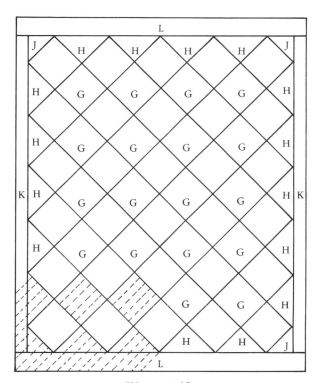

Diagram 12

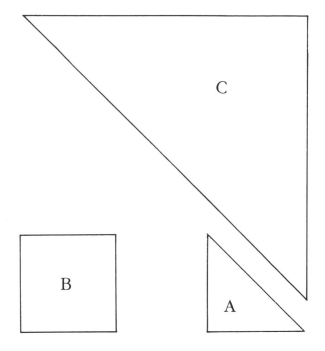

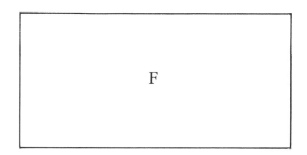

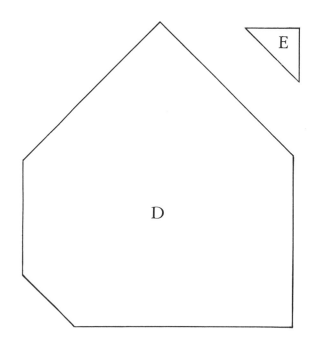

plain G blocks to form a checkerboard pattern. You can turn all the trees sideways as shown on the quilt, or position them straight up if you wish. Fill in the side edges with the H triangles. Fill in the corners with the J triangles.

15. Note that the quilt is constructed in diagonal rows. Stitch the blocks together in rows starting with the middle ones and working outward. Be sure to sew an H or a J triangle to each end of each row.

16. Stitch the rows together, matching seams carefully at the intersections.

17. Sew the K borders to each side of the patchwork.

18. Sew the L borders to the top and bottom of the patchwork to complete the quilt top.

19. To make the quilt back, sew the two fabric pieces together along the long edges; press the seam allowance to one side.

20. Assemble the quilt top, batting/wadding and back as directed on page 113.

Finishing

21. Outline-quilt all the edges of the dark pieces on the patchwork blocks.

22. Quilt straight parallel lines on the G, H and J pieces as shown in Diagram 12. Continue the lines of H and J onto the border strips.

23. Bind the quilt with a separate binding as directed on page 115.

Note: These pattern pieces **do not** include seam allowance.

SNAIL TRAIL

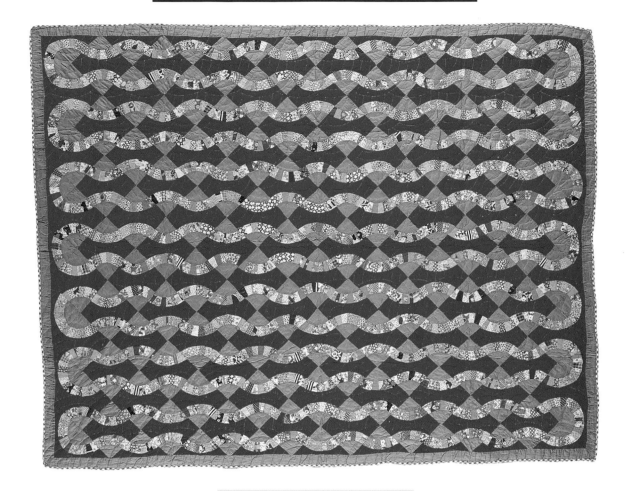

Red and green have long been favorite color combinations for quilters. This fanciful 1940s quilt is made with bright red and green glazed cottons. It is hard to determine the dominant feature on this quilt – the meandering Snail Trail pattern itself or the dazzling color ensemble.

Skill Level: Intermediate

Size

Block is 6½ inches/16.5 cm square
110 blocks and 32 side triangles are needed for finished quilt
Finished quilt is 67⅜ × 85¾ inches/171 × 218 cm

Materials

Note: For clarity, the actual colors used in the quilt in the photograph have been listed in parentheses below.

● 4 yards/meters dark fabric (red) for patchwork blocks and side triangles
● 2½ yards/meters medium fabric (green) for

patchwork blocks, side triangles and borders
● Total of about 3½ yards/meters different bright fabrics for patchwork blocks and side triangles

Note: The quilt shown in the color photograph is actually a scrap quilt – different fabrics were used for the A pieces on each patchwork block, and the wonderful, almost dancing movement of the 'snail trail' is achieved through the use of a wide variety of fabrics. The yardage given here is the total amount you'll need for the A pieces, but it is recommended that you use wildly different scraps for the best effect.

● 4⅞ yards/meters coordinating fabric for back of quilt
● ⅜ yard/meter coordinating fabric for binding
● 68 × 86¼ inch/172.7 × 219 cm piece of batting/wadding

Cutting (per quilt)

Note: All measurements include a ¼ inch/6 mm seam allowance.

BACK OF QUILT

Cut two pieces coordinating fabric, each 34¼ × 86¼ inches/87 × 219 cm

BORDERS

Two **E** strips 2 × 86¼ inches/5 × 219 cm, medium fabric

Two **F** strips 2 × 67⅞ inches/5 × 172.4 cm, medium fabric

BINDING

Cut coordinating fabric into seven 1½ inch/4 cm wide strips across the full width of the fabric and sew together to measure 8½ yards/meters long

PATTERN PIECE	NUMBER OF PIECES

Note: Number of pieces for a single block is shown in parentheses. It is essential that you place the templates with the arrows on the straight grain of fabric when marking and cutting out the patchwork pieces.

Snail Trail Block		
A	(12)	1320 bright
B	(2)	220 medium
C	(1)	110 dark
Side Triangles		
A	(6)	192 bright
B	(1)	32 medium
D	(1)	32 dark

Piecing

SNAIL TRAIL BLOCKS

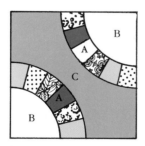

Block Assembly Diagram

1. Sew six different A pieces together to form a curve as shown in Diagram 1. Construct a second A curve in the same manner.

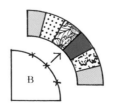

Diagram 1   **Diagram 2**

2. Sew a B to the inner edge of each of the A curves as shown in Diagram 2, matching the Xs on B to the first, third and fifth A seams. (See page 111 for instructions on sewing curves.)

3. Sew a B–A unit to each side of C as shown in Diagram 3, matching the dots on C to the first, third and fifth A seams.

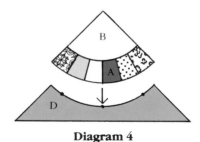

Diagram 3

4. Construct 109 more Snail Trail blocks in the same manner.

SIDE TRIANGLES

5. Following Diagrams 1 and 2, construct an A–B corner unit for each side triangle.

6. Sew the curved A edge of the corner unit to D as shown in Diagram 4, matching the dots on D to the first, third and fifth A seams.

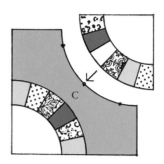

Diagram 4

7. Construct 31 more side triangles in the same manner.

Assembly

8. Working on a large flat surface, arrange the patchwork blocks following Diagrams 5 and 6 (next page). The edges of the A pieces should meet, forming a continuous 'snail trail'. Fill in the sides and corners with the side triangles as shown in Diagram 5 to create a continuous curve at the top and bottom edges of the quilt.

9. Note that the quilt is constructed in diagonal rows. Stitch the blocks together in rows starting from the middle and working outward. Take care to match the edges of the A pieces. Be sure to sew a side triangle to each end of each row.

Diagram 5

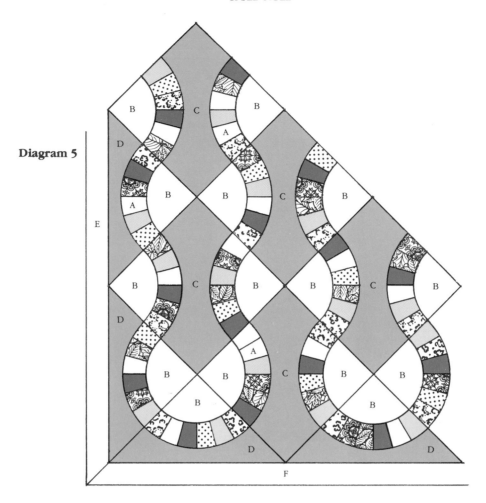

Diagram 6

10. Stitch the rows together, matching seams carefully at the intersections and the edges of the A pieces.

11. Sew an E border strip to each side of the patchwork, allowing the ends of the strips to extend evenly above and below the patchwork.

12. Sew an F border strip to the top and bottom of the patchwork, allowing the ends of the strips to extend evenly beyond the sides of the patchwork.

13. Miter the corners of the E and F strips together to complete the quilt top. (See page 112 for instructions on mitering corners.)

14. Following the directions on pages 108–9, enlarge the wave quilting design and make a quilting template. Following the instructions on page 113, use the template to mark the wave pattern across the entire quilt top, including the borders.

15. To make the quilt back, sew the two fabric pieces together along the long edges; press the seam allowance to one side.

16. Assemble the quilt top, batting/wadding and back as directed on page 113.

Finishing

17. Quilt the marked wave design.
18. Bind the quilt with a separate binding as directed on page 115.

Note: These pattern pieces **do not** include seam allowance.

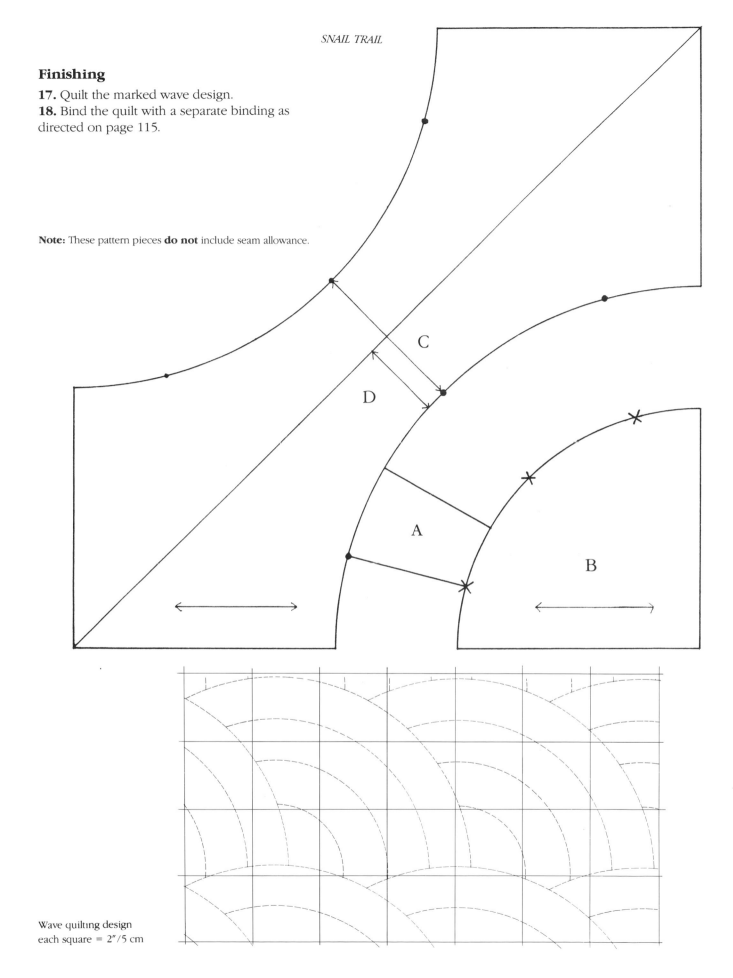

Wave quilting design
each square = 2″/5 cm

RAILROAD

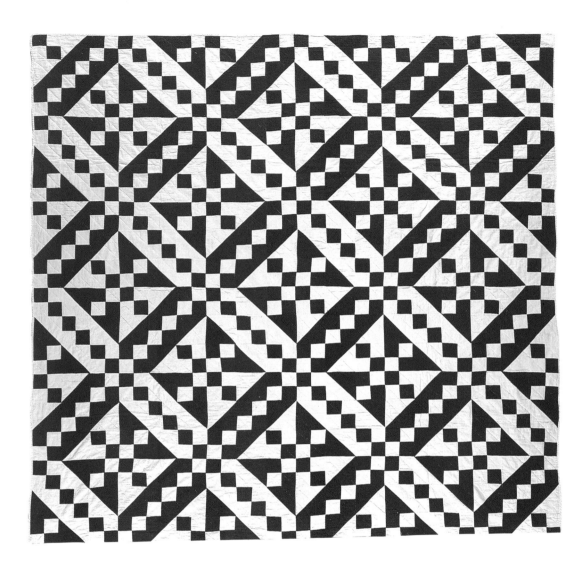

*Two-color quilts became popular during the middle of the
nineteenth century. This Railroad Quilt, probably made in the
1870s or 1880s, is a sophisticated example of the growing Victorian
interest in optical illusion which accompanied the refinement of
photographic techniques. The fast-piecing method of construction
given here makes this quilt very quick and easy to assemble.*

Skill Level: Easy

Size

Block is 15 inches/38 cm square
36 blocks are needed for finished quilt
Finished quilt is 90 × 90 inches/228.6 × 228.6 cm

Materials

● 4⅝ yards/meters light fabric for patchwork blocks
and binding
● 4¼ yards/meters dark fabric for patchwork blocks
● 7½ yards/meters coordinating fabric for back of
quilt

● 90½ × 90½ inch/230 × 230 cm piece of batting/wadding

Cutting (per quilt)

Note: All measurements include a ¼ inch/6 mm seam allowance.

BACK OF QUILT

Cut three pieces coordinating fabric, each 30½ × 90½ inches/77.4 × 230 cm

BINDING

Cut light fabric into nine 1½ inch/4 cm wide strips across the full width of the fabric and sew together to measure 10 yards/meters long

This quilt can be made very quickly and easily without the use of templates. You can use a rotary cutter and ruler to cut the strips, or you can mark the fabric with a pencil and ruler and cut the strips using scissors. See the instructions on page 110 for using a rotary cutter. Be extremely accurate with your cutting so that the pieces fit together perfectly.

All the measurements that follow assume that your fabric is 45 inches/114.3 cm wide; cut off ½ inch/13 mm at each selvage edge for a total width of 44 inches/111.7 cm. All measurements include a ¼ inch/6 mm seam allowance.

BLOCK UNITS	NUMBER OF PIECES
Note: Number of pieces for a single block is shown in parentheses.	
Checkerboard squares	(5) 180 light/dark
Triangle squares	(4) 144 light/dark

Piecing

RAILROAD BLOCKS

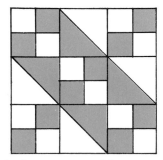

Block No. 1 Assembly Diagram

1. To construct the checkerboard squares, measure and cut twenty-six strips, each 3 inches/7.6 cm wide, across the entire width of each of your light and dark fabrics.

2. Following Diagram 1, sew each light strip to a dark one; press the seam allowances toward the dark fabric.

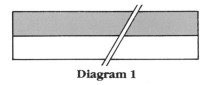

Diagram 1

3. Following Diagram 2, measure and cut fourteen strips, each 3 inches/7.6 cm wide, from each width of pieced fabric, until you have a total of 360 light/dark strips.

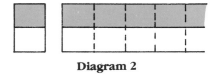

Diagram 2

4. Following Diagram 3, sew a pair of strips together, turning one of the strips so that the dark and light pieces are opposite one another. You will end up with a 5½ inch/14 cm square. Construct 179 more checkerboard squares in the same manner.

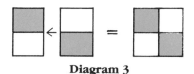

Diagram 3

5. To construct the triangle squares, measure and mark eighteen 11⅞ inch/30 cm squares on the light fabric. Three of these squares will fit across your yardage, so you will need six rows of squares. Cut out each square along the marked lines.

6. Following Diagram 4 and using a pencil and ruler, mark diagonal lines on the wrong side of each of the squares. Then mark horizontal and vertical lines as shown, dividing the block neatly and accurately into eight triangles.

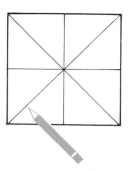

Diagram 4

7. Use each square as a pattern to cut a matching square from dark fabric. With right sides facing and all raw edges even, steam-press a light and dark fabric square together so that they will cling to one another without shifting.

8. Following Diagram 5, sew a seam ¼ inch/6 mm away from each side of each of the marked diagonal lines. The seams will cross one another in the middle.

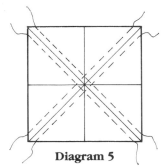

Diagram 5

9. Following Diagram 6, cut the fabrics apart along the marked diagonal lines.

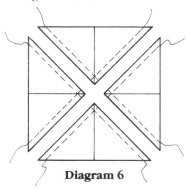

Diagram 6

10. Following Diagram 7, cut the triangles apart along the marked horizontal and vertical lines.

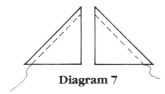

Diagram 7

11. Open up the fabrics to reveal a 5½ inch/14 cm square as shown in Diagram 8. Press the seam allowances toward the dark fabric. You will have a total of 144 triangle squares.

Diagram 8

12. To make the top row of Block No. 1, sew two checkerboard squares to opposite sides of a triangle square, positioning the colors as shown in Diagram 9. Construct another row in the same manner for the bottom row.

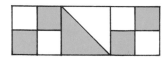

Diagram 9

13. For the middle row of Block No. 1, sew two triangle squares to opposite sides of a checkerboard square, positioning the colors as shown in Diagram 10.

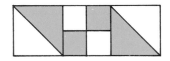

Diagram 10

14. Sew the top and bottom rows to opposite sides of the middle row, matching seams carefully and positioning the colors as shown in the Block No. 1 Assembly Diagram, to complete Block No. 1. Construct a total of 18 No. 1 blocks.

15. To make the top row of Block No. 2, sew two checkerboard squares to opposite sides of a triangle square, positioning the colors as shown in Diagram 11. Construct another row in the same manner for the bottom row.

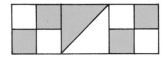

Diagram 11

16. For the middle row of Block No. 2, sew two triangle squares to opposite sides of a checkerboard square, positioning the colors as shown in Diagram 12.

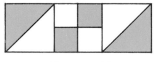

Diagram 12

17. Sew the top and bottom rows to opposite sides of the middle row, matching seams carefully and positioning the colors as shown in the Block No. 2 Assembly Diagram, to complete Block No. 2. Construct a total of 18 No. 2 blocks.

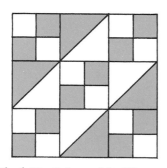

Block No. 2 Assembly Diagram

19. Stitch the blocks together in rows, matching seams carefully.

20. Stitch the rows together, again matching seams carefully, to complete the quilt top.

21. To make the quilt back, sew the three fabric pieces together along the long edges; press the seam allowances to one side.

22. Assemble the quilt top, batting/wadding and back as directed on page 113.

Assembly

18. Following Diagrams 13 and 14, and working on a large flat surface, arrange the patchwork blocks, alternating the No. 1 and No. 2 blocks as shown, in six rows with six blocks in each row. (Diagram 14 shows the position of the four blocks in the upper left corner of the quilt.)

Finishing

23. Quilt diagonal lines across the quilt as shown in Diagram 14.

24. Bind the quilt with a separate binding as directed on page 115.

2	1	2	1	2	1
1	2	1	2	1	2
2	1	2	1	2	1
1	2	1	2	1	2
2	1	2	1	2	1
1	2	1	2	1	2

Diagram 13

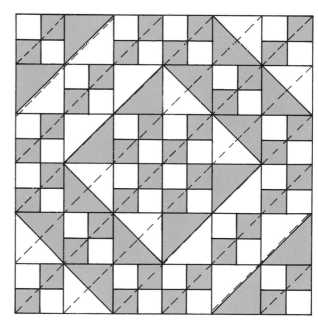

Diagram 14

UNION ARMY ENCIRCLED STAR

This mesmerizing, almost iridescent quilt is said to have been made at a 'Bee' for a fundraising auction to aid the Union Army, c.1860. The design is unique and has defied all well-intentioned efforts to find an appropriate pattern name. The sixteen blocks are beautifully held together by strong, navy-blue sashing with well-proportioned cheddar-colored diamonds. The straight edges in the design motifs are in stark contrast to the curvilinear 'wave' quilting pattern.

Skill Level: Advanced

Size

Block is 17⅜ inches/44 cm square
16 blocks are needed for finished quilt
Finished quilt is 77 × 77 inches/195.6 × 195.6 cm

Materials

Note: For clarity, the actual colors used to make the quilt in the photograph above have been listed in parentheses below.

● 2¾ yards/meters white fabric for patchwork blocks and back of quilt
● 3 yards/meters bright fabric (cheddar) for patchwork blocks
● ½ yard/meter medium fabric (dark maroon) for patchwork blocks
● 3⅝ yards/meters dark fabric (navy) for patchwork blocks, sashing and borders, and binding
● 77½ × 77½ inch/197 × 197 cm piece of batting/wadding

Cutting (per quilt)

Note: All measurements include a ¼ inch/6 mm seam allowance.

BACK OF QUILT

Cut two pieces white fabric, each 39 × 77½ inches/ 99 × 197 cm

SASHING AND BORDERS

Twelve **G** strips 2 × 17⅞ inches/5 × 45.5 cm, dark fabric
Five **H** strips 2 × 74½ inches/5 × 189 cm, dark fabric
Two **J** strips 2 × 77½ inches/5 × 197 cm, dark fabric

BINDING

Cut dark fabric into seven 1½ inch/4 cm wide strips across the full width of the fabric and sew together to measure 8¾ yards/meters long

PATTERN PIECE	NUMBER OF PIECES	
A	(4)	64 bright
	(4)	64 dark
B	(8)	128 white
C	(16)	256 bright
	(8)	128 medium
	(16)	256 dark
D	(16)	256 white
	(8)	128 dark
E	(8)	128 white
F	(4)	64 bright

Note: Number of pieces for a single block is shown in parentheses.

Piecing

UNION ARMY ENCIRCLED STAR BLOCKS

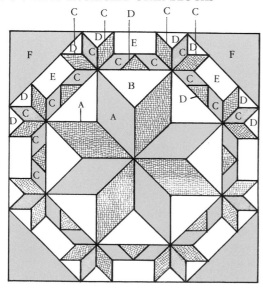

Block Assembly Diagram

1. Sew a bright A to a dark A to form a pair as shown in Diagram 1. Make three more pairs in the same manner.

Diagram 1

2. To form the central star, sew four A–A pairs together, matching seams carefully in the middle as shown in Diagram 2.

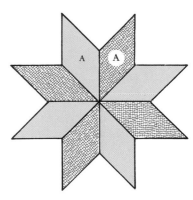

Diagram 2

3. Inset a B into each angled edge of the central star as shown in Diagram 3. (See page 111 for instructions on insetting.)

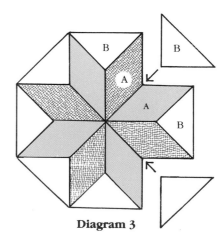

Diagram 3

4. Next make the strips that surround the central star. Sew a bright C to each side of a dark D as shown in Diagram 4 (next page). Construct 7 more C–D–C strips in the same manner.

231

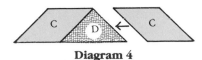

Diagram 4

5. Sew four C–D–C strips to alternating edges of the central star as shown in Diagram 5.

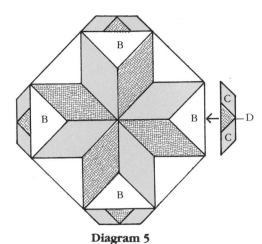

Diagram 5

6. To form the corner flowers, sew two dark Cs to each side of a medium C as shown in Diagram 6.

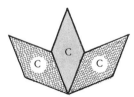

Diagram 6

7. Following Diagram 7, inset a white D into the two angled edges of the corner flower. Construct 7 more corner flowers in the same manner.

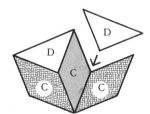

Diagram 7

8. Following Diagram 8 carefully, sew a corner flower to each side of a C–D–C strip. Repeat three more times for a total of four corner strips.

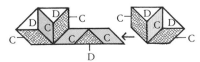

Diagram 8

9. Following Diagram 9, inset an E into the opening formed between the corner flowers. Repeat for the other three corner strips.

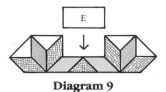

Diagram 9

10. To complete the corner unit, sew an F to the straight edge formed by insetting the E piece as shown in Diagram 10. Repeat for the other three corner strips.

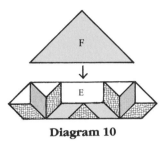

Diagram 10

11. Sew a corner unit to each corner of the central star as shown in Diagram 11.

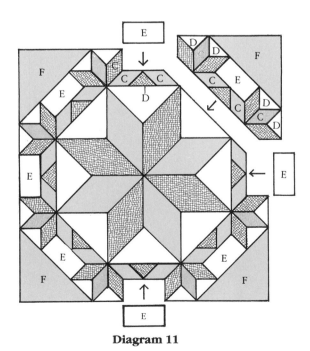

Diagram 11

12. Inset an E into the four remaining openings as shown in Diagram 11 to complete the block as shown in the Block Assembly Diagram.

13. Construct 15 more Union Army Encircled Star blocks in the same manner.

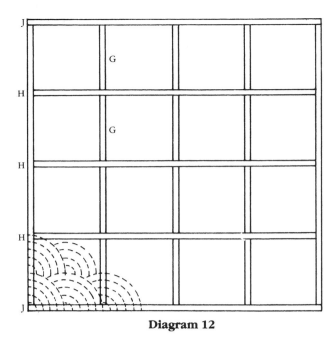

Diagram 12

15. Sew the G sashing strips between the blocks to form four horizontal rows.

16. Sew the patchwork rows to each side of the H sashing strips as shown in Diagram 12.

17. Sew an H border strip to each side of the patchwork.

18. Sew a J border strip to the top and bottom of the patchwork to complete the quilt top.

19. Following the directions on pages 108–9, enlarge the wave quilting design given on page 225, and use the enlarged pattern to make a quilting template. Following the directions on page 113, use the template to mark the wave design across the entire quilt top, including the borders.

20. To make the quilt back, sew the two fabric pieces together along the long edges; press the seam allowance to one side.

21. Assemble the quilt top, batting/wadding and back as directed on page 113.

Assembly

14. Following Diagram 12 and working on a large flat surface, arrange the patchwork blocks with the sashing strips in four rows with four blocks in each row.

Finishing

22. Quilt the marked wave design.

23. Bind the quilt with a separate binding as directed on page 115.

Note: These pattern pieces **do not** include seam allowance.

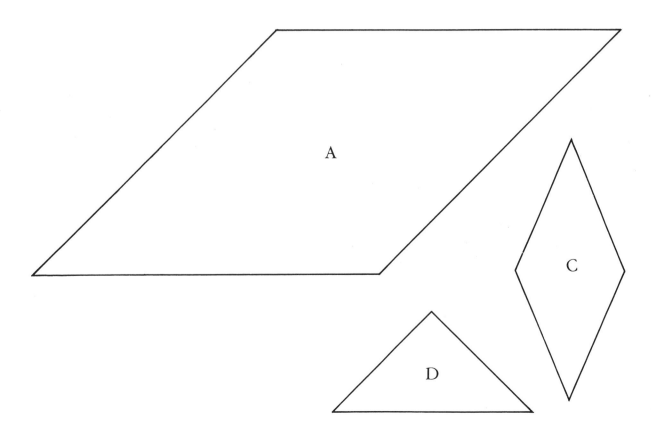

233

Note: These pattern pieces **do not** include seam allowance.

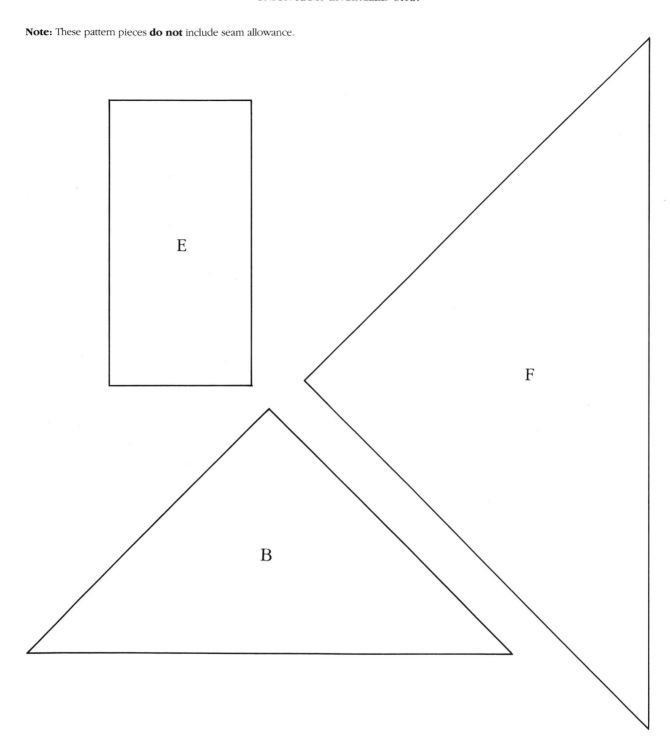

MISSOURI FOLK ART LILY

This exquisitely detailed quilt was made in Missouri sometime during the middle of the nineteenth century. The border is composed of triangles in three harmonious shades. Smaller triangles representing flying geese are repeated in the central thirty blocks. The thirty-five pieced lilies in the same colors as the border add a wonderfully eclectic touch to the entire piece. The beautiful quilting itself completes the picture.

Skill Level: Advanced

Size

Blocks are 7⅞ inches/20 cm square
35 No. 1 blocks, 30 No. 2 blocks and 5 No. 3 blocks are needed for finished quilt
Finished quilt is 73 × 95½ inches/185.4 × 242.5 cm

Materials

Note: For clarity, the actual colors used in the quilt in the photograph have been listed below.

● 8¼ yards/meters white fabric for patchwork blocks Nos. 1, 2 and 3, and back of quilt
● 2⅞ yards/meters navy fabric for patchwork blocks Nos. 2 and 3, and binding

- 1¾ yards/meters brown fabric for patchwork block No. 1 and border triangles
- 1½ yards/meters beige print fabric for patchwork block No. 3 and border triangles
- 1⅛ yards/meters green fabric for patchwork blocks Nos. 1 and 2, and border triangles
- ¾ yard/meter orange fabric for patchwork blocks Nos. 1 and 2
- 73½ × 96 inch/186.7 × 244 cm piece of batting/wadding

Cutting (per quilt)

Note: All measurements include a ¼ inch/6 mm seam allowance.

BACK OF QUILT

Cut two pieces white fabric, each 37 × 96 inches/94 × 244 cm

SIDE P TRIANGLES

From brown fabric, cut five 12½ inch/31.7 cm squares; cut each square diagonally into four quarters to make twenty side triangles; use one triangle as a pattern to cut one additional triangle for a total of twenty-one

From beige print fabric, cut nine 12½ inch/31.7 cm squares; cut each square diagonally into four quarters to make thirty-six side triangles; use one triangle as a pattern to cut one additional triangle for a total of thirty-seven

From green fabric, cut five 12½ inch/31.7 cm squares; cut each square diagonally into four quarters to make twenty side triangles

CORNER Q TRIANGLES

From brown fabric, cut one 6⅝ inch/16.7 cm square; cut in half diagonally to make two corner triangles

From beige print fabric, cut one 6⅝ inch/16.7 cm square; cut in half diagonally to make two corner triangles; use one triangle as a pattern to cut one additional triangle for a total of three

From green fabric, cut one triangle using a beige corner triangle as a pattern

BINDING

Cut navy fabric into eight 1½ inch/4 cm wide strips across the full width of the fabric and sew together to measure 9½ yards/meters long

PATTERN PIECE	NUMBER OF PIECES	

Note: Number of pieces for a single block is shown in parentheses.

Block No. 1 (Missouri Folk Art Lily)

A	(1)	35 orange
	(2)	70 brown
A reversed	(1)	35 orange
	(2)	70 brown
B	(3)	105 white
C	(2)	70 white
D	(2)	70 white
E	(2)	70 white
F	(1)	35 green
G	(1)	35 green
G reversed	(1)	35 green

Block No. 2 (Wild Goose Chase Variation)

H	(12)	360 navy
J	(24)	720 white
K	(4)	120 orange
L	(8)	240 white
M	(1)	30 green
N	(4)	120 navy

Block No. 3 (Variation of Block No. 2)

K	(4)	20 beige print
L	(8)	40 white
M	(1)	5 navy
N	(4)	20 navy
O	(4)	20 white

Border Triangles (see cutting notes above)

P		37 beige print
		21 brown
		20 green
Q		3 beige print
		2 brown
		1 green

Piecing

BLOCK NO. 1: MISSOURI FOLK ART LILY BLOCKS

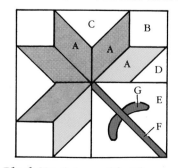

Block No. 1 Assembly Diagram

1. For each lily, use two pairs (an A and a reversed A) of brown A 'petals' and one pair of orange A petals. Sew a pair of brown A petals together as shown in Diagram 1. Then sew each remaining brown A to an orange A in the same manner.

2. Inset a B into the corner of each A–A pair as shown in Diagram 2. (See page 111 for instructions on insetting.)

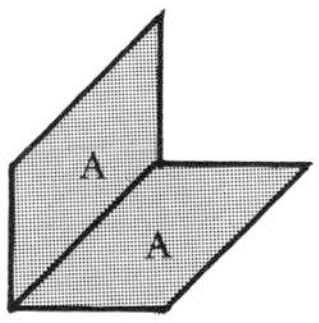

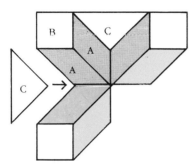

Diagram 1 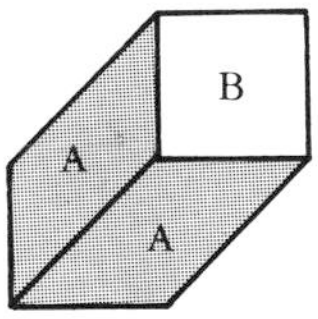   **Diagram 2**

3. Following Diagram 3, sew the three pairs of A petals together so that the orange petals are at the base of the flower. Then inset two Cs between the brown A petals as shown.

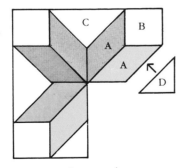

Diagram 3

4. Sew a D to each orange A as shown in Diagram 4.

Diagram 4

5. Following Diagram 5, appliqué a G and a reversed G leaf onto two E triangles, matching the raw straight edge of the G leaf to the raw edge of the E triangle. (See page 112 for instructions on how to appliqué.) Then sew the E triangles to each side of an F stem to form a square, enclosing the raw edges of the appliqués in the seams.

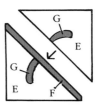

Diagram 5

6. Inset the square just made into the petal portion of the block as shown in the Block No. 1 Assembly Diagram.

7. Construct 34 more Missouri Folk Art Lily blocks in the same manner.

BLOCK NO. 2: WILD GOOSE CHASE VARIATION

Block No. 2
Assembly Diagram

8. Sew a J to each side of an H to form a rectangle as shown in Diagram 6. Repeat eleven more times for a total of twelve rectangles.

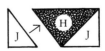

Diagram 6

9. Sew three J–H–J rectangles together to form a long rectangle as shown in Diagram 7. Repeat three more times for a total of four rectangles.

10. Sew an L to two adjacent edges of an orange K square as shown in Diagram 8. Repeat three more times for a total of four corner units.

          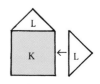

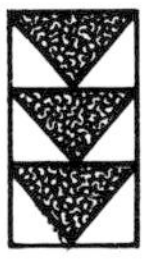

Diagram 7   **Diagram 8**

237

11. Following Diagram 9, sew a corner unit to each of the J–H–J rectangles. Sew the J edge of two rectangle strips to each side of a green M square to complete the central strip.

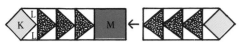

Diagram 9

12. Following Diagram 10, sew an N triangle to each side of the remaining two rectangle strips.

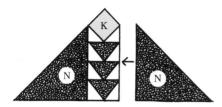

Diagram 10

13. Sew the triangles just made to each side of the central strip, completing the block as shown in the Block No. 2 Assembly Diagram.
14. Construct 29 more Wild Goose Chase blocks in the same manner.

BLOCK NO. 3: VARIATION OF BLOCK NO. 2

**Block No. 3
Assembly Diagram**

15. Following Diagram 8, sew an L to two adjacent edges of a beige K square. Repeat three more times for a total of four corner units.
16. Following Diagram 11, sew a corner unit to one end of an O rectangle. Repeat three more times for a total of four pieces.

Diagram 11

17. Following Diagram 12, sew a K–L–O strip to opposite sides of a navy M square to complete the central strip.

Diagram 12

18. Following Diagram 13, sew an N triangle to each side of one of the remaining two K–L–O strips. Repeat to make a second triangle in the same manner.

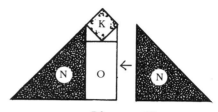

Diagram 13

19. Sew the triangles just made to each side of the central strip, completing the block as shown in the Block No. 3 Assembly Diagram.
20. Construct 4 more blocks in the same manner.

Assembly

21. Working on a large flat surface, arrange the patchwork blocks as shown in Diagram 14, following the marked numbers for the position of blocks 1 through 3. You can turn all the lilies sideways as shown by the arrows on the diagram, or position them straight up if you wish. Fill in the sides and two opposite corners with the beige P triangles. Fill in the remaining two corners with the beige Q triangles as shown.
22. Note that the quilt is constructed in diagonal rows. Stitch the blocks together in rows starting with the middle ones and working outward. Be sure to sew a P or a Q triangle to each end of each row.
23. Stitch the rows together, matching seams carefully at the intersections.
24. Arrange the remaining P and Q triangles to form a border around the quilt as shown in Diagram 14. You will need a total of fifteen P triangles and one Q triangle for each of the two side borders. For the top and bottom borders you will need a total of twelve P triangles and two Q triangles for each. You can exactly copy the quilt in the photograph, in which case, follow the diagram faithfully. The three white

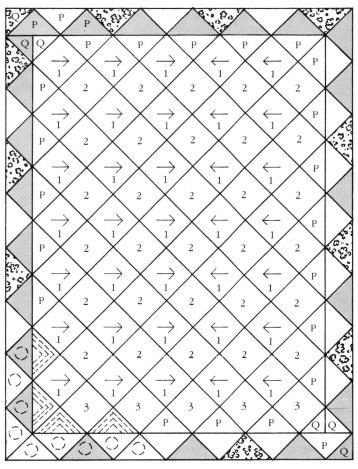

Diagram 14

triangles (lower left corner) do not show the beige print so that you can see the quilting pattern. Or, you can make up your own color arrangement of the triangles.

25. When you are satisfied with your arrangement, sew the triangles together to form four strips. Sew the side strips to the patchwork first, then sew the top and bottom strips to the patchwork, mitering the upper right and lower left corners of the quilt. (See page 112 for instructions on mitering.)

26. To make the quilt back, sew the two fabric pieces together along the long edges; press the seam allowance to one side.

27. Assemble the quilt top, batting/wadding and back as directed on page 113.

Finishing

28. Outline-quilt the petals, stem and leaves of the lily on each Block No. 1.

29. Refer to the photograph and quilt horizontal, vertical and diagonal lines across each of the No. 2 and No. 3 blocks. Then, outline-quilt each M triangle.

30. Outline-quilt each individual block.

31. Quilt the beige P triangles at the ends of the rows with rows of echo quilting as shown in Diagram 14, spacing the lines about ¾ inch/2 cm apart.

32. Outline-quilt each of the P and Q triangles along the border, and then quilt a 3 inch/7.6 cm diameter circle in the middle of each triangle as shown in Diagram 14.

33. Bind the quilt with a separate binding as directed on page 115.

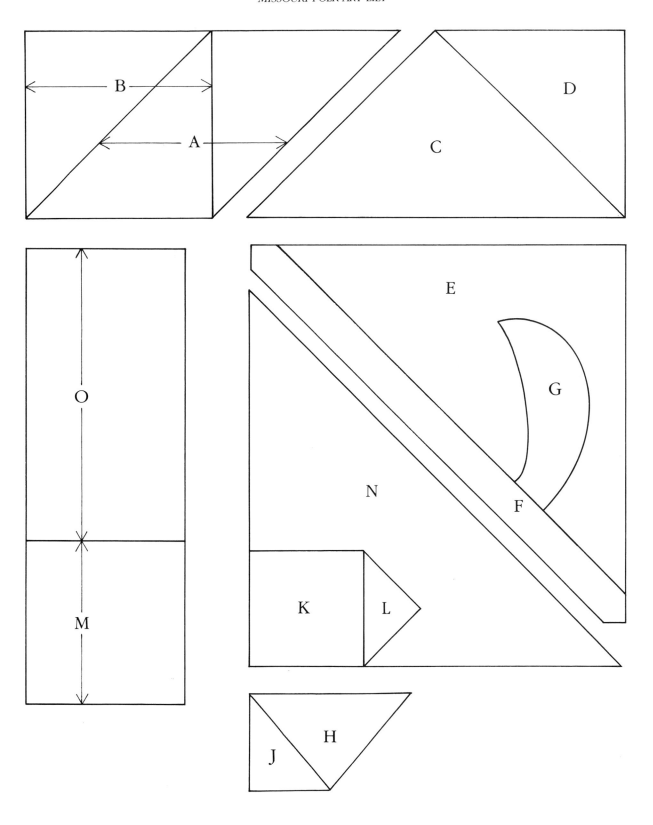

Note: These pattern pieces **do not** include seam allowance.

MAPLE LEAF

It's hard to imagine this strikingly modern-looking quilt as having been made by a Holmes County, Ohio, housewife around 1880. Chrome orange and Turkey red were in fact popular color combinations during this period. There is a three-dimensional quality to this quilt. The quilting on the border is finely stitched in a rope pattern.

Skill Level: Easy

Size

Block is 15 inches/38 cm square
16 blocks are needed for finished quilt
Finished quilt is 66 × 72 inches/167.6 × 183 cm

Materials

● 8 yards/meters light fabric for patchwork blocks, back of quilt and self binding, and borders
● 1¾ yards/meters medium fabric for patchwork blocks
● 1¾ yards/meters bright fabric for patchwork blocks
● 66½ × 72½ inch/169 × 184 cm piece of batting/wadding

Cutting (per quilt)

Note: All measurements include a ¼ inch/6 mm seam allowance.

BACK OF QUILT AND SELF BINDING

Cut two pieces light fabric, each 34¼ × 73½ inches/ 87 × 186.7 cm

BORDERS

Two **E** strips 3½ × 60½ inches/9 × 153.6 cm, light fabric

Two **F** strips 6½ × 66½ inches/16.5 × 169 cm, light fabric

PATTERN PIECE	NUMBER OF PIECES

Note: Number of pieces for a single block is shown in parentheses.

A	(16) 256 light
	(8) 128 medium
	(8) 128 bright
B	(4) 64 light
	(6) 96 medium
	(6) 96 bright
C	(2) 32 medium
	(2) 32 bright
D	(8) 128 light

Piecing

MAPLE LEAF BLOCKS

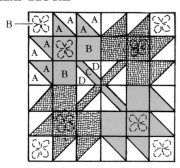

Block Assembly Diagram

1. Each Maple Leaf block is composed of four Maple Leaf squares, sewn together with the stems matching in the middle. The following directions will first instruct you to make a Maple Leaf square, then the entire block.

2. Sew a light A to a medium A along the diagonal edge to form a square as shown in Diagram 1. Make three more A squares in the same manner.

Diagram 1

3. For the top row, sew two A squares together, then sew a light B to left edge as shown in Diagram 2.

Diagram 2

4. For the middle row, sew two medium Bs together, then sew an A–A square to the left edge as shown in Diagram 3.

Diagram 3

5. For the bottom row, first sew a D to opposite sides of a medium C as shown in Diagram 4. Then,

Diagram 4

following Diagram 5, sew an A–A square to the left side of a medium B and the C–D square to the right side.

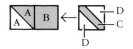

Diagram 5

6. Following the marked square in the Block Assembly Diagram, sew the three rows together, matching seams carefully, to complete one medium Maple Leaf square.

7. Make another medium Maple Leaf square and two bright Maple Leaf squares in the same manner, substituting the bright pieces for the medium pieces in steps 2–5. Arrange the four squares on a flat surface with the stems meeting in the middle, and alternating the medium and bright leaves. Stitch together in two rows, then stitch the rows together, matching seams carefully, to create one Maple Leaf block as shown in the Block Assembly Diagram.

8. Construct 15 more Maple Leaf blocks in the same manner.

9. Following the instructions on page 108, make a quilting template for the flower given on the B template. Following the instructions on page 113, use the template to mark the quilting design on each of the B squares indicated on the Block Assembly Diagram (mark a flower on the central B square of each *bright* Maple Leaf as well).

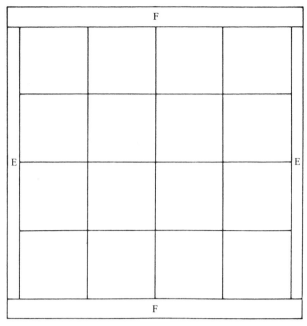

Diagram 6

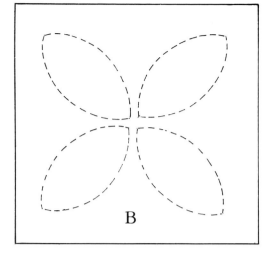

Flower quilting design

Note: These pattern pieces **do not** include seam allowance.

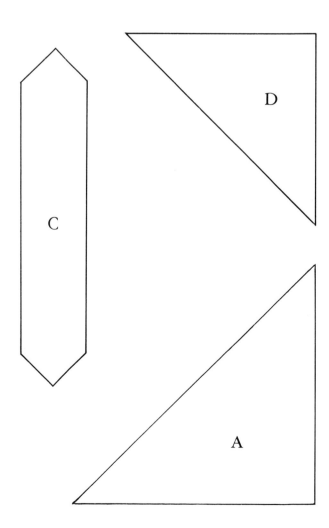

Assembly

10. Following Diagram 6 and working on a large flat surface, arrange the blocks side by side, alternating the medium and bright leaves as shown in the color photograph.

11. Sew the blocks together in rows, matching seams carefully.

12. Sew the rows together, matching seams carefully at the intersections.

13. Sew the side E borders to the right and left edges of the quilt top.

14. Sew the F borders to the top and bottom of the quilt top.

15. To make the quilt back, sew the two fabric pieces together along the long edges; press the seam allowance to one side.

16. Assemble the quilt top, batting/wadding and back as directed on page 113, centering the top and batting/wadding on the back which will be larger.

Finishing

17. Quilt the marked flowers on all the B squares.

18. Work diagonal quilting lines across the rest of the quilt; do not quilt on the squares with the flowers.

19. Quilt a lozenge border design similar to the one on page 217 on each of the borders.

20. Following the directions on page 116 for a self binding, wrap the fabric from the back over onto the top of the quilt and bind off neatly.

PENNSYLVANIA DUTCH FOLK ART

Phosphorescent-like vegetable dyes and mid-nineteenth-century printed cottons contribute to the visual excitement of this quilt from the Pennsylvania German community. The appliqué motifs of hearts, curvilinear shapes, oak leaves, and pieced stars and triangles present the legacy of a folk heritage rich with symbolism. The rick-rack border hand-stitched onto a darker green background creates a firm sense of proportion and overall harmony.

Skill Level: Advanced

Size

Block is 13½ inches/34.3 cm square
12 patchwork blocks, 6 appliquéd blocks, 10 appliquéd side triangles and 4 appliquéd corner triangles are needed for finished quilt
Finished quilt is 75½ × 95¾ inches/191.7 × 243 cm

Materials

Note: For clarity, the actual colors used in the quilt pictured in the photograph above have been listed below, except for the light, medium and dark fabrics in the patchwork blocks which are varied.

● 8¼ yards/meters white fabric for patchwork blocks and back of quilt
● 2⅜ yards/meters solid green fabric for corner star block and border

- 1¾ yards/meters green print fabric for appliqué block, side triangles and corner triangles
- 1⅜ yards/meters brown print fabric for patchwork blocks
- ⅞ yard/meter red print fabric for patchwork block and border appliqué
- ⅝ yard/meter light fabric for patchwork blocks and border appliqué
- ⅝ yard/meter red fabric for appliqué blocks and binding
- ⅜ yard/meter medium fabric for patchwork blocks
- ⅜ yard/meter dark fabric for patchwork blocks
- 13 yards/meters red rickrack, ¼ inch/6 mm wide
- 80 × 96¼ inch/203 × 244.5 cm piece of batting/wadding

- Make templates (see page 108) for the following pieces (measurements include a ¼ inch/6 mm seam allowance):
G: 5½ × 5½ inches/14 × 14 cm square
K: 14 × 14 inches/35.5 × 35.5 cm square
C1: 3½ × 3½ inches/9 × 9 cm square

Cutting (per quilt)

Note: Read the appliqué instructions on page 112 before marking and cutting out the appliqué pieces. All measurements include a ¼ inch/6 mm seam allowance.

BACK OF QUILT

Cut two pieces white fabric, each 40¼ × 96¼ inches/102 × 244.5 cm

BORDER

Two **S** strips 7½ × 62 inches/19 × 157.5 cm, green fabric
Two **T** strips 7½ × 82¼ inches/19 × 209 cm, green fabric

SIDE N TRIANGLES

From green print fabric, cut two 20¼ inch/51.4 cm squares; cut each square diagonally into four quarters to make eight side triangles; use one triangle as a pattern to cut two additional triangles

CORNER P TRIANGLES

From green print fabric, cut two 10½ inch/26.7 cm squares; cut in half diagonally to make four corner triangles

BINDING

Cut red fabric into eight 1½ inch/4 cm wide strips across the full width of the fabric and sew together to measure 9½ yards/meters long

PATTERN PIECE	NUMBER OF PIECES	
Note: Number of pieces for a single block is shown in parentheses.		
A	(4)	48 white
B	(4)	48 red print
B reversed	(4)	48 red print
C	(1)	12 red print
D	(4)	48 white
E	(4)	48 light
	(4)	48 medium
	(4)	48 dark
F	(12)	144 white
F reversed	(12)	144 white
G	(4)	48 brown print
H	(1)	6 white
J	(4)	24 red for appliqué blocks
	(1)	10 red for appliqué side triangles
	(1)	4 red for appliqué corner triangles
K	(1)	6 green print
L	(1)	6 red
M	(1)	10 white
N	(1)	10 green print (see **Cutting** above)
O	(1)	4 white
P	(1)	4 green print (see **Cutting** above)
Q		16 red print
R		16 white
		16 light
A1	(4)	16 white
B1	(4)	16 green
B1 reversed	(4)	16 green
C1	(1)	4 green
D1	(4)	16 white

Piecing

PATCHWORK BLOCKS

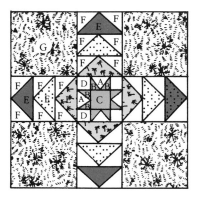

Block Assembly Diagram

1. Sew a B and a reversed B to each side of A to form a rectangle as shown in Diagram 1. Make three more rectangles in the same manner.

Diagram 1

2. To make the central strip, sew a B–A–B rectangle to each side of C as shown in Diagram 2.

Diagram 2

3. For the top and bottom strips, sew a D to each side of the remaining two B–A–B rectangles as shown in Diagram 3.

Diagram 3

4. Sew the top and bottom strips to each side of the central strip to complete the star as shown in the middle of the Patchwork Block Assembly Diagram.
5. Following Diagram 4, sew an F and a reversed F to each side of a dark E to form a rectangle. Make three more dark E rectangles, four medium E rectangles and four light E rectangles in the same manner.

Diagram 4

6. Following Diagram 5, sew a strip of dark, medium and light F–E–F rectangles together. Make three more strips in the same manner.

Diagram 5

7. For the central strip, sew an F–E–F strip to each side of the star with the tips of the triangles pointing outward as shown in Diagram 6.

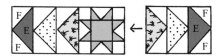

Diagram 6

8. For the top and bottom strips, sew a G to each side of the remaining two F–E–F strips as shown in Diagram 7.

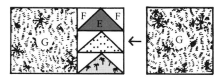

Diagram 7

9. Sew the top and bottom strips to each side of the central strip with the tips of the triangles pointing outward to complete the patchwork block.
10. Construct 11 more Patchwork Blocks in the same manner.

APPLIQUÉ BLOCKS

11. Prepare pieces H and L for appliqué as directed on page 112. Lightly mark the four J hearts on the right side of H, then mark a seam allowance ¼ inch/ 6 mm *within* the marked heart outlines; cut out the interior of the hearts along the inner marked line. Clip into the seam allowance all around each heart as shown in Diagram 8.

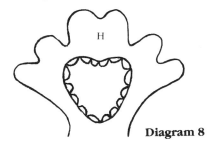

Diagram 8

12. Fold the clipped seam allowance to the wrong side and press carefully. Then baste a J heart *behind* each opening in H as shown in Diagram 9. Using white thread and making tiny stitches, stitch the appliqués together; this is called 'reverse appliqué'.

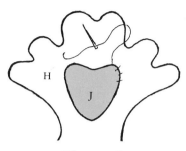

Diagram 9

13. Following Diagram 10, position H in the middle of the background K square. Baste in place, then appliqué H to the background (see page 112 for instructions on how to appliqué).

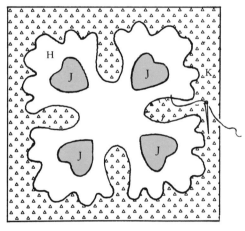

Diagram 10

14. Following Diagram 11, position piece L in the middle of H, matching the tips of L to the edges of H as shown. Appliqué L to H.

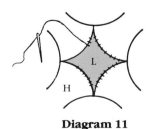

Diagram 11

15. Construct 5 more Appliqué Blocks in the same manner.

APPLIQUÉ SIDE TRIANGLES

16. Prepare piece M for appliqué as directed on page 112; you do not have to turn the straight bottom edge under because the raw edge will be hidden in the seam. Treat the curved 'half-heart' areas by clipping and turning the seam allowance to the wrong side as you did in step 11.

17. Following the instructions in steps 11 and 12, reverse-appliqué one J heart to the center top of M.

18. Following Diagram 12, position M in the middle of the long edge of a side N triangle, matching the straight raw edges. Baste in place, then appliqué M to N. Appliqué the 'half-heart' curves to the background as well.

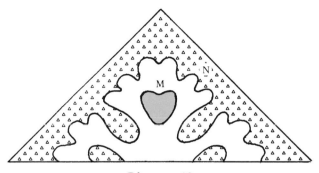

Diagram 12

19. Construct 9 more Appliqué Side Triangles in the same manner.

APPLIQUÉ CORNER TRIANGLES

20. Prepare piece O for appliqué as directed on page 112; you do not have to turn the straight bottom edge under because the raw edge will be hidden in the seam.

21. Following the instructions in steps 11 and 12, reverse-appliqué one J heart to O.

22. Following Diagram 13, position O in the middle of the long edge of the corner P triangle matching the straight raw edges. Baste in place, then appliqué O to P.

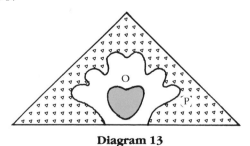

Diagram 13

23. Construct 3 more Appliqué Corner Triangles in the same manner.

APPLIQUÉ BORDERS

24. It is easier to appliqué the borders before sewing them to the quilt top; just take care not to fray the edges of the fabric borders. You may wish to zigzag-stitch the edges to keep them from fraying while you work.

25. First work on the top and bottom S borders. Following Diagram 14 and using a compass, mark ten 5½ inch/14 cm diameter circles on the right side of the fabric, centered between the top and bottom edges. The left edge of the first circle should start 3½ inches/9 cm away from the left end of the S border strip.

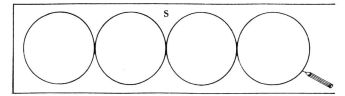

Diagram 14

26. Begin applying rickrack to the border. When you start, align the raw edge of the rickrack with the raw edge of the border. Make a graceful curve away from the raw edge to the first marked circle as shown in Diagram 15 and the color photograph on page 244. Following Diagram 15, run the rickrack along alternate sides of the marked circles, hand-stitching it in place with matching thread as you go. When you have reached the end of the circles, run the rickrack gracefully off to the raw edge as you did at the beginning and cut off the remaining length of rickrack, even with the raw edge of the border. Press the rickrack in place very carefully so that the curves are smooth. Repeat for the other S border.

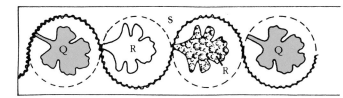

Diagram 15

27. For the T border, follow Diagram 14 to mark fourteen 5½ inch/14 cm diameter circles on the right side of the fabric, centered between the top and bottom edges. The left edge of the first circle should start 2⅝ inches/6.4 cm away from the left end of the T border strip.

28. Apply the rickrack to the border as you did for the S borders. Repeat for the other T border.

29. Prepare the Q and R leaves for appliqué as directed on page 112, turning all edges under because the leaves will not be placed beneath the rickrack but will just touch them.

30. Following Diagram 15 and the color photograph, position the leaves on the S and T borders, pinning them in place as shown. Note that there are two R leaves between each Q leaf. You will need ten leaves for each S border, and fourteen leaves for each T border. Once you are satisfied with their position, appliqué the leaves to the borders.

CORNER STARS

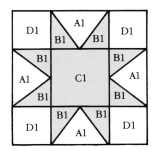

Corner Star Assembly Diagram

31. Following the Corner Star Assembly Diagram and using templates A1, B1, C1 and D1, construct four corner stars as directed in steps 1 through 4.

Assembly

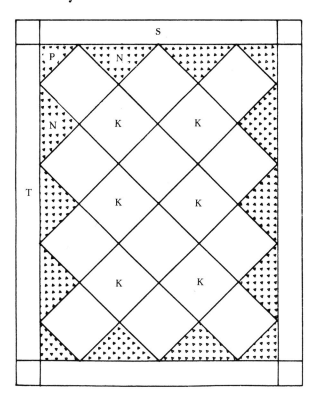

Diagram 16

32. Following Diagram 16 and working on a large flat surface, arrange the patchwork blocks with the appliquéd blocks and side and corner triangles.

33. Note that the quilt is constructed in diagonal rows. Stitch the blocks together in rows starting with the middle ones and working outward. Be sure to sew an N or P triangle to each end of each row.

34. Stitch the rows together, matching seams carefully at the intersections.

35. Sew an S border to the top and bottom edges of the quilt top.

36. Sew a corner star to each end of each T corner.

37. Sew the T/star borders to each side to complete the quilt top.

38. To make the quilt back, sew the two fabric pieces together along the long edges; press the seam allowance to one side.

39. Assemble the quilt top, batting/wadding and back as directed on page 113.

Finishing

40. Quilt the patchwork blocks as follows: Outline-quilt the central star and the F and the G pieces. Quilt diagonal lines across the G pieces.

41. Outline-quilt each of the appliqués on the K squares, and the N and P triangles. Outline-quilt the J hearts.

42. Following Diagram 15, quilt along the edges of the circles that do not have rickrack. Outline-quilt each of the leaves.

43. Outline-quilt each of the corner stars.

44. Bind the quilt with a separate binding as directed on page 115.

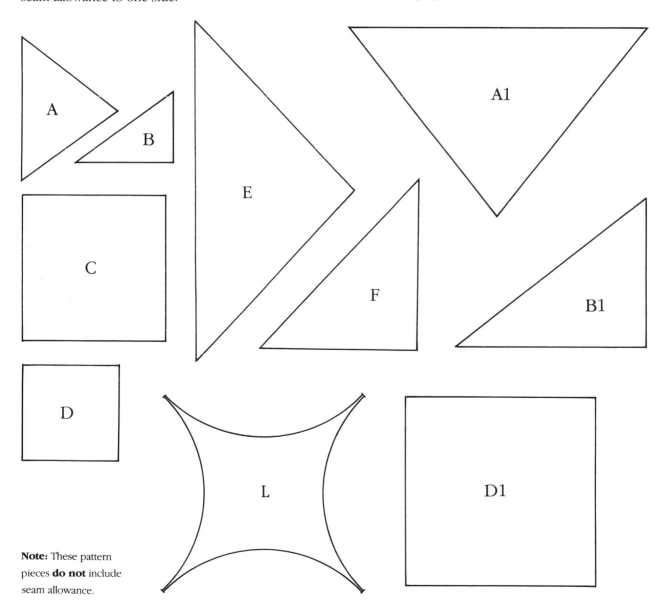

Note: These pattern pieces **do not** include seam allowance.

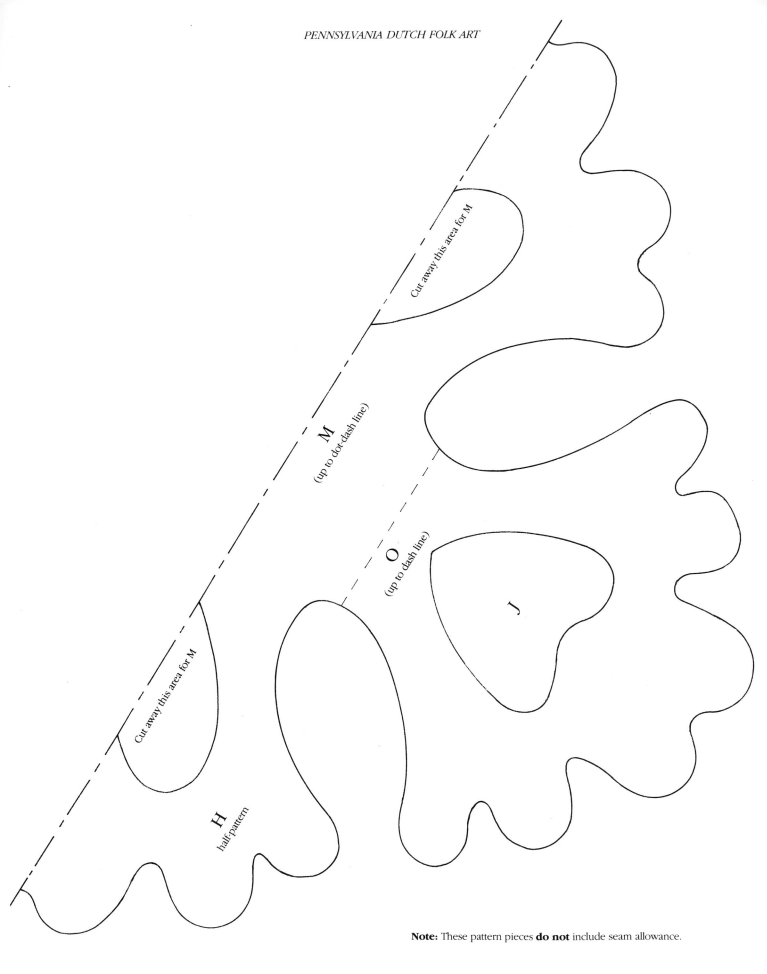

Cut away this area for M

M
(up to dot-dash line)

O
(up to dash line)

J

Cut away this area for M

H
half pattern

Note: These pattern pieces **do not** include seam allowance.

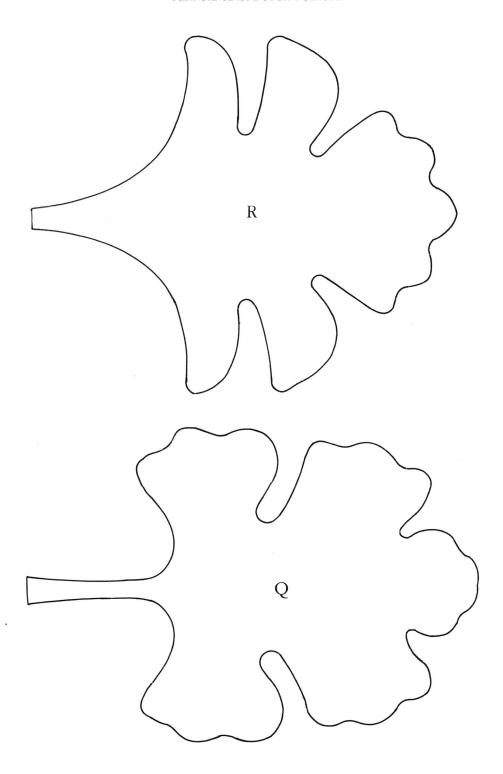

Note: These pattern pieces **do not** include seam allowance.

Bibliography

American Quarterly. Vol. 18, 1966.

Antique Collecting. Vol. 23, No. 4, 1988.

Allan, Gloria Seaman. *First Flowerings; Early Virginia Quilts*. DAR Museum, Washington D.C. 1981.

Bank, Mirra. *Anonymous Was A Woman*. St Martin's Press, New York. 1979.

Becker, Jane S. and Barbara Franco. *Folk Roots, New Roots*. Museum of our National Heritage, Lexington, Massachusetts. 1988.

Benson, Adolph B. (Ed.). *America of the Fifties: Letters of Frederika Bremer*. New York. 1924.

Bishop, Robert and Carter Houck. *All Flags Flying: American Patriotic Quilts As Expressions Of Liberty*. E.P. Dutton, New York. 1986.

Bishop, Robert and Elizabeth Safanda. *A Gallery of Amish Quilts*. E.P. Dutton, New York. 1976.

Blum, Dilys and Jack L. Lindsey (Eds.). *Philadelphia Museum of Art Bulletin: Quilts*. Vol. 85, Nos. 363-4, Fall 1989.

Boorstin, Daniel J. *The Americans: The Colonial Experience*. Pelican, New York. 1958.

—— *The Americans: The National Experience*. Cardinal, New York. 1965.

—— *The Americans: The Democratic Experience*. Cardinal, New York. 1973.

Bordin, Ruth. *Women and Temperance: The Quest for Power and Liberty 1873-1900*. Rutgers University Press, New Brunswick. 1990.

Brackman, Barbara. *Clues in the Calico*. EPM Publications, Inc., McLean, Virginia. 1989.

Brogan, Hugh. *The Pelican History of the United States of America*. Penguin Books, Ltd, Middlesex. 1985.

Bullard, Lacy Folmar and Betty Jo Shiell. *Chintz Quilts: Unfading Glory*. Serendipity Publishers, Florida. 1983.

Colby, Averil. *Patchwork*. B.T. Batsford, London. 1958.

—— *Quilting*. Charles Scribner's Sons, New York. 1971.

Cott, Nancy F. *The Bonds of Womanhood: 'Woman's Sphere' in New England 1780-1835*. Yale University Press, New Haven. 1977.

Douglas, Ann. *The Feminization of American Culture*. Avon Books, New York. 1977.

Epstein, Barbara Leslie. *The Politics of Domesticity: Women, Evangelism and Temperance in Nineteenth-Century America*. Wesleyan University Press, Middletown, Connecticut. 1981.

Ferrero, Pat and Elaine Hedges, Julie Silber. *Hearts and Hands: The Influence of Women & Quilts on American Society*. The Quilt Digest Press, San Francisco, California. 1987.

Finley, Ruth. *Old Patchwork Quilts and the Women Who Made Them*. J.B. Lippincott Company, Philadelphia. 1929.

Fisher, Laura. *Quilts of Illusion*. The Main Street Press, Pittstown, New Jersey. 1988.

Garoutte, Sally and Laurel Horton (Eds.). *Uncoverings*. American Quilt Study Group, Mill Valley, California. Vols. 1-10, 1980-89.

Garraty, John A. and Robert McGaughey. *The American Nation: A History of the United States*. (7th edition) HarperCollins Publishers, Inc., New York. 1991.

Garvan, Beatrice and Charles Hummel. *The Pennsylvania Germans: A Celebration of Their Arts 1683-1850*. The Philadelphia Museum of Art, Philadelphia. 1982.

Granick, Eve Wheatcroft. *The Amish Quilt*. Good Books, Intercourse, Pennsylvania. 1989.

Hall, Carrie A. and Rose G. Kretsinger. *The Romance of the Patchwork Quilt in America*. Bonanza Books, New York. 1935.

Hall, Eliza Calvert. *Aunt Jane of Kentucky*. R. & E. Miles, San Pedro, California. 1986. Facsimile of 1907 Little, Brown, & Co. Edition.

Holmes, Kenneth L. (Ed.). *Covered Wagon Women: Diaries & Letters From the Western Trails 1840-1890*. Arthur H. Clark, Glendale, California. 1983.

Holstein, Jonathan. *The Pieced Quilt*. New York Graphic Society Press, Greenwich, Connecticut. 1973.

—— (Ed.). *Kentucky Quilts 1800-1900: The Kentucky Quilt Project*. Pantheon Books, New York. 1982.

Ickis, Marguerite. *The Standard Book of Quiltmaking & Collecting*. Dover Publications, Inc., New York. 1949.

Katzenberg, Dena S. *Baltimore Album Quilts*. The Baltimore Museum of Art, Baltimore, Maryland. 1981.

Kerber, Linda K. and Jane De Hart Mathews. *Women's America: Refocusing the Past*. Oxford University Press, New York. 1982.

Kiracofe, Roderick and Michael Kile (Eds.). *The Quilt Digest*. (5 Vols.) The Quilt Digest Press, San Francisco, California. 1983-87.

Larcom, Lucy. *A New England Girlhood*. Peter Smith, Gloucester, Massachusetts. 1973.

Larkin, Jack. *The Reshaping of Everyday Life 1790–1840*. Harper and Row Publishers, New York. 1988.

Lasansky, Jeannette. *In the Heart of Pennsylvania: 19th & 20th Century Quiltmaking Traditions*. Oral Traditions Project, Lewisburg, Pennsylvania. 1985.

—— *In the Heart of Pennsylvania: Symposium Papers*. 1986.

—— *Pieced by Mother: Over 100 Years of Quiltmaking Traditions*. 1987.

—— *Pieced by Mother: Symposium Papers*. 1988.

—— *A Good Start: The Aussteier of Dowry*. 1990.

—— *Bits and Pieces: Textile Traditions*. 1991.

Little, Frances. *Early American Textiles*. The Century Company, New York. 1931.

Mintz, Steven and Susan Kellogg. *Domestic Revolutions: A Social History of American Family Life*. The Free Press, New York. 1988.

Montgomery, Florence M. *Textiles in America: 1650–1870*. W.W. Norton and Company, New York. 1984.

—— *Printed Textiles. English and American Cottons and Linens: 1700–1850*. Viking Press, New York. 1970.

Nelson, Cyril and Carter Houck. *A Treasury of American Quilts*. E.P. Dutton, New York. 1982.

Orlofsky, Patsy and Myron. *Quilts in America*. McGraw-Hill Book Co., New York. 1974.

Petit, Florence H. *America's Printed & Painted Fabrics: 1600–1900*. Hastings House Publishers, New York. 1970.

Peto, Florence. *American Quilts and Coverlets*. Chanticleer Press, New York. 1949.

Phillips, Christopher. 'The Radical Crusade'. *Gateway Heritage*. Missouri Historical Society Quarterly. Vol. 10, No. 4. Spring 1990, pp.22–43.

Pottinger, David. *Quilts from the Indiana Amish: A Regional Collection*. E.P. Dutton, New York. 1983.

Rae, Janet. *The Quilts of the British Isles*. Bellew Publishing, London. 1987.

Riley, Glenda. *The Female Frontier: A Comparative View of Women on the Prairie and the Plains*. University Press of Kansas, Lawrence, Kansas. 1988.

Schlissel, Lillian. *Women's Diaries of the Westward Journey*. Schocken Books, New York. 1982.

Schlissel, Lillian, Byrd Gibbens and Elizabeth Hampsten. *Far From Home: Families of the Westward Journey*. Schocken Books, New York. 1989.

Seward, Linda. *The Complete Book of Patchwork, Quilting and Appliqué*. Mitchell Beazley, London. 1987.

Shi, David E. *The Simple Life: Plain Living and High Thinking in American Culture*. Oxford University Press, New York. 1985.

Stratton, Joanna L. *Pioneer Women: Voices from the Kansas Frontier*. Touchstone, New York. 1981.

Taylor, Joshua. *America as Art*. Harper and Row Publishers, Inc., New York. 1976.

Thompson, E. P. *William Morris: Romantic to Revolutionary*. Merlin Press, London. 1955.

Vlach, John Michael and Simon J. Bronner (Eds.). *Folk Art and Art Worlds*. UMI Research Press, Michigan. 1986.

Waldvogel, Merikay. *Soft Covers for Hard Times: Quiltmaking & The Great Depression*. Rutledge Hill Press, Nashville, Tennessee. 1990.

Webster, Marie D. *Quilts: Their Story and How to Make Them*. Doubleday, Page & Co., New York. 1915.

Weissman, Judith Reiter and Wendy Lavitt. *Labors of Love: America's Textiles and Needlework 1650–1930*. Knopf Publishers, New York. 1987.

Wentworth, Judy. *Quilts*. Bracken Books, London. 1989.

Woodard, Thomas K. and Blanche Greenstein. *Twentieth-Century Quilts 1900–1950*. E.P. Dutton & Co., New York. 1988.

—— *Crib Quilts and Other Small Wonders*. E.P. Dutton, Inc., New York. 1981.

Index

*Page numbers in italics refer to illustrations and their captions. Page numbers in **bold type** refer to practical quiltmaking techniques and projects.*